Separation

of

Sins

A Novel by David R. Phillips

(Author of For Reasons Unknown)

Fictional Characters

The story in this book, in its entirety, is a work of fiction. Several names within the story are names of real people, but there is no intention to link these names to the actual characters or the story. Simply put, these are real names that I found interesting. The purpose of including real peoples' names was an attempt to honor these individuals as friends, colleagues, or family members. If you don't want to risk being a character in my next novel, you should either stop being my friend, change your name to something uninteresting (like David Phillips), or request in writing on thermal fax paper (good luck finding that) not to be included.

Enjoy!

Acknowledgements

There are so many people who I could thank for helping and encouraging me to complete this book. You know who you are and I am forever in your debt.

This book was edited by the incredibly talented writer Cortney Meriwether, who also happens to be my daughter. She taught me more than I could have ever learned in an academic setting and I am a better writer thanks to her efforts.

I also wish to thank Laurie Brown for her cover design. The picture on the cover is of the Jefferson Memorial in Washington DC. After reading this novel, you will realize just how significant Thomas Jefferson was in establishing this country as a haven of religious freedom. Many brave soldiers have died to preserve that freedom and, unfortunately, many more will have to give their lives in the future. In a very real sense, this book is an acknowledgement of those who have fought to protect our freedom to follow our faith without threat of persecution by our government. Freedom of religion is part of the foundation of the United States of America and must be respected and defended. Thanks to all who serve, or have served to protect this basic human right.

Dedication

This novel is dedicated to another writer who has inspired me my entire life, my mother, Nancy Lail (Phillips). She pushed me as a child to overcome some learning disabilities and limitations, and without her love, support, and encouragement, I would not possess the confidence needed to complete a novel. Today, I'm just trying to keep up with her as a writer. Go read her books *Mayhem at Mahem: A Collegiate Conundrum* and *Stalked Again*.

Love you, mom!

Author's Note

In the United States, we have freedom of religion, but not freedom from religion. That means you can decide what faith, if any, you wish to follow, and so can I. To fulfill the vision of our Founding Fathers, we need to become better at tolerating those with different beliefs than our own.

This book is an attempt to give readers a bit of context around the issues and problems that arise when religion and politics are mixed. That does not mean that man's laws and governments have to be devoid of religious principles; rather, it means the opposite. General religious principles are the foundation of all laws and societies. However, when men use religious laws to govern countries, freedom is destroyed.

Each religion decides what it considers to be a sin and those whose beliefs align with that religion's moral expectations voluntarily "follow." In a similar fashion, people are basically free (limitations exist) to live in whatever country they want, based on the defined set of secular sins (laws) of that country. In a perfect world, people would be allowed to decide what moral laws (religion) they wish to follow and what set of societal laws (government) to which to subjugate themselves.

Unfortunately, the world is not perfect, nor should we expect it to achieve such a lofty standard. When humans enforce religious laws with the power of government, freedom is trampled. To have a free society, we must keep separate what we consider to be religious sin from what society has determined to be secular sin. Both are critical to every culture, and when applied with a balanced approach, create a harmonious society. When applied unevenly, an environment of fear, suppression, and hate is fostered.

Almost all human wars can be traced to a society where religion and government have been combined. Nazi Germany, Northern Ireland, the Middle East, and our own Revolutionary War are all examples from the past that still linger today. Peace is a result of keeping separate what we consider to be the sins of God (religion) and the sins of man (government).

Don't worry, the story in this book is much more interesting and entertaining than the issue discussed above. Read on and enjoy!

David R. Phillips

Chapter 1

It is amazing what humans can do when motivated by revenge. Jonathan Hill was about to give the world an extreme example of the power of hatred combined with the need to even the score. His life was over, had been over for almost 15 years, and now he was going to serve justice on those who had taken his life.

Over the years his own reality had morphed and rationalized to a point that he now believed the Bible was calling him to seek revenge. He had not read the Good Book since the day his soul was first destroyed, but he remembered part of a verse in Matthew that called for "an eye for an eye and a tooth for a tooth."

He had been dealt a killing blow that had slowly and painfully extinguished his life. His last act would be to take the three lives that had taken his life away.

For the past two months, he had obsessively plotted his grand exit. Tonight was the night the world, his world, would be justified. It would cost three people's lives, which was more than an eye for an eye, but his 15 years of suffering seemed worth three lives. Besides, he could not determine which of the three deserved to die more than the others.

A strong breeze rustled through the tree limbs that were just starting to show the new life of spring. The noise made his movement silent as he slowly moved toward the small compound. Jonathan was not worried about the half dozen security cameras that guarded the perimeter of the residence. By the time the police saw his deed on the recording, he would have already ended his own life.

He gave a final scan of the area to make sure no one was around to interfere. The only signs of life were the lights in windows of the nearby mansions. Like a cat, he quickly scaled a tree and easily stepped onto the flat top of the high brick wall that guarded the courtyard behind the residence. He'd been using this vantage point to stalk his prey and had noticed several routines he could exploit. The glowing dial on his watch said 8:55. He knew it was time to move.

After slightly adjusting the straps of his small backpack, he lowered himself over the wall and dropped to the ground. The sound of his landing was covered by the noise of a breezy night. With practiced movements, he worked his way to a large bush near the back door that opened onto a large brick patio. Swiftly, he removed his backpack and extracted an air-pressured dart gun. The dart was loaded with a powerful tranquilizer that would knock out its target in a matter of seconds.

Checking his watch was not necessary, but like a nervous twitch, he did so anyway. Any time now the Archbishop's aide would appear and call for Faith, the fat honey-colored tomcat, to come in for the night. Sensing movement on the other side of the large frosted glass door, Jonathan readied for the attack. Exactly as expected, a slightly built, yet handsome young man emerged and stepped out onto the patio. He was dressed in all black except for the white priest's collar.

"Here kitty, kitty," he called before dropping hard to the patio with a dull thud.

The duct tape was already out of Jonathan's backpack before the aide hit the bricks. Within 60 seconds, the tape had been applied to the aide's mouth, wrists, and ankles. The tranquilizer would wear off soon enough, but it would be hours before he would be able to free himself. By then, it would all be over.

Jonathan entered the house quietly and paused to listen for any sign of trouble. His recognizance had revealed only the Archbishop and his aide generally occupied the house during the evening and the Archbishop spent the evening in his study until he went upstairs to bed. Just in case, the dart gun was ready to silence any unexpected visitors. Hearing nothing, he proceeded toward the study, hoping his target was still there.

The old wood floors creaked under his feet, but detection was not a concern right now. Having never been in the house before, he only knew the general direction of the study. By process of elimination, he settled on a large, ornate wooden door with light seeping out from the half-inch gap near the floor. There was no pause to his motions or hedging of his intentions as he turned the glass doorknob and entered the room to face his demon.

The Archbishop was sitting in a large armchair reading an old bible. As he looked up to see who had interrupted his solitude, a hint of fear crossed his face. Jonathan crossed the room and stood silently in front of the older man, the dart gun hanging casually at his side. The old priest did not seem to recognize Jonathan, but he was sure the priest could feel the hatred in his eyes. The few seconds of silence as they faced each other seemed like a lifetime.

"Who are you?" The Archbishop's voice was calmer than Jonathan had expected.

"I wondered if you'd recognize me."

"Justin," he yelled, presumably calling for his aid.

"It's just you and me, just like the old days. You used to like being alone with me."

"The old days? Am I supposed to know you?"

"Maybe you'd recognize me if I dropped my pants."

"What? Who are you?"

Jonathan was very calm, considering the situation. Revenge is sweet, he thought, and then made a conscious decision to take his time and enjoy it. "Since you still do not know who I am, despite that clue, I can confirm I was not the only one."

"The only one . . . what are you talking about?"

"Tell you what, Father . . . I'll let you live if you just stop the bullshit and apologize for what you did to me and all the others."

"Look here, young man," he stated as he pushed himself up out of the big chair. Jonathan's foot smashed into the Archbishop's chest and sent him back to the chair with such force the chair fell over backwards. The younger man stepped forward and put his foot on his tormentor's throat with enough pressure to keep him from breathing.

"Last chance. Let me hear your apology or I'll crush your throat and you will die slowly trying to catch your breath. I'm gonna take my foot off and you will either apologize, or die."

After having the foot removed, the defeated priest shook his head and held his hand up to ask for time to catch his breath. "Okay," he said after a while, still breathing heavily. "I apologize for what I did to you."

"What about the others?

"Them too. I'm a weak man and can't help myself."

"You're not weak, you're a scum bag who likes to ruin the lives of little boys," the younger man stated evenly.

"No! I loved those boys," pleaded the priest. "You don't understand."

"No, I don't understand," he said calmly. The past 15 years had been a search for the answer. "Why? How could you do that to us?"

"It was for the good of the church."

"What?" That was not an answer he expected.

"Yes, as a servant of the Lord I give so much to others, to the church. God knows it's difficult on a priest to always give love, so He provides love for us. Man cannot always give love, he needs love in return. The boys were my love. They gave me the strength to serve the church. I loved those kids."

"Kids? Girls too? How many were there?"

"I don't know. Dozens of boys, but only a few girls. The girls were harder to convince."

He looked down at the terrified old man lying on the floor with his arms up defending his face. He was beyond being capable of feeling any pity for this man, or the other two that he would deal with soon. Now he had the answer he had come for, even if it was a ridiculous rationalization of a terrible sin. He did not even try to understand how this evil man had separated reality from his sins. The only thing that remained now was to make this man pay for his sins by inflicting fifteen years of revenge on him. Thoughts of this moment had often crossed his mind. Sweet, sweet revenge.

***

It was just after 8:00 a.m. when Nate was awake enough to consider the time of day. Normally Saturdays were just like any other day in his line of work, but this one had a special twist to it. He was coming off a hard week of work, long hours and a tough case. Actually, it had been an eight-day week and he was looking forward to a real weekend.

He heard the sound of her door shutting and the tapping of her running shoes as they ascended the flight of steps that ran parallel to his. He had declined her offer to go for a run this morning since sleep was more of an urgent need than exercise. Now that he had finally enjoyed a good night's sleep, he was second-guessing that decision.

He had only been dating Trista for a little over four months. It was sometimes awkward dating the girl who literally lived next door, but they had set ground rules provided clear boundaries. They both knew that everyone needs their own space from time to time, especially in a new relationship. That's why he had woken up in his loft apartment alone . . . boundaries. The thought of her made him second-guess that decision as well.

Grabbing the remote from the bedside table, he clicked the television to life and turned the volume up higher than necessary. The loud volume was a signal to Trista that he was awake and if she wanted to call, she could. They had briefly discussed going to breakfast at a small cafe down the street that served the best peanut butter and banana French toast in the world, or so their menu claimed.

Rolling out of bed, he flipped on the coffee pot before heading to the bathroom for his morning routine. When his phone rang, he knew it was her.

"Good morning, you sleep well?" she asked. He could hear the smile in her voice.

"Mornin'. Yep, like a ton of bricks."

"You up for some breakfast?" she asked. "I think I had dreams about peanut butter and banana French toast."

"Not sure I dreamed at all, but I'm hungry. How long you need?"

"'Bout 45 minutes. Just finished a run. Gonna jump in the shower. Trust me, you'll be glad I did."

"Maybe I'll hop over and join you," he said flirtatiously.

"If you do, it will be more than 45 minutes until breakfast and I'm hungry."

"Suit yourself. Buzz me when you're ready." They didn't bother saying goodbye.

Fifty minutes later he got the call she was ready to go get breakfast. He walked out his front door and, as it closed behind him, he couldn't help but smile. He'd never forget their first meeting, which featured him holding a newspaper in nothing but his bathrobe after being locked out when the door blew closed. She had shown off her lock picking skills, let him back in and they had been together ever since.

The café was not very crowded, which was unusual. They slipped into a booth and gave their orders to the waitress as she poured coffee. It was not a fancy place, but the food and the service were good.

The French toast arrived and they paused their lively discussion about the latest stupid off-season move the Redskins had made. Conversation came easy to them and Nate knew he was falling for this petite blond with the big southern accent. She was the only person he'd even known from Alabama and she never ceased to amaze him. She was smart, funny, beautiful, and could pick a lock as quick as any burglar.

If there was a stumbling block between the two, it was their jobs. A DC Homicide Detective and a reporter were a natural mismatch. Nate's job often took him away from her without a moment's notice and she worried for his safety. Cops naturally held a disdain for reporters, but the focus of Trista's job was the real source of Nate's disgust. She was the lead political reporter for *The Washington Post* and Nate hated *The Post* and considered politicians to be a step below the scumbags he locked up.

Like the relationship boundaries they had set up as neighbors, they had mutually agreed to avoid detailed discussions about their jobs. Nate always sugarcoated the truth about the dangerous situations he faced daily. Such details would just worry her. Avoiding the discussion of politics in Washington, D.C. was difficult, but they rarely talked about what story Trista was working on.

Nate often checked the byline on *Post* articles looking for her name, but rarely read the story. He had made a game of the placement of her articles and always congratulated her on making the front page. He actually liked that she sometimes exposed evil deeds by the corrupt political system, but he hated that her job exposed her to these people. The first and only time she had taken him to a political event she was covering had not gone well.

Some things are best kept apart and he knew how hard it would be to build a lasting relationship with such a divide.

"Whatcha wanna do today?" he asked, right before shoveling another bite into his mouth.

"Would it be terribly unromantic to suggest the Holocaust Museum?"

"Yes, but we can do it anyway."

She smiled with a flirtatious intent. "How 'bout I make it up to you by cooking you dinner tonight?"

"Ah, that sounds good. Are you on the menu?"

"Maybe, but first I'm going to take a big risk."

"Yeah, what?"

"Well, Nate Romano," she said with emphasis on his last name. "This southern gal is going to make Italian."

"Oh, that is gusty. Do I have to clean my plate before I get dessert?"

"As long as you don't say it's not as good as your mother used to make, you'll probably be okay."

Their laughter was interrupted by the chirping of Nate's cell phone. The playful mood they were enjoying ended. Duty was calling

***

There are some people in this world who would not be missed if they disappeared and the vast population of homeless people in Washington, DC were among them. Most simply ignored the homeless, but Jake Rivers saw opportunity in the despair.

Rivers was on the hunt. His white passenger van cruised the early morning streets slowly and deliberately. Few other cars were on the road this early on a Saturday morning. Like other animals, early morning was a good time to hunt the homeless. If you slept on the streets, morning was time to relocate from your secret hiding place which was often compromised when the city awoke.

Rivers saw what appeared to be a mother and two scraggly looking girls and knew he had an easy score. He pulled his van over to the curb and rolled down the window. "Good morning ladies and God bless. Can I offer you a ride over to the mission for a hot breakfast and a place to shower?"

The mother looked at Jake and then glanced at the side of the van obviously reading "Capitol Area Mission" written on the side.

"Capitol Mission? Where's that?" asked the mother.

"We're located on 13th Street North-west. We're operated by New Age Christ Ministries. I'm Jake, a volunteer, out looking for folks who need some help. We have some decent food and a nice place to clean up."

"It's kinda far away. Will you bring us back here later?"

"Sure. Hop on in."

The van was warm and comfortable and Jake knew the thought of a real shower was dreamlike for the girls. He needed to know everything about their desperate situation and he gently probed the mom on their way to the Mission. How long had they been on the street? Did they have any family in the area? Where did they stay at night? She politely answered his questions as she helped the two girls unzip their coats.

Her name was Kristen Carr and her two young girls were 6-year old Sarah and 4-year old Mini. They had been on the street for a year and Kristen seemed determined to get their life back on track. Her husband's suicide, after pissing away every nickel they had in an Atlantic City casino, had taken her life away in an instant. She had never worked before and had trusted her husband to take care of everyday needs. She'd been on the street a year now, and seemed quite proud she had mastered the art of surviving. She even confided in him that getting off the streets was next on her to-do list.

After 15 minutes on the quiet morning streets of DC, the van pulled into a large garage door in the back of a warehouse. The automatic door clicked to life and closed before he had come to a complete stop. The garage was large, but mostly empty. Another van with the same name painted on the side was parked next to them.

"Here we are. Why don't we get you some food and then you can get cleaned up?" Jake offered.

He led them to a door that would take them into the Mission. He held the door for them and Kristen led the way while holding Sarah and Mini by the hand. The door led to a small, windowless room with another door on the opposite wall with a sign taped to it that said, "Welcome to Capitol Area Mission." They moved slowly towards the other door, but they never made it.

The canister bounced across the floor as the gas hissed from the small cap. Kristen looked back just in time to see the door shut, trapping the three of them inside. She dropped the girl's hands and tried the door with the Mission sign. Locked. She ran to the other door, but it was also locked.

Jake listened outside the door. Jake could tell panic was setting in as she banged on the door in a futile attempt to save them. He could hear the girls coughing but soon that stopped and all was quiet. Jake smiled as he thought about how easy it was to manipulate people.

***

Senator Terry McDermott had just finished a CNN appearance to discuss his latest bill – his latest attempt to purge any reference to God in American doctrine. This time it was the phrase "In God We Trust" from all U.S. currency. His argument had been compelling, although not popular. As an atheist, he said the phrase was an obvious attempt to have the government convert him away from atheism. If America was truly going to stand for religious freedom, even unpopular religions like Atheism must be protected.

He had not always been an Atheist and the good people of Missouri would not have elected him had they known. Actually, he was not an Atheist when he was elected. He had converted, if you can call it that, when a tornado had ripped through his hometown of Joplin and killed his parents, wife, and two daughters. If there were a God, he would never have allowed such devastation.

While most understood how Senator McDermott could lose faith after such a horrific event, very few supported him in his effort to rid America of any and all mentions of God. After all, some surveys showed as many as 95% of Americans believed in God. But McDermott was not deterred. He was on a mission.

Senate Bill 1363 had been nicknamed Bill 666 by many Republicans. That was particularly upsetting because Senator McDermott was a member of the Republican Party. There had been a few attempts to oust him from the Party, but to do so meant the loss of a vote. The Senate was evenly divided between the two parties and any loss of a vote could be politically devastating.

There were no co-sponsors of his bill from either party. The best he hoped for was to get it out of committee and put to a vote on the Senate floor. If he could just have his day for debate, he had convinced himself, the righteousness of his cause would prevail. Most believed the Bill would never see the light of day in Committee, much less the Senate floor.

While he was on his own in the political realm, there was some support from outside Washington, D.C. Unfortunately, none of that support was from his constituents in Missouri. In fact, the process of a recall election had begun. McDermott knew his time was short and he needed to push hard if he was going to have any success.

The most important supporter of Senator McDermott was Jill Demetri from Massachusetts. She was a rather eccentric lady, but worth billions of dollars thanks to her late husband. She was giving the Senator millions of dollars to make sure this issue did not die. No one seemed to know why she supported this cause; most chalked it up just to her being nuts.

McDermott had discovered that the best way to stir up debate on the issue was to be hostile to the religious community. He had offered amendments to take away the tax-exempt status of all religious institutions and his Foundation for Religious Freedom, backed by Mrs. Demetri, had initiated dozens of lawsuits against school systems that allowed the Pledge of Allegiance or any type of prayer.

Privately, he chuckled at how easy it was to rile the churches. They were his best source of publicity. He would never have been asked to appear on CNN this morning if the well-known TV preacher Reverend Jerry Allen had not gone ballistic when the Foundation for Religious Freedom sued almost every jurisdiction in Pennsylvania for carrying a copy of the Bible and Koran in public libraries. Every time he enraged the powerful religious establishment, he got more free publicity.

Hell may have no fury like a woman scorned, but heaven has no nemesis like a man devastated.

***

Amir Assad was enjoying an Egyptian tea at the Wired Puppy Specialty Coffee and Tea Shop in City Center, Boston. He had never acquired a taste for coffee, but coffee shops had provided him a good place to observe American culture. It was amazing how stupid these infidels were, spending $3.00 on a cup of caffeine. Then again, life was pretty good here.

In his heart he knew he had sold out to the luxuries of life in America. The finer things were not part of his country's culture and his leaders believed the very luxuries he had grown to appreciate were the trappings of all the evil in America. No matter – he could separate right from wrong and considered it a necessary part of his job to embed himself in the extravagant culture of his enemy. Or, at least, he had convinced himself this was true.

In an hour, he'd have to deal with the other side of reality when he met with his handler before returning to DC. Amir knew his new assignment would be significant, but he did not know what that meant yet. He had noticed the communications he had read from the Muslim leadership had recently started to emphasize this was a religious war he was helping to fight. The sooner America realized that fact, the sooner his country would be victorious.

This new rhetoric worried Amir. He knew the citizens of America would not be as easy to manipulate if they realized their religion was being attacked. He had read about the brutality Christians and Jews had displayed for centuries when they felt their religions were being challenged. America was a relatively new nation and had not been in a religious war since the Revolutionary War had separated them from the Church of England. Most Americans did not think of that war as a religious war either, but Amir saw the root of that war to be the battle of religious freedom verse state control.

In his mind, this same issue of state control of religion was the basis of the current world war between Muslims and Christians. His religion was not only the guiding light of his personal life, but also that of his government. The Christian countries had proven themselves to be morally corrupted. By separating the principles of religion from their governments, they had allowed their citizens to spin out of control.

These corrupt and immoral countries were a threat to Muslim nations. If his people were exposed to the spiritually bankrupt way of life in Christian nations, it would lead them down a path away from Allah. Amir realized this because it was exactly what he was experiencing sitting in this coffee shop sipping a three-dollar cup of the drug that made America work. He had been exposed to a lot of wealth and luxury in the 18 years he had lived in this country and he knew he had been corrupted. He had given his life to evil so he could protect his people from it. It was a sacrifice he considered to be his duty.

America was not the only country that threatened the Muslim Nation, but it was the big fish. Defeat America and the rest of the Christian empire would fall. 'Defeat' was not a military term, but a cultural assault. Amir and his other spiritual warriors would not be satisfied until America was run under Muslim law. The further they could drive out Judeo/Christian ideals from Government, the easier it would be to insert the purity of Muslim law.

Amir had already scored a political defeat of America when it came to protecting Muslim control on the world's energy supply; he assumed his next assignment would be to send the western world a message that Muslim law was the law of the land, even in America. Stopping America from harvesting its rich oil reserves in ANWR and other places would be easy compared to the next step in this religious war.

Chapter 2

When the caller ID on Nate's phone showed Pete's name, Nate knew his plans for the day were about to be changed. Pete Marcus was a veteran Detective in the DC police force. He was the chosen one to tackle all the politically sensitive cases, and in DC, there were many.

"Hey Pete, what's up?"

"Nate. Sorry."

"It's all right," Nate replied, even though it did not feel "all right" to him.

"Got a big one. A really big one. Need some help."

"Sure," he replied, fighting off the urge to scream. He didn't mind the work, but he did hate to have to cancel his day with Trista. "What ya got?"

"The simple version: three dead priests, high-ranking priests. But that's just the tip of the iceberg."

Trista had left the breakfast table and gone to the ladies room when Pete had called. When she returned, he was paying the check. His disappointed expression was enough to let her know their trip to the Holocaust Museum would have to wait.

"You gotta go?"

"Yep, sorry."

"Any chance we're still on for dinner and dessert?" she added as an enticing afterthought.

"Not sure. This case sounds pretty bad. Three dead priests. Can I check-in later to let you know?"

"Yikes, that sounds awful. Just keep me posted and we'll see if it all works out."

***

There was a lot of activity on the street as Nate pulled up to the Archbishop's compound. The full crime team had been called out on this Saturday morning and the area was abuzz with activity. Also present were, of course, the news media. Nate's natural hatred of the media was tempered now that he was dating Trista, but it was hard to suppress his annoyance on a crime scene.

There were three satellite trucks doing live broadcasts, probably to an international audience given the reach of the Catholic Church. From past experience on big cases like this, Nate knew they were simply broadcasting something was happening, but they were not sure what.

He had to park more than a block away from the scene, and even then the only space available was in front of a fire hydrant. He successfully avoided the press and made it past the crime scene tape to the front door. Pete was there just inside the door issuing orders to crime scene techs and uniform officers. He acknowledged Nate with a head nod and continued directing traffic. Nate waited patiently for his opening.

"Hey Nate. Thanks for coming."

"No problem," he lied. "Whatchu need?"

"First, you need to see the crime scene and the video."

"Video?"

"Yep, the killer left a video. It kinda explains everything. Rather disturbing and amazing at the same time."

"Okay, then what?"

"I want you to handle the non-crime-scene stuff. We have plenty on the killer. Basically, the video is a full confession and if he is true to his word, we will find him dead. There are some rather amazing accusations of a cover-up by the church and very high-ranking politicians. That's what I want you to dig into."

It went without saying anything and everything Nate discovered would come back to Pete and only Pete would be talking to the press, or anyone else. This case was going to be very complicated and sensitive. Nate was happy to let the savvy Pete Marcus handle the lead.

"Got it." Nate started to walk away to see the crime scene and let Pete return to directing traffic.

"Nate," he called and waited for Nate to turn around. "Thanks," Pete said to complete the thought.

Nate simply nodded his head and went to find the crime scene. The swirl of activity down the hallway made it easy to locate. As he entered the door to the Archbishop's office, the gruesomeness of the scene was remarkable. There was not a lot of blood, but the position of the body and the object protruding from it were disturbing.

The Archbishop's torso was lying face down on the large desk and his pants were pulled down to his knees. The handle end of an umbrella was sticking up toward the ceiling with the pointed end jammed into his ass. Nate took in the entire scene and determined the leader of the CSI team – a middle aged forensic scientist with a hardened scowl and colored brown hair. Nate recognized her from other crime scenes and knew she was all business.

"Cheryl," he began. "Not exactly your standard crime scene."

She turned to notice him. "Oh hey, Detective Romano. Yeah, this isn't just a normal day in the office."

"Can you give me the short story and tell me about the video?"

"Sure. This is a very staged crime scene. The vic was killed and then placed in this position. Initial cause of death appears to be strangulation, but I'd wait on the ME to call that. Plenty of prints, so it does not seem there was any intent to cover up evidence. The video, according to Marcus, is a confession, so I'm guessing the umbrella means something."

"Yeah, good call. Who's seen the video?"

"Just Detective Marcus as far as I know."

"Where is it?"

"On a flash drive in a baggie with the rest of the evidence," she said pointing to a pile of stuff in the corner. "It's been dusted, so feel free to take it."

"Thanks." Nate resisted his natural curiosity to examine the crime scene more closely and stuck to his assigned task. He retrieved the flash drive and borrowed one of the CSI laptops to watch it. He found a quiet place and plugged in the flash drive. The video auto-loaded and started to play. Twenty minutes later, Nate sat in stunned silence, blown away about what he had just watched. "Holy crap!" were the only words he could muster.

***

The fog was slowly lifting from Kristen's brain. She blinked her eyes, but they refused to focus. When she tried to rub her eyes to clear them, she realized her hands had been bound behind her back. A flashback to the locked room and the gas canister filled her with sudden panic. Sarah, Mini? Where were her girls?

She struggled to free her hands, but there was no give. There was a cutting feeling against her wrist – handcuffs, she guessed. Her feet were free and she used them to swing herself into a sitting position. Her scream was muffled by the gag she now realized was restraining her mouth.

The room was becoming gradually clear as her eyes came into focus. She felt unsteady, rather dizzy in fact, and decided not to risk standing just yet. The initial panic she had felt was subsiding and her street-smart demeanor was returning. She was still alive and that meant all was not lost yet.

Looking around the room, she started to plan her next move. There were no windows and the ceiling and walls were plaster. The door looked to be metal and sturdy. She decided to try the handle even if it was almost certainly locked.

Rising slowly, she stood still for a few seconds to gain her balance. Feeling reasonably solid on her feet, she shuffled over to the door, turned her back so her hands could reach the handle. It did not budge. Looking around, she saw no options. A lesser-willed person might have been overcome by frustration and dissolved into tears. The street had taught her to fight. There was no time to waste on worthless emotions. Instead, she got angry.

The first blow from her foot against the door made the entire room vibrate. She screamed as best she could, but it wasn't much. The second kick was not quite as hard as the first, but made plenty of noise. Pausing for a second to listen for any activity outside her cell, she gave her mind time to think. The door handle was a lever style and could work to free her mouth.

She bent over and tried to hook the edge of the gag on the handle. The cloth had been tied very tight, but she managed to force the point of the handle between her cheek and the gag. She twisted her jaw and used the door handle to try to pull the gag loose. There was great pain in what she was doing, but she was determined to make some progress. After a few minutes of struggle, she finally worked the gag over her chin, but before she could unhook it from the door handle, the door burst open slamming her head so hard she saw stars. The gag stayed hooked to the door as her knees buckled and left her hanging, literally.

Just as she was about to blackout completely, she felt a strong pair of hands grab her and lift her off the hangman's noose. Before she could recover her footing, she was thrown on the floor face down with enough force to let her know who was in charge. Feeling she had little to lose, she verbally lashed out screaming, "Let me go, you son-of-a-bitch!"

Before she could start a second round of verbal assault, she felt the needle plunge into her arm. She managed to scream, "Where are my girls?" before the effects of the strong sedative started to hit her. The words were still being said clearly in her head, but the words that escaped her mouth were incomprehensible. Seconds later she lay still, sedated into oblivion.

***

Amir crossed the street and headed towards the rundown grey brick office building. This is what Americans refer to as the "bad part of town," but compared to the poorer sections of Saudi Arabia, his homeland, it was in good shape. He patted the right side of his jacket and felt his holstered 45 and felt safe. Americans were sometimes thugs, but they were no match for his culture when it came to violence.

The office building was vacant, but according to the address he'd been given, this was the place he was to meet his handler. He had not seen the man, known only as Murdock to him, for three years. In fact, he had seen him only once, with all other communications coming via a secure satellite phone. Amir was expecting to get his new mission today; all he had been told was that it was a significant change in his duties.

He casually looked around and found no other sign of life on the street. The area was mostly abandoned office buildings and closed businesses. The building he was told to enter looked closed and abandoned, but in better shape than many of the surrounding properties. An uneasy feeling swept over him, starting in his stomach and working its way into his throat.

After a deep breath to try to calm his nerves, he grabbed the handle of the door and pulled it open. He was almost surprised that it opened. Reaching below his jacket, he released the safety on the 45. There was no light inside and he could barely see by the dim glow coming through the glass door and a window toward the back of the building. Taking two steps in, he stopped and listened. Nothing.

There was a lit exit sign he could see towards the back of the building. Other than that, the building was devoid of furnishings and lights. He walked slowly toward the back of the building and the exit sign. The building opened from the narrow entrance hallway into a large vacant room. At first Amir didn't see the dark figure of a man in the corner of the large room, but the slow movement of the man stepping out from the corner caught his eye.

"Hello my friend," said the dark figure.

"Hello to you, my friend. I heard this building is for sale," Amir replied.

"Everything is for sale, at the right price."

"That is true, my wise friend." With that, the rehearsed password dialog was completed and the two men move forward and embraced.

"It really is good to see you, Amir."

"And you, too, Murdock. It has been a long time."

"Yes, it has. And you have been doing great work. Your people are very grateful, or at least they would be if we could tell them of your success."

"Doing Allah's work is my pleasure. Praise Allah."

"Indeed, praise Allah. Now, let's discuss your next assignment in our war against the evil Americans and their weak god."

Thirty minutes later, Amir left the building with a flash drive full of information and a head full of thoughts. He could not believe his responsibilities had advanced this far. His comfortable life in the confines of America's capital city was coming to an end, and if they were to be successful, many others' comfortable lives would be coming to an end. Finally, America would realize they were in a religious war, even if they did not want to admit it.

***

Nate's assigned job was to find out if there was any truth to the many allegations he'd heard in the killer's video. Experience had taught him the best method to finding the truth was to start in the center of the situation and work his way out from there. The center of this labyrinth of conspiracy and cover up was the Catholic Church – although, he suspected that was more like the beginning of a long chain rather than a true center.

He had called ahead to let the Archdiocese of Washington know he was coming. He had been connected to Auxiliary Bishop David Charron, who had already heard of the murders and was audibly shaken by the loss of three close colleagues. Bishop Charron was essentially second in command at the Archdiocese, until today. Now, with the murder of Archbishop Patrick Reilly, he was forced to assume the lead role in the worst possible circumstance. Nate had not bothered to tell Bishop Charron there was more to this case than the murders. Such news was best delivered in person so he could read the reaction on his face.

The headquarters for the nearly 600,000 Catholics in the DC area was located in Hyattsville, MD, just outside the District. Nate pulled up to the small brick guardhouse at the Archdiocese and let down his window. The wrought iron gates leading to the compound were closed. There was a Maryland State Police car just inside the gate and a uniformed officer guarding the front door. The guard at the gate was armed and understandably tense. Nate was an expected visitor, but his credentials were carefully checked and verified before the gates were opened.

An older nun, Sister Mary Elizabeth, greeted him at the doorway and led him to an ornate parlor with furniture that could have been borrowed from Buckingham Palace. He was informed Bishop Charron was on a conference call and would be a few minutes. A glass of water was offered, but he declined and pulled out his phone so he could use this free time to get a few things done.

Nate had to suppress his instinct to charge full speed ahead on this case. Normally his cases involved drug dealers, or some hothead who murdered his cheating spouse. Such cases required his hard-charging, direct approach. This case involved high-ranking politicians and religious leaders, and he could expect every move of the investigation to be criticized and analyzed. He was going to have to hold tight to some of the accusations on the video for longer than he liked or this case would get crazy. Sooner or later, he knew, it was going to get crazy, but for now he needed to control things as best he could.

He decided to send a text to Pete Markus to recommend he not share the contents of video with anyone until they had a chance to discuss strategy. He got an almost instant response with a simple "Good idea" on the screen.

Next, he sent a text to Trista to see if they could still meet for dinner. Unfortunately, it would be a working dinner now. He was going to need her help on the political side of things. Her contacts and familiarity with the politicians mentioned in the video would save him hours of work. He just had to figure out how to convince her to help without letting her write a story about it. Her job at *The Washington Post* would be greatly enhanced by uncovering a story like this. To ask her to help and not let her write about it was not fair, but giving your girlfriend a story like this would likely get him removed from the case. He'd figure it out, but not until dinner.

A smile appeared on his face as he read her reply: *Sure. Just dinner? ;-)*

Before he could reply, Sister Mary Elizabeth was back. "Bishop Charron will see you now."

Without another word, she turned and left the room. Quickly he slipped his phone back into the breast pocket of his sports coat and followed her across the entrance foyer and down a hall toward the back of the building. He was having trouble keeping up until the Sister suddenly stopped at a large wooden door. With a hand on the doorknob she knocked three times firmly on the door with the other. Her ear was almost touching the door as if waiting for a verbal command. Nate never heard the command, but the sister opened the door and stepped back to let him in to what he assumed was Bishop Charron's office.

"Thanks, Sister," he managed to say, just before she shut the door behind him.

Bishop Charron rose from behind his desk and approached Nate with his hand extended. There was a sad, drawn look to his face, except for his eyes, which were clear and focused.

"Good morning, Detective Romano. Bishop Charron," he announced himself.

"I wish it was a good morning, Bishop. Sorry for your loss."

"Thank you. It is tough day for many. God works in mysterious ways, ours is not to question why."

"Actually—" Nate stumbled with his words. "It is my job to find out why. This is not the best time for you, but I need to ask you a few questions."

"I understand, Detective. You need to find out why one man has followed a path of evil. Maybe along the way we will discover God's will."

For the next 45 minutes, Nate questioned Bishop Charron on his duties, his relationship to the victims, and the church's knowledge of the killer, Jonathan Hill. He left with more questions than answers and a promise from Bishop Charron to fully cooperate and turn over any records of Mr. Hill's interaction with the church.

Stepping out into the mid-day sunshine of a beautiful spring morning in the Nation's Capital, Nate looked around to get his bearings and consider his next move. There were so many loose ends to follow-up on he knew he would need to prioritize them and stay focused. It was too soon to pursue the political aspects of the case, so he decided to work on the killer's history to see what that could tell him.

Chapter 3

Jill Demetri was used to getting what she wanted. She had married the love of her life in her early twenties and had enjoyed the many spoils as she watched her husband grow his business and their personal fortune for more than 40 years. His death eight years ago had left a huge hole in her soul and her search to fill this void had led her to Senator Terry McDermott and his cause of ridding the United States government of religion.

Massachusetts was a small state, but power in Washington, DC was measured by the size of your bank account. In Jill's case, power was measured by her willingness to spend large amounts of her wealth in the political arena. She had bankrolled several causes, most of them far outside mainstream politics. Most insiders considered her nothing more than an eccentric fool, but no one wanted to be on opposite sides of an issue with her.

Money has the power to intimidate; foolish money scares everyone who is not a fool.

She knew Senator McDermott rarely returned to his home state of Missouri and for good reason. His constituents were more likely to organize a recall vote for him than support his cause of forcing religious separation in America. In the time she'd known him, he'd made more trips to Massachusetts to visit her, than to his home state.

Their relationship was more of a game than a real kindred bond. They both knew he wanted her money and to get it, he needed to butter her up. She was lonely and craved company, but she was also wise about the relationship between money and politics. They both knew he was not simply conning a confused old lady out of her fortune. She knew his issue and understood even her vast riches would not cause real change in Congress.

Real change, as she saw it, would come from the other way laws were made in this country – the courts. Money worked in Congress to maintain the status quo, but no politician had the guts to lead the way in changing even less controversial issues, like reforming the US Postal System. Getting re-elected was the only thing that really mattered to a DC politician and changing the status quo was a sure-fired way to get voted out of office.

Senator McDermott was different. She no longer considered him a DC politician. After his family had been killed, his perspective had changed. He was now on a mission and was not concerned about getting re-elected.

He politely stood as she entered the parlor of her Massachusetts mansion. "Good afternoon, Jill."

"Sit, sit, sit," she commanded pointing to the chair he had just vacated. "I may be old and rich, but you don't have to treat me like the queen, for goodness sake."

"I see you're still as fiery as ever."

"'Fiery' is a nice word. Most just think I'm an old bitch."

"And they think I'm a fool. We make a rather odd team I suppose."

"Screw those spineless wimps. A fool and a bitch can get more done in a day than the whole worthless bunch combined. That's why those idiots are scared of us."

She watched him as he looked off into the distance. "Senator, what's that look on your face?"

"Sorry, just lost in thought. Can I ask you a personal question?"

"Ask what you want, I'm not promising any answers."

"I should have asked you this before. Why? Why are you as passionate about this issue as I am?"

She looked off to her right and stared at the picture of her late husband that hung majestically on the wall. "Fair question. Damn you for asking, but fair question. Someday, I'll answer it. Not today; we have important things to discuss." She waved her hand dismissively, as if to fan away smoke. "Richmond. Tell me about Richmond, Senator."

"Sure. Could be a big one, or at least the start of a big one. I was contacted by a man name Scott Willard who owns a few health clubs in Virginia. He saw me on MSNBC one day and said he wanted to join the fight. To make a long story short, he is mad at the politicians in the Charlottesville area for subsidizing a YMCA that competes with him."

"A YMCA? What's wrong with that?"

"Most people forget, but the 'C' in YMCA stands for Christian."

"Of course. Funny how we forget things like that."

"Also, because they are a religious organization, they get a nice tax advantage over Mr. Willard's business. We are preparing a lawsuit to be filed in the Federal Court in Richmond. I had trouble finding a major law firm to represent us, but Willard introduced me to an independent lawyer who used to be a player in one of the biggies, but had some issues."

"Issues? Anything to worry about?"

"Not for us. He had a drug habit and a gambling problem. He lost his job, had a messy divorce and hit bottom. Bankruptcy, suspended by the VA BAR for six months. He's clean now and needs business. Our case will be much needed for him. He's very good, or at least he was. Won some big cases before his life fell apart. Seems to have it back together again."

"What's his name?"

"Max Pigman."

"Ha," she chuckled. "Sounds like our type of guy. How much do you need?"

He gazed at the ceiling as if he was adding up numbers in his head. "A million."

Now it was her turn to be dramatic. She broke his eye contact and was quiet for a moment. Without looking at him, she said, "Whatever you need. I love this case, mostly for the business angle. It could blossom into the courts taking away the tax-exempt status of churches. That would be sweet justice."

They both smiled, but Jill knew they were pleased for different reasons.

***

Sarah and Mini were both scared, but neither showed it. Living on the street had taught them showing fear was a weakness that did not help you survive. They sat huddled next to each other on the floor of the windowless empty room, tucked away in a corner farthest from the one door.

Sarah was the older of the two, having just turned six years old last month. There had been no birthday celebration, but her mother had made the day as special as she could. They had used one ticket to get all three of them onto the Metro and spent most of the day inside the underground mall at Crystal City.

Sarah could remember life before the street and knew what they were going through was not normal. Mini, on the other hand, was only four and was oblivious to the hardship of living on the street. To her, it was just normal life.

The one thing both girls knew was Mommy was not there and something bad was happening. It was not normal for them to be apart. Rule number one for them on the street was always stick together. The only times Mommy had ever left them alone was when she had to go talk to men and when that happened, she had always made sure they were in a safe spot.

This was not a safe spot; it was a jail cell. They had woken up here and no one had checked on them for hours. They were hungry, but that was normal. Speaking had been avoided because they did not want anyone to know they were awake. They had whispered a few times, but their throats were so dry and tight even that had hurt.

A noise outside the room startled them. They heard a key being inserted in the door and knew it was not their mommy. The darkness of the room was pierced by a bright light as the door opened slowly. The girls huddled tighter together, blinking their eyes trying to get them to focus on the danger at the door.

The silhouette of a man was all they could see. He moved slowly towards them. "Would you girls like to see your mother?"

That got their attention, but neither girl moved except to huddle closer together. Sarah's arms instinctively wrapped around her little sister to protect her. The man stood over them now and Sarah could see his face. It was the man who called himself Jake, from the van.

"Who are you and why did you take our mommy?" Sarah asked softly.

The man dropped to one knee in front of them and offered a seemingly pleasant smile. "I'm helping your mommy. She wants, more than anything, to get a nice home for you two. I'm going to help you get that new home. Do you want to go see her now?" he asked again.

Sarah nodded her head without hesitation.

"Okay, grab your sister's hand and follow me."

Sarah stood and extended her hand. Mini gave her a concerned look, but reached out anyway and took her sister's hand. They did as asked and followed the man out of the room. The lights were brighter out here and the girls squinted while trying to look for their mommy. They went down a plain looking hall and turned right into a larger room with furniture. It looked like a normal family room, as well as Sarah could remember, until she realized it had no windows.

Becoming more cautious, she stopped moving forward. "Where's my mommy?" she asked.

"I'm going to get her now. You girls sit on that couch and enjoy that bowl of fruit while I go get your mom."

They had been too scared to think about food, but the sight of the big bowl of grapes and bananas got their attention. Jake moved towards a door at the other end of the room, which provided the girls a clear path to the couch and fruit. They slowly edged their way, keeping one eye on this man and the other on the fruit.

"Good girls. I'll be right back with your mommy," he said, as he turned and left the room.

Sarah thought about trying to escape, but the fruit and the thought of seeing her mommy was more powerful.

***

Nate entered the killer's apartment slowly, absorbing every detail with his trained detective eyes. Jonathan Hill was not a rich man based on the shabby old apartment building and the rough neighborhood. The crime lab team had finished collecting evidence and was packing up their gear. They looked up as he entered.

"Detective Romano," he announced, as he flashed his badge. He recognized all three members of the team, but couldn't remember their names.

A young woman in army boots and hospital scrubs removed her latex glove and extended her hand in greeting. "Laurie Ganz, Detective. We're just wrapping up, can we turn the scene over to you?"

"Sure. Can you give me a quick summary?" Nate sized her up quickly using his detective superpowers. She was young, but confident beyond her years. Maybe she had already seen more of life than most people her age, or maybe there was some hardship she'd overcome that had molded her. However it had happened, she now exuded a deft professional confidence that said, "I'm different, but I'm good, so deal with it."

"Yeah. You the lead on this case?"

"No, Pete Markus is. I'm working the back story tryin' to figure out what made this nut crack."

"You mean who, not what," she said nodding her head towards the back of the apartment. "He seems to have an obsession with politicians and priests. Whole room full of photos back there."

"What else?"

"We took his computer and smart phone. Have to wait on the results for that. Lived alone. Unis' talked to the neighbors, but you'll have to read their report. The body was on the bed. No visible signs of cause. He was just lying there, fully clothed." She quickly scrolled through the pictures on her camera until she found the images of the body to show him.

"M.E. have any guesses?"

"Said it might be sleeping pills cause he looked so calm and at peace. That and the empty prescription bottle in the bathroom," she added with a smile.

"What else you guys taking back?"

"Backpack. A couple weapons. Very simple scene for us. Heard the other scenes were pretty ugly."

"Yeah. Disturbing is the word I'd use for the one I saw."

"That's it. We'll be out of your way in five."

"Thanks, Laurie."

Nate wandered to the back room to see the photos. It was the extra bedroom of the small two-bedroom apartment. The walls were literally covered with photos and newspaper articles. He noticed right away they were all men.

Many of the faces were familiar to Nate, but he did not know their names. As he focused his attention to the scene, he realized many of the pictures had newspaper articles tacked to the wall behind them. He removed a picture of a familiar looking silver haired man that appeared to have been printed from the Internet. The newspaper article behind it had a picture of the same man standing behind a podium. The caption read, "Senator Mike Stiano (R, Indiana) speaks out against Obamacare's birth control requirement."

Nate recognized the name from the killer's video. He'd have to watch the video again to see what part Stiano had played in the alleged conspiracy to protect the Catholic Church. He panned the room and realized the pictures were not just randomly pinned to the wall. There was a pattern, a hierarchy of sorts, to how they were placed.

It was a safe bet the names of these men were going to be the same names in the video. It was also a safe bet Nate would get to know these men very well.

***

Father Charron was a good man, a true man of the cloth. He had never really wanted to be a leader in the church, but his talents had been recognized early in his career. He had flourished as the leader of a nice parish in the DC suburbs in Maryland and had quickly been promoted to the Basilica of the National Shrine of the Immaculate Conception, the largest church in America.

Now Father Charron was the Auxiliary Bishop, the second highest-ranking leader in the Greater Washington Catholic Diocese. Even with his fast rise to lofty positions in the church, he remained a humble man. This was not the path he had chosen; it was the path God had chosen for him.

Now, with Archbishop Reilly dead, he had assumed the lead role in the Diocese, at least on an interim basis. His faith in God's divine ways gave him the strength to do what he must now do to serve the church.

It had been eight hours since he had first learned of the tragic death of his three colleagues. He had still not had time to progress past the first step in the grieving process – denial. He had been too busy dealing with crisis to even think about allowing himself to think about the fate of his friends and mentors.

The door to his office was closed and locked and he sat at his desk all alone. He had instructed his secretary to go home and the nuns to leave him alone for the remainder of the evening. The enormity of the situation settled on him like fog on the mountain. Slowly his brain unwound and allowed his duties to be obscured by the thoughts of the situation.

A feelingly of helplessness overcame him. Had his mentor, the Archbishop, really been a child molester? How could a holy man have succumbed to such evil and, more importantly, how could he have not seen this evil in his mentor? Tears flowed down his cheeks and his jaw retracted to allow the sobs to flow freely.

Anger is something he had learned to control very early in his service to the church, but this was not something he could suppress. He was not really sure if he was angry with the Archbishop or the killer, Jonathan Hill. Maybe it was both.

An hour later, exhausted from the rage that had overcome him, he wiped away his last tear and pulled himself together. The church needed him to be strong and he reached out to the Bible in front of him with a caressing touch. When he needed strength, he had always found it in the Holy Scriptures.

He opened the book to a random spot in the middle pages and looked down. "For we can do nothing against the truth, but for the truth." (2 Corinthians 13:8)

The truth was what he'd have to find out before he could move forward.

***

They had agreed to meet for dinner at 7:00 p.m. Nate would bring the wine to go with the tortellini and sausage she was making. Trista's homemade sauce was simmering on the stove by the time she heard him walking up the wooden steps to his adjacent loft apartment just after 6:00 p.m.

She was a bit nervous about making Italian for a man whose mother was born in Italy, but she had done her homework. The menu she'd selected was more of an American version of Italian cuisine, heavy on pasta and meat, but the sauce was the real test. With the Internet and the Food Network at her disposal, she had learned many secrets about making sauces.

The key to sauces, as with most foods, was to use fresh ingredients. She had made a special trip to an authentic Italian grocery and had even purchased wooden spoons to stir the sauce because someone on the Food Network had mentioned metal spoons affected the taste. She had selected a simple red sauce with basil and oregano and the wonderful smell now filled her apartment.

A smile crossed her face as she contemplated his reaction to her efforts. Their relationship was comfortable and natural, but still fresh and exciting. She did not know where they were going as a couple, but she was sure they were falling in love.

Her grandmother had always told her love was when you found someone you liked better than yourself. Nate was very likeable to her. He was smart, handsome, and very funny. Despite being born in DC, he was a southern gentleman to her, which she knew was Nate's attempt to charm her pants off.

His charm had worked on her, despite her best efforts to play hard to get. There was a very strong physical attraction that had remained fresh after months of lovemaking. He was a giving lover and always took care of her needs. Tonight, she had needs and the thought of them between the sheets brought a coy smile to her face.

At 6:55 p.m. she heard Nate enter the door at the bottom of the steps that led to her loft apartment. Her unit was literally a mirror image of his and they had shared keys a few months ago, but not until their ground rules were well-established. Living next door to your lover was both convenient and inconvenient. Setting boundaries early in their relationship had worked out well.

"Hey there! Sure smells good in here," he commented upon reaching the top step holding a bottle of red wine.

"Thanks." She had noticed he was freshly showered and had a freshly pressed shirt on with his jeans. She appreciated his efforts to look good for their date.

Without another word she pointed at the apron she was wearing over her jeans and simple red blouse. The apron proclaimed, "Kiss the Cook!" He took her suggestion and they eased into a gentle, yet passionate kiss. His eyes were still closed as she pulled back and there was a big smile on his face.

"Mmm. That was nice," she breathed softly.

"Just doing what I was told." He nodded towards her apron.

"Dinner's all ready. Just need to plate it up. Pour a gal a glass of wine?"

"Sure thing. Looks like you've already started," he said, nodding toward a mostly empty wine glass on the counter.

"Cocktail hour waits for no one."

"Fine by me. Just gets you one step closer to getting drunk so I can take advantage of you," he said with a playful smile.

"Ha, ya think so, do you? Pretty sure you won't need to get me drunk." With that they embraced in another long kiss. Her arms went around his neck and pulled him gently into her. His hand grabbed her waist and pulled her hips into him as she subtly grinded into his crotch. His right hand slipped down to her left butt cheek and gave a good squeeze.

After a few seconds they broke apart and looked at each other, both with large smiles on their faces. She searched his eyes to see if this was just foreplay, or if dinner was going to have to wait. He seemed to be contemplating the same thing.

"Would it ruin your dinner if we didn't eat for a while?"

"I don't think so. How much longer?" she asked with a coy smile.

"Ten minutes at least."

"Ten minutes? Is that all you can muster. How about we take our time and then I'll have an excuse if dinner is not up to your standards?"

"Deal." They kissed briefly as if to seal the deal. His hands untied her apron and she slipped it over her head, letting it drop to the floor. She looked up to his face with a very happy smile. His hands started to work on the buttons of her blouse until it was completely open. Her black lace bra was peeking out and her hands were working on his belt. Not wanting to continue in her small kitchen, she took his hand and led the way to the bedroom.

An hour later the sausage was a bit over-cooked and dry, but otherwise the meal was a big hit. It had worked out well that they had had "dessert" before dinner because the dinner conversation was not very romantic. Nate had been guarded, almost secretive as he asked her for background on a half dozen members of Congress, including Indiana Senator Mike Stiano. He had explained his need to be mysterious and apologized for talking business on a date. She pretended she didn't mind the change of atmosphere for their evening.

She had not known much about all of them, but had given him some good tips about where to dig and what to look for. He apologized for having to pry her for information and promised her he'd do what he could to give her a heads up when the story was about to go public. It didn't make up for derailing their romantic evening, but she did a fine job of hiding her disappointment.

Chapter 4

The Catholic Church kept amazing records because it considered itself to be both the center of history and the curator of the future. Bishop Charron, like every other priest, had been trained to document everything, so history could be recorded accurately. As with any historic documentation, accuracy was in the hands of those who recorded it.

He felt a bit guilty searching through the private records of Archbishop Reilly, but he was driven by the need to find the truth. He had prayed and contemplated about where the facts might take him, but he accepted his role as leader of the church and was prepared for the burden the truth might carry.

He had not slept well and was up before any of the nuns who ran the Diocese. The Archbishop's private office was neat and tidy, but well used. The large roll-top desk had many battle scars and historical blemishes. This desk had likely been used by every Archbishop of the Diocese and may have originally been shipped in from the Vatican.

The office was not very large and he could swivel around in the desk chair to reach both of the files cabinets with little effort. Unfortunately, both cabinets were locked. They were not as old as the desk, but were made of solid wood. Turning back to the desk, he looked in the main center drawer for a key to unlock the files. Finding nothing, he moved to the next drawer without bothering to shut the first. The second drawer would not open and he thought it was locked at first. He shut the first drawer and then tried a third. It opened easily.

When no key was found, he shut it and retried the second drawer. It opened easily. A search found no key. He repeated the process on the remaining four drawers and found nothing. Leaving the last drawer opened, he leaned back in his chair and tried to think of where such a key would be hidden. In addition to being passionate historians, the church loved secrecy and mystery just as much.

Out of frustration, he opened the center drawer to look again. Shuffling paperclips and memo pads around to see if it was hidden had the same results. He even ran his hand along the underside of the drawer to see if they key had been taped there. Nothing.

Leaning back in the chair with a frustrated groan, he considered his options. He could probably find a way to pry the cabinet open, or call a locksmith to open it. He did not like either of these options and paused to ask God for help and guidance. Leaning forward he slammed the two open drawers shut at the same time with a little more force than he intended. Without warning the panel that ran along the front edge of the desk where the upper part meets the desktop popped open.

He leaned forward and peered into the dark space behind the panel and found a small key ring with a half dozen keys attached. Before grabbing the keys, he paused and looked to heaven with grateful amazement.

The third key he tried opened one of the cabinets. There were many files inside, all neatly labeled and filed alphabetically. Some were names he recognized as priests from the various churches in the Dioceses, but others looked older and were unfamiliar names. Surprisingly, there was even a file for Archbishop Reilly.

Laying the legal sized manila file folder on the desk, he took a deep breath and then opened it and started his search for the truth. An hour later, he leaned back and tried to digest everything he had learned. He was not sure what was worse, knowing the truth, or wondering if the accusations were true.

***

A relationship had not been part of the assignment for Amir, at least not a serious one. But, it had happened anyway. He had never planned for things to get serious and he understood he would have to break it off at some point. Now, knowing his new assignment, he was going to have to face the inconvenient conflict between his duty and his heart.

Debbie Neuberger was not American born and still spoke with a German accent despite being in the states for 10 years. Her job at the German Embassy as attaché to the Ambassador was intriguing, but a little scary to him. There was likely a file on her at the CIA and she might be "observed" from time to time by the US government. Then again, the CIA probably had a file on him, too.

They had met in a coffee shop and hit it off right away. Her short skirt and fit legs had gotten his attention, but her spunky attitude had been what really attracted him to her. She was a blond, not too tall, but carried herself with a confidence he found both challenging and exciting.

He'd asked her out that first day they met and to his surprise, she had said yes. They had agreed to meet for dinner and the evening went well until she asked him why a Google search for him had come up empty. While admiring her directness, he had not prepared for this question. He tried to play dumb, which wasn't a stretch, and she fed him a few possible explanations.

In the end they decide his name was very common and his lack of social media participation pushed him well down the list of a Google search. She had asked him where he worked and how long he'd been in the country. Both of these facts would be used to verify him, no doubt using the German Embassy computers to dig into his cover. He was reasonably confident she would buy into his created background after her deep search.

He had helped her into a cab at the end of the evening and she had given him a quick kiss to assure him she'd like to go out with him again. He promised to call and watched as she drove off in the cab looking back at him through the rear window. He stood there for a few long minutes trying to sort out what had just happened. His heart and his head seemed to be in an intense debate.

Six months later, his heart seemed to be winning the debate. He had flown back from Boston late Sunday evening. She had suggested he come over for a late night drink and plan to stay. It was an easy invitation to accept.

She did not need to leave for work until mid-day and he had hoped to sleep late, but Amir had awoken at 7:30 a.m. with thoughts of his new mission. He had still not processed it all, but knew he'd have to soon. She was still sound asleep and he propped up on one elbow and watched her. The covers were gathered around her waist and legs leaving her torso exposed. She was lying naked on her side, facing him, with her face partially covered by her long blond hair.

To avoid thinking about his new assignment, he focused on the curve of her breasts and the memory of making love into the early morning hours. She was as quirky and energetic in bed as she was in life and he had given in to her. Normally, he was in control at all times, but she was the lion tamer in the relationship.

***

The fog in her head had been slowly lifting for what seemed like hours. Kristen had drifted in and out of consciousness several times and was finally able to stay awake. Her vision was starting to clear, but her mind was still drowsy and confused.

As her mind cleared, she started to remember she was a prisoner. There was no panicked feeling in her head thanks to the strong sedative he had given her. Her survival instincts and determination were awakening and she started forming a plan before she could physically lift her head off the hard floor.

After a few minutes, she was able to sit up and lean against the wall. Her head was light and dizzy and a powerful thirst had closed her throat to a point it was hard to breath. She tried to lick her lips, but there was no moisture.

Looking around the room, she noticed only two things, a camera in the corner of the ceiling and a heavy door. She remembered her effort to get the gag off and almost hanging herself. The gag was gone now and her hands and feet were no longer tied. For that, she was grateful.

Her new plan was based on outwitting her capturer instead of trying to overpower him. She would be the model prisoner, even showing appreciation to her captor, and wait for an opening to escape or gain an advantage. Living on the streets had taught her patience and cunning were the most effective tools for survival.

The door started opening, but she did not move. His name, she seemed to remember was Jake. He was about to start losing the upper hand in this situation, but he'd never see it coming until it was too late. At least, that was her plan.

She tried to give him a smile, but her lips were so dry her entire mouth would not work. He approached her cautiously and twisted the cap off a bottle of water before handing it to her. She swirled a mouthful to re-hydrate her tongue and cheeks before swallowing. It was both painful and wonderful. Ignoring him, she downed the entire bottle over the next few minutes.

"Thanks," she croaked, her vocal cords still not ready for action.

"Would you like another?" he asked, holding out a fresh bottle.

She nodded her head and took the bottle from him. This time he left the cap on. She tried to think about how she could use the bottle as a weapon, but decided the fluid was more important right now.

"I'm a mess," she said running her fingers through her short, dark hair. "Any chance I could visit the bathroom?"

"Sure. In fact, let's get you a bath and something to eat. You've had a rough night."

"Are my girls okay?"

"They are doing well. Maybe we can let you see them in a bit." She sensed he was giving her hope as a good way to keep her in line.

"That'd be great," she said with restrained excitement.

***

Nate was up early and getting ready to leave when he heard Trista moving around in the apartment next door. He had not spent the night because that was part of their boundary agreement. If either of them had to work in the morning, they would not sleep together. Since it was a Monday morning, they both were heading in to work.

He had regretted turning their nice evening into a working dinner. Things had started out very well, but discussing business had ruined the mood. He knew she was not happy with him, but appreciated her effort to hide her feelings and let him do his job. He'd have to bring her some flowers this evening to make up for being a jerk.

He decided to start the apology process by sending her a text to let her know he was sorry about messing up the date. Her first reply was a simple smiley face. Her second reply said, "I'll let you make it up to me," and included a winking smiley face. Forgiveness is a sweet gift.

Nate's day would start out at the office following up on the details of the case and checking some of the resources Trista had suggested. The puzzle had many missing pieces and he was energized by the challenge. If he were lucky, he might even get to take down a few politicians along the way.

***

She couldn't stay mad at him. Actually, correcting her own thought, it was not helpful to stay mad at anyone, or anything. She had learned at any early age anger was more harmful to the angered than to the person it was directed. Her grandmother had once told her that you should forgive your enemies because it would drive them nuts. She had found it worked on boyfriends as well.

The smile on her face was coy and playful. Dating was a game to her and she was good at it. Because of her petite frame and strong southern accent, men had always underestimated her. Nate was different. He had learned there was more to her than meets the eye from the first time they met. When she had picked the lock on his front door in under ten seconds, he had quickly realized she was a complex bundle of contradictions.

Nate, like most men, was not complicated. He was the type of man she had always been attracted to, strong, protecting and kind. She felt safe and comfortable with him and that worried her sometimes. She was ready to settle down, but not willing to settle. Was Nate the right guy for her? Did she like him better than she liked herself?

***

News of the three murdered priests had become a worldwide whirlwind. The Pope had issued a statement saying the church was saddened by the deaths, but it had not addressed the rumors of child molestation had been speculated as a motive. The DC police had released very few facts, so the newsies just repeated the basic facts over and over. There was also an endless parade of "experts" who speculated on a wide variety of things. The Pope should resign, some proclaimed. Others championed the need for mental health reform or suggested parents should talk to their kids about inappropriate touching.

The press was also having a field day dragging up the old scandals that involved priests molesting kids. Unfortunately for the church, there were many cases in the past that were once again being highlighted. Social media was being more honest than the news media because who needs a fact checker on Twitter?

By noon the church was under full attack from everyone. The press, feeling left behind by bloggers, was jumping on the bandwagon, and calling for the Pope's resignation. The Vatican was on lockdown and the Cardinals from all over the world had been alerted a trip to Rome might be needed soon.

The burden of dealing with the scandal and tragedy had fallen on Auxiliary Bishop Charron's shoulders. TV trucks had surrounded the Diocese since dawn and a small mob had formed at the front gate. Bishop Carron peeked through a small crack in the heavy shades covering his office window. He could see the front gate and the growing circus. Now that he knew the truth, he was being crushed by his responsibility.

The Vatican had told him to sit tight and say nothing until they could formulate an official response. He was expecting another call from them any minute with marching orders. He had not shared what he'd learned by reading the files on the three dead priests. He suspected they knew, but they did not know he was now fully informed on the past of his three fallen colleagues.

A soft knock at the door startled him. "Enter, please."

"Bishop Charron, the Vatican is on line five."

"Thanks, Sister Mary Elizabeth."

Line five was a special secure line directly connected to the Vatican. The other four lines of the Diocese had been busy all morning. The staff was making an attempt to answer every call, but the volume had all but overwhelmed the system.

"This is Auxiliary Bishop Charron," he said, holding the phone to his ear while easing into his office chair.

Thirty minutes later he had been told by Cardinal Jespers, the spokesperson for the College of Cardinals, to categorically deny the accusations and redirect the sympathies of the world to the real victims. In addition, he was told the Pope was considering making him Archbishop and he should be prepared to assume that role. The insinuation was clear, play along with the church's plan and the promotion was his.

After being spoken to for the entire call, it was now his turn to talk. He knew the gravity of the situation and knew the crosshairs of history were aimed directly at him. The words he'd read last night rang in his head: "For we can do nothing against the truth, but for the truth." This was the ultimate test of his faith. Was he going to place his faith with God as he had encouraged so many to do, or was he going to put his faith in the church? Until today, he had thought the two went hand-in-hand.

"Cardinal Jespers, we have a problem. This morning, I read the personnel files of the three deceased priests. After doing so, I cannot continue to perpetrate this lie. The path of righteousness, I believe, is the only course that will allow the church to heal. Not only for the church, but we owe the truth to the hundreds of children who were harmed by these monsters."

"Bishop Charron!" There was panic in the Cardinal's voice, but it was quickly replaced by arrogance. "The 'truth,' as you call it, is more complicated than can be explained. As you know, the church, like any large organization, has good and bad people. You have to consider the big picture. The church does so many good things that far outweigh the bad. To bring this much attention on the bad would have a devastating effect on the millions of innocent people who rely on the church. Clearly you do not wish to bring harm to so many, do you?"

"No, Cardinal, I do not, but I cannot be party to the evil deeds of this church, no matter what the consequences."

"Your character is without question, Archbishop Charron," the Cardinal said, taunting him with the thought of a promotion. "Let's take some more time to think this over. For now, you can release a simple statement about how saddened you are with this tragedy and that the church is fully cooperating with the police investigation." This sounded like a command rather than a suggestion.

"For now, that is wise. Emotions are running too high." He heard his words and realized he was rationalizing his actions. He knew that did not make them right, but it didn't make them wrong. He needed to buy some time and make sure what he was doing was the right thing...although, he considered, it might be too late to do the right thing.

Chapter 5

After a morning of research and digging, it was time to meet with Pete Marcus, the lead detective. Nate's part of the investigation was getting ready to get tricky and political. Pete was going to have to deal with the press and likely some significant political pressure. This was DC, after all.

Despite Nate's first instinct, he knew he could not just walk in a Congressman's office and start demanding answers and slinging accusations. He could try to get a warrant to search their emails and documents, but he was going to need more proof before any judge would end their career to let him go fishing around a congressional office.

"Hey Pete. Ready for me?"

"Sure, Nate. Come on in. Grab a seat and I'll be with you in a second." Pete's keyboard clicked a few more times and then he sent the email he had been working on.

"So," Pete started. "Break it to me easy. Is this as ugly as I think?"

"'Fraid so. We've got three members of Congress who might be involved in a cover-up as well as the entire Catholic Church. We might have to indict the Pope himself if this has legs."

Pete's head dropped and his shoulders slumped. "Shit! Mixing religion and politics is never a good idea, but in this town it is a disaster. Tell me what ya got."

"I spoke with Bishop Charron who is now the head of the Church here in DC since the Archbishop is gone. Seems like a good guy, but a bit overwhelmed right now. I'm going back to see him this afternoon and pick up some files. I might want a warrant, but wanted to check with you before I did."

"Not sure we have a choice, Pete replied. "Let's try to keep it quiet, but if they stonewall you in any way, get tough. Based on history, the church is in this up to the Pope's nose. I'd tell you to try to treat this like every other case, but we know it's not."

"Gotcha. What about the political guys? That's gonna be a tough nut. I haven't even started with that yet."

"Yeah. We gotta find something to tie one of them to the church. This is probably a house of cards and we just need to make sure we are not underneath when it comes crashing down. Let's leave the politicians out of it for now. The press is all over the church, so we keep working that and then see if we can link the others. The killer's video is not enough. We need more."

"Sounds good. How's the press treating you?"

"Not too bad so far, but they are going to want more soon. I'm not planning to release the video until the trial. Keep me posted." Pete turned back to his computer and Nate rose to leave.

"Pete, do you think we need to worry about folks who know too much?"

Pete looked up at Nate and then off to the corner of the room in contemplation. "Yeah, probably. Maybe even ourselves." He looked back at Nate and said, "Let's be careful and trust no one. If you need security for someone, let me know."

***

The Vatican had called line five three times before noon. Each time it had been Cardinal Jespers, who was talented in talking in innuendo and vague threats. Some religions spoke in tongues, but the Catholic Church spoke in a dialect that was easy to understand and hard to prove in court.

Bishop Charron had played their game to this point, but he was skilled enough in *Vaticanspeak* to hold his own with the Cardinal. He had not decided what to do yet, but doing nothing was not something he would consider. Even if he tried, the police already had enough to launch a full investigation.

At 1:00 p.m., Detective Romano would be back and he was expecting some answers. Cardinal Jespers had suggested he should "clean up" his files while he was doing the research the detective had asked. "No sense wasting the police's time with irrelevant documents that are not related to the murders," the Cardinal had added.

Bishop Charron had not done as the Cardinal had suggested. Instead, he had compiled a one-inch thick folder with copies of documents that implemented the three dead priests and even the Vatican in a cover up of a culture of pedophilia and other acts of child molestation. He had not decided what to do with this information just yet, but he was determined to find justice.

The documents were probably not enough to make a court case against the church by themselves because like the Cardinal's phone call, the documents had been laced with subtleties and code words that were masterful. Any defense lawyer could find a reasonable explanation for the emails, letters and reports that had been filed.

A few dozen of the documents were records of bank transfers to different members of the church in the DC area. Each record had been accompanied by a letter making the transfer seem like a donation to the family to help their son get professional help for an unmentioned problem. Each of the letters were almost identical.

If each of these documents represented a child who had been molested, how could this many parents have been convinced to keep quiet? The payoffs were only in the $5,000 to $10,000 range, which did not seem like enough to qualify as hush money. There must be another explanation.

***

Amir slipped out of Debbie's apartment unnoticed. He had work to do and Debbie liked to sleep late. He'd left a note he hoped to see her later that day and to call when she woke up.

He had only been given a few weeks to complete his mission, which was not a lot of time to be ready to change the world. Most of the groundwork had already been laid and others were covering the violent parts that would take many innocent lives. His role was to inflame the American people and their government into war with radical Muslim states. His country, Saudi Arabia, would not be implicated in the attacks, assuming he carried out his mission well.

He also felt remorseful, not for the people who would lose their lives, but for himself. His comfortable life would no longer exist, assuming he was alive at all, and his relationship with Debbie would be over. He could not risk trying to enroll her in his plan and he would probably have to break up with her soon. Not only was she a risk to the secrecy of his plan, she would also take up too much of his time.

The plan was masterful in its simplicity. If successful, it would start a religious war. In the end, his country would benefit when the powerful U.S. military eliminated Iran, Iraq, and Syria and left his country as the most powerful Muslim based country in the world. More importantly, it would drive up the price of oil on the world market and bring great wealth to his homeland.

***

It had been less than 48 hours since the Catholic Priest killings and already Senator McDermott had found a way to use the sensational story to advance his cause of eliminating all religion in government. He had sent out a press release condemning the Catholic Church as the perfect example of a corrupt religious state and followed this up with a speech from the floor of the Senate.

There was no one present during his speech except the C-Span camera that broadcast his message around the world. It was a common practice in both the House and Senate to make speeches in this manner. The politicians loved the idea because it allowed them to go on record with their point of view without wasting valuable time while in session to hear the babbling speeches of others.

In reality, the international press was about the only ones who watched C-Span anymore. The Voters were so fed up with Congress that C-Span's rating had fallen off the map after the Clinton Impeachment. Fake speeches, like the one Senator McDermott had given, were just another reason for the public to be disgusted with Congress.

Lunchtime in Washington, DC was also a time to make a political statement. Who you were eating with in a public restaurant was often more newsworthy than a politician's position on any policy. No member of Congress wanted to be seen dining with Senator McDermott. Being linked to him was like poison in the veins for anyone who needed to get re-elected. Max Pigman was on a short list of people who would actually benefit from being seen with Senator McDermott in a public place.

Max was not a small man, standing tall at six foot four inches and weighing in excess of three hundred pounds. His legal career had hit rock bottom over the last two years and he had just recently been allowed to start practicing law again. Simply put, being seen with Senator McDermott would not drag his career any further down.

According to the research McDermott had done, a few down years in his otherwise successful career had not shaken Max's confidence. His car was no longer a Mercedes and his mansion was now a small apartment, but his ego/confidence was reportedly still larger than his enormous body.

"Thanks for coming on short notice, Mr. Pigman."

"It's Max and it's not a problem. Glad I was able to fit you in my schedule," he added with a sarcastic smile. "Frankly, my schedule has more holes than a golf course."

"Okay, Max. Here comes the waiter, so let's order a drink and then we can talk."

Five minutes later the waiter left with their drink orders and a promise to bring fresh rolls. Senator McDermott eyed the big man for a few seconds before opening the conversation. "So, I assume you've had the opportunity to look into the case . . ."

"Never good to assume, Senator, but yes. Suing a city is not an easy task because they have all kinds of exemptions from liability, but the separation of church and state is an interesting angle. Not a lot of case law to help us, but the Constitution is vague enough on this to give us some room to run."

"The Constitution is vague? In many ways you are correct, but the public believes the constitution clearly calls for a separation of church and state."

"Senator, in this case, it is going to be more important to consider what a judge believes. Or, more precisely, judges. Even if we win the first case, this is going through appeals, and if you are up for it, probably all the way to the Supreme Court."

"I agree. Tell me, do you know where the term 'separation of church and state' comes from?"

"Senator, I'm from Virginia and I went to Mr. Jefferson's University for both undergrad and law school. I have been to the library at Monticello and viewed the original letter from Mr. Jefferson to the Baptists of Danbury where the phrase 'wall of separation between church and state' first appears.

"I know this issue well and even wrote about it in college," he added. "The Constitution, despite popular belief, does not include this phrase. Nor does the Doctrine of Religious Freedom Jefferson wrote for Virginia." Max leaned back in his seat apparently satisfied with his answer.

The Senator nodded in agreement and showed his respect with a smile. "Impressive Max. So, tell me what you will use to win this case."

Max leaned back in and lowered his voice to a near whisper. "Politics, Senator. Good old fashion politics."

"Oh? I know a few things about politics. How can I help?"

"Senator, no offense, but you need to stay out of this. You are toxic on this issue. Your efforts in Congress, as I'm sure you are aware, are the politics that will backlash and lose this case. As you know, I'm in no position to turn this case down. I need the work. But, if I were in a better position, I'd tell you I would not work this case unless you stayed away from it. Except to write the checks," he added with a playful smile.

The Senator fell silent and looked away. He had planned to use this case to hammer his point home in DC. He understood the rationale for staying away, but his term would be over before this case was finished. Was it worth the wait? Would this case be the one that brought about real change, even if it was after he had left the Senate?

"Tell me, what type of politics are you planning to use?" he asked, stalling.

"The politics of yesterday will not work today with these issues. We have to use what we have in front of us. If we argue this case on a political issue that is over 200 years old, we will lose. Even if we are right, we will likely lose."

"We are right."

"Yes, Senator, we are, but that is not the way the courts work today. Especially the Supremes. Judges are appointed by politicians in Virginia and most were appointed because of politics. Not because they were good judges, but because they played the political game with the politicians."

"Okay. But what does that mean for us?"

"The politics of today are, like the politics of yesteryear, based in ideology. The First Amendment was written because England had tried to force the King's religion on us. This was one of the most fundamental objections to English rule. In fact, I'd say we'd still be her Majesty's loyal subjects if not for the religious freedom issue.

"Of course today, that is not an issue in America. Well, except for you, Senator, making it an issue. Most Americans are happy with their freedom to practice whatever religion they want and making a case that the government is taking away religious freedom is going to be tough. Instead, we will use the ideology of today, to win the case for the ideology of the founding fathers."

"And that is what?" the Senator asked.

"Government vs. private enterprise. Big government vs. the free market. We have to show who churches are competing in the free marketplace, but they have unfair advantages like tax breaks and subsidies."

"Well that shouldn't be hard to prove," snorted the Senator.

"I agree, but getting a ruling in our favor is more difficult, and very political. That's why, again no offense, you need to stay the hell away. If any judge sides with you, his career will be over. If a judge sides with the business community over government, however, they will become the darling of conservatives everywhere."

"Okay, I get that, but how does that help me fix the problem on a national level?"

"Senator, in case you hadn't noticed. Nothing gets 'fixed' in Washington anymore. It's about the judges, the Supremes and the courts. It's the only way real change takes place anymore. At least on the big issues. A favorable ruling that stands up on appeal will cause real change. But, I will not win this case if I get tied to you. Frankly, it is a little risky being seen with you today."

"You don't beat around the bush, do you?" The Senator looked away, reflecting on his dilemma. "Here's my problem. It will take years to get this through the courts. My term will run out before that, and as you might guess, my chances for re-election are slim. I don't have the luxury of time."

"It's up to you Senator. I'm expecting to get paid either way, but the only way I'm gonna win is if we do it my way."

The waiter arrived with their drinks and breadbasket. "You gentlemen made a decision yet, or do you need more time?"

The Senator looked up at the waiter and smiled at the timing and irony in his question. "Not yet, give us a few minutes."

Chapter 6

The steaming hot water felt wonderful on Kristen's skin. It had been a while since she had enjoyed the luxury of a hot shower. When you live on the street, showering becomes a low priority. She tried to allow herself to get lost in the pleasure and not think about her girls, but it was a futile effort.

What was this goon up to? Was he a pervert who molested little girls? Was he some religious whacko who used kidnapping to recruit members to his flock? It was hard to defeat an enemy when she didn't know his goal, so she resolved to make the next step. "Know thy enemy," she whispered to herself.

She was still toweling herself dry behind the shower curtain when she heard the door open. "Who's there?" she asked, without trying to look.

"Just me. I brought you some clean clothes. I hope they fit."

Keeping an enemy off balance was always a good idea, so she decided to get bold. The shower curtain whipped open and startled her kidnapper. She made no attempt to cover her nakedness and he stepped back and diverted his eyes, but not until after he had seen her.

"Thanks," she said flatly as she stepped out of the shower towards him. "By the way, you told me your name was Jake, right?"

"Stay back, please," he pleaded, obviously uncomfortable by her brashness.

"Oh sorry. Does my naked body bother you? Do you prefer men? I sure hope you don't prefer little girls."

"No! No, of course not."

"No to which one, men or little girls?" She was pressing, but knew she had probably reached the limit for being aggressive with this jerk.

"Neither," he said, as he started to recover from her move. He turned and faced her, but kept his eyes high at her face. "I have some other sizes if these don't fit," he stated, as he turned and left the room.

She heard the door lock behind him and knew she was trapped once again. She tried to decide what she had just learned about him. He did not seem like a monster, nor did he seem like a pervert or psychopath. That seemed like a positive development, but it did not help her know more about him.

The clothes were a simple pair of jeans and a sweatshirt. He had not left her any underwear so she put her old ones back on. It was not the first time she had worn dirty underwear. She pulled the sweatshirt on and momentarily thought about the last time she had worn a bra. It had been months.

After toweling her hair dry and working out a few of the tangles with a brush she found on the sink, she went to the door and knocked. "Hello, I'm done."

The door quickly unlatched and opened slightly. She grabbed the handle and slowly opened it. He was there in a room that looked like the foyer of an office standing ten feet away. He did not have a gun, but he was much bigger than she was and she dismissed any idea of rushing him.

"What now?" she asked, to break the awkward silence. "Can I see my girls?"

"If you continue to be cooperative, we'll see. First, let's get you something to eat."

"I'll do whatever you want, just don't hurt my girls."

"They're fine." He motioned for her to go through the door to her right and she obeyed. The door led to a family type room she remembered walking through on the way to the shower. There were no windows, but otherwise it looked like a normal waiting room in a doctor's office.

"Have a seat and help yourself." There was a pile of grapes and bananas and several granola bars on a coffee table in front of the couch. Without hesitating, she sat down and started to fill her need. She didn't even notice he had left the room.

After 10 minutes of an almost frenzied consumption of food, Kristen looked up at him. He was just staring at her, not smiling or showing any emotion. Time for her to push a little more.

"So, Jake. What's this all about? What's going to happen to me and my girls?"

"You don't beat around the bush, do you?"

"Life's short. How short seems to be in your hands right now. So why waste time?"

"Your life is in God's hands. I am just his servant."

"Okay, what is God up to?"

"I assure you what God has in store for you is better than a life on the street."

"That's a pretty low bar."

"Exactly. We are going to find a place for you to live and not be hungry every day. How does that sound?"

"Suspicious." She decided to stay quiet and see how far he would reveal his plans.

"Let's just say there is travel and new adventures ahead for you."

She shrugged her shoulders to encourage him to continue.

"For now, let's just leave it at that. I assure you you'll enjoy your new life. I need your cooperation, but I do not want to harm you."

"Will I be with my daughters in this new life?"

"Yes." She knew he was lying.

"Can I see my girls now?"

"Yes, but only for 10 minutes. Then I'm going to need you to return to your room."

"You mean my cell?" She regretted the words as soon as they left her mouth.

"It does not seem like you are ready to see your girls after all. Please stand up and turn around."

"I'm sorry," she pleaded, her voice sounding desperate.

"Sorry, but you are not ready to cooperate just yet."

"No, I am! I swear I'll do whatever you want, just let me see my girls!" Tears were forming in her eyes.

"Stand up and turn around. Now! Or you'll never see your girls again."

"Okay, okay. I'm sorry Jake, I'll do whatever you say."

He handcuffed her hands behind her back and led her back to the same room she had been held in before. He guided her into the room, quickly removed the handcuffs and pushed her forward. She turned to face him. His stare was hard and cold and he turned and left without saying a word. She heard the door lock and she sunk to the floor in tears.

***

It was almost lunchtime and Nate was regretting skipping breakfast. He had to have some fuel and whenever he thought of food, Trista seemed to be connected. They had occasionally met for lunch, but typically their schedules did not match.

Lunch? Where r u, read his text.

Hill. Senate in session, no can do ☹, she replied.

Dinner?

Business or pleasure? She responded, reminding him he owed her one after ruining last night.

Pleasure, promise. I'll call you later ;-) He had wanted to suggest more pleasure than just dinner, but knew he was pushing his luck and still had one foot in the doghouse.

He left the office and headed for his favorite street vendor to get a couple of hotdogs. Not the best meal, but quick, easy, and cheap. Ten minutes later he was in his car working his way across town to visit Bishop Charron. Traffic, as usual, was horrid, but the side roads and shortcuts provided a clear path to those who knew how to navigate the complicated road patterns in DC.

His phone rang and he touched his Bluetooth earpiece to answer it. "This is Nate."

"Hey Nate. Laurie Ganz from the lab. Wanted to give you a heads-up on some stuff we found. Might be important."

"Thanks, whatcha got?"

"Interesting stuff on both the computer and the phone. Lots of pictures of the three murder scenes. He had done his research. But that's not what's so interesting. He was also quite a writer. I've looked through his documents and communications for the past six months. Tells quite a story and implicates several members of Congress."

"Yeah. I've seen the movie."

"Since you said you were working the back story, I thought you should know."

"Laurie, have you shared this with anyone else? Anyone?"

"No. I've been alone all morning. The rest of the team is at a scene."

"Good. Here's the deal. This stuff is obviously very sensitive. We can't let the political stuff get out to the press before we are ready or all hell's gonna break loose. Know what I mean?"

"No shit. I'll keep it between us."

"Pete Marcus is the only other person who has seen the video and knows everything. That's already three too many people who know this. Shit like this spreads quickly in the underground DC channels. We don't want these bastards to see us comin' for 'em."

"Mum's the word. Do you want to start background searches, money trails, and digging on any of them?"

"At some point, but I could use your help for something else first. I'm headed over to the Diocese with a search warrant. You interested in searching their computers while I look for other evidence?"

"Sure. Just need to check with my director. Shouldn't be a problem." He gave her the address and she promised to be there as soon as possible.

"After I get done there, I'll finish my report on Hill and get them over to you as soon as they are done."

"No rush. The church is the hotter angle right now with the press all over it. We better get our digging done before they destroy evidence. Thanks, see you soon." He clicked the phone off and turned down another quiet side street to get around the traffic jam that was Dupont Circle.

***

Sister Mary Elizabeth had delivered a nice lunch to his office, but Bishop Charron had barely touched it. He had spent most of the morning praying, except for the multiple phone calls with Cardinal Jespers from the Vatican. After every call, he felt a greater need to pray, hoping for a divine solution to his problem. God had not answered yet.

Bishop Charron had made one decision . . . he would require the detective to have a warrant, but once he legally requested the information, the church would hand it over. Some secrets were not meant to be kept.

There was a soft knock on his door and he glanced at the ornate clock on the fireplace mantel. 1:00 p.m., it was time to meet with Detective Romano. He took a deep breath and exhaled loudly to help relieve his tension. "Come in, please."

The door appeared to magically open as Sister Mary Elizabeth skillfully stayed out of sight. The detective stood in the doorway and the men made eye contact briefly before Bishop Charron motioned him to enter. "Good afternoon, Detective."

"And to you, Bishop Charron," Detective Romano said in a formal tone that seemed to fit the moment. "I know this a very tough time and I appreciate you seeing me. How are you holding up?"

The question was a surprise and he had to regroup quickly. "Ah, thank you for your concern. While this is a difficult time for us all, God only gives us what we can handle. This too shall pass."

"Indeed it will," the Detective agreed. "The press is a little out of control right now. Let's hope that part passes sooner than later. Any word from the Vatican?"

"Oh yes," he said with a feigned smile. "The Vatican, as you can imagine, is monitoring the situation."

"Were they aware of any of the accusations against the Archbishop, before his death?"

"Detective, as you can understand, I'm sure, this is a serious criminal investigation we are discussing and I would be ill-advised to speak without the church's legal counsel present. I will cooperate with you fully, but I must do so in an appropriate manner."

"Of course. May I ask if you had the opportunity to check your files for anything related to Jonathan Hill and any ties to the . . . ah . . . deceased?" he asked stumbling a bit.

"Again, Detective. I'm sure you understand, but I'm not at liberty to share any of the church's records at this time."

"Of course, I understand. And I'm sure you understand I have to perform my duties as an officer of the law." He reached into the inside pocket of his blue blazer and pulled out a document. "Bishop, this is a search warrant. It provides me the legal right to search this entire building for evidence related to this crime. You are welcomed to accompany me while I perform my duties, but I will need full access to whatever I need to see."

"Detective," the Bishop started in a very calm voice, "I'm sure you are aware we have a great deal of personal information on innocent people that cannot be shared."

"As you are aware, we have three murders and a suicide that need to be investigated," the detective countered. "I will be as discrete as possible."

The Bishop smiled and looked the detective in the eyes. There was a quiet confidence and resolve in his body language. "Detective, I have not slept much since we last met. I felt a need to find out a possible explanation for this tragedy, so I searched all the relevant files, including the Archbishop's private records. I have created this folder," he patted the inch thick folder. "I would suggest you start your search here."

Nate looked at the Bishop and then at the folder with obvious confusion on his face.

"Detective, I see you are a bit confused. I was not at liberty to share these documents with you, no matter if I *wanted to* or not. When you produced the search warrant, which gave you the legal right to search our files and discover this information, it was no longer up to me. I have simply saved you the time."

"How do I know it's all there?"

"I suppose you don't, but I think you will be very satisfied with what you see."

"I'm sensing another motive here."

"Two, actually. First, I want to see justice served, and I am also hoping that providing this information to you will satisfy you enough that you will not have to explore the private records of the hundreds of innocent people the church helps."

Nate looked down at the file and seemed to be deciding if he should trust the Bishop.

"I tell you what, let me look through that file and see what I think after seeing what you've got."

"That's fair. May I interest you in a cup of tea while you work? It took me all night and half the morning."

"No thanks, but one other thing. I have someone from the lab coming to look over the Archbishop's computer. Her name is Laurie Ganz. Can you notify security to let her in?"

***

Amir was a rare combination of talents. He was a very savvy people person, with great ability to manipulate, and technically brilliant when it came to computers. His role in this latest game would feature the latter of his skills.

His apartment featured more electronic equipment and Internet connections than most businesses. As he pulled out three laptops from the closet he referred to as "the computer room," he smiled at how small technology had become. Fifteen years ago he would not have been able to operate this much computing power without a real computer room and a million dollars' worth of equipment.

His goal for the day was to set up fake terrorist chats on multiple international social media sites. The three computers would be able to emulate dozens of different users, each with a different IP address. That would make US Homeland Security think there was excessive terrorist chatter. His plan was to push the discussion just enough to get Homeland Security's attention without causing the threat level to be raised from orange to red on the silly color code system they used.

Essentially he would be chatting with himself, but thanks to his Random IP Generator program, he would appear to be several suspicious characters sharing hatred for the United States. The hardest part for him was keeping straight which character he was playing in this elaborate scheme.

An hour into his fake chats he noticed he'd picked up a few other participants on one of the sites. He could not tell if they were real radical Muslims or very good imposters. He engaged them by sending messages from several of his characters. His focus was intense as he darted between the three laptops and three-dozen IP addresses.

A soft ding from his computer startled him and broke his focus. It was a notification he had received a text message, probably from Debbie. The thought of her distracted him and he cursed his weakness for this beautiful German girl. Giving in, he opened the chat with her and messaged her back.

hey babe, good morning ☺ wish you were here ☹ you home?, read her message.

yep, working

whats your new cell #? For security reasons, he changed cell phones every few months.

202 788 2386

going shopping, I'll call when done

He thought about telling her he loved her, but instead closed the program and went back to his other chat. The discussion on the one site had become heated without his help, so he decided he'd caused enough trouble for now.

Chapter 7

It had taken almost three hours for Nate to read the entire file Bishop Charron had given him. He guessed it was two hundred pages. Thankfully, the Catholic Church was big on documenting everything, but he was not sure why. Were they historians or narcissists? Either way, it made his job a lot easier.

Archbishop Reilly's files had yielded the most evidence. There were many letters from years ago, and emails from recent years appeared to be an attempt to document some sort of incident. Unfortunately, the Catholic version of "document" was laced with complex innuendos and code words. You could tell both the author of the letter and the receiver knew what was being said, but an outsider, or police detective, would have gaps in the facts could easily be defended in a court of law.

After reading one letter for the third time, he actually took a second to admire the Archbishop for his crafty writing. He knew the letter was an apology to the parents of Jonathan Hill, but without the background knowledge he'd seen on the killer's video, the letter said almost nothing.

The sad part was he found dozens of similar letters with vague apologies. Now that the Archbishop and his fellow molesters were dead and the secret was public, he suspected many of these families would stop hiding the truth and join the inevitable lawsuits against the church. They would also make great witnesses in a criminal trial, but first he needed to find someone to charge who was still alive.

The documents yielded plenty of evidence and leads to support Jonathan Hill's allegations about the three priests, but there was no reference to the politicians. He needed to find that link, assuming there was one, before he'd be able to compel a judge to sign a search warrant on a member of Congress.

Nate checked his watch. Four o'clock already? Where had the afternoon gone? He slipped the entire folder of documents into a large evidence bag and removed his latex gloves. It was time to check on Laurie Ganz's efforts to search the Archbishop's computer files.

"Hey Laurie," he announced, as he entered the Archbishop's private office. "Find anything?"

"Yep, but not because the Archbishop was sloppy. His computer was very clean. There were only five messages in his inbox and his deleted folder had been emptied just hours before he was killed."

"Sounds like he was a bit paranoid."

"Sure does. But, fortunately, he was not computer savvy. Most people don't know that even an email that has been permanently deleted still has a digital footprint."

"People like you scare me. Sure glad you're on our team."

"Best rule for hiding something is to never type it. Once you do, there is a record no matter how hard you try to hide it."

"So, what'd you find?"

"A string of erased emails from last October with Senator Stiano. Not a smoking gun, but a fit with Hill's story. Stiano was one of the main characters in his manifest on the cover-up." She handed him the printout of the email string and waited for him to read it.

"Well…that's a start. We're gonna need more. Anything else?"

"Some possible related links with deleted emails to a Cardinal Jespers. Not sure, but he might be from the Vatican."

"Great, the Vatican. Can this case get any more dicey? Fuck!" As soon as the word left his mouth he realized it was inappropriate. "Sorry, probably should not be dropping F-bombs in this place. And, in front of a lady," he added with a smile.

She returned his smile and for the first time he realized the young lab tech was quite beautiful. Her smile lit up her face. "I must not be much of a lady, 'cause I didn't even notice until you said something."

He must have been staring at her a little too long because she looked back to the computer to hide her blushing face. His mind drifted as he watched her clicking the mouse and pecking on the keyboard.

He had never noticed her attractiveness probably because every time he'd seen her she had been wearing a Crime Lab windbreaker and had her long blond hair pulled back in a ponytail. Her jacket was now tossed over a chair and her hair was loosely hanging over her shoulders.

His phone chirped, indicated a text message had arrived. The screen showed the face of the sender and a guilty feeling smacked him in the heart as he looked at Trista's beautiful face.

***

One of the best things about living in the nation's capital was the food. No matter which part of the city you were in, there were plenty of great restaurants and the variety of cuisines was the best in the world. DC was the ultimate global community and the restaurant scene reflected that. Restaurants were highly specialized to showcase a particular country or even region within a country.

There was the typical fare like northern Italian, but you could also find a restaurant that featured Ethiopian cuisine or traditional delicacies from Columbia. Amir had greatly expanded his tastes while living in this city for the last six years and had developed a half-dozen favorite places to eat.

Tonight, he had plans with Debbie to go back to the little German restaurant she had suggested for their first date. She had claimed it to be "real" German food and it had not disappointed. The place was called Döner Bistro and the hip setting in the Adams Morgan neighborhood was one of the things he would miss about America.

The restaurant scene in DC was also amazing for the crowds. It could be a Tuesday night in February and you'd still have a busy restaurant. Tonight was no exception and the Döner Bistro was filled enough to make Amir wondered if Americans even knew how to cook for themselves.

"Why aren't you looking at the menu?" Her question jolted him back from his reflections on the DC restaurant scene.

"I was thinking of trying something different tonight," he responded with a coy smile and a raised eyebrow.

"Yeah?" She smiled back indicating she knew he was not talking about food. "Did you have something in mind?"

"I was hoping you'd make a recommendation."

"You were, huh. Well, I love the Wiener schnitzel, but for you," she paused to look at the menu, "The Currywurst would be a spicy treat."

"Spicy is good. I'll look forward to it." They shared a knowing smile and moved on. "How was your day at the Embassy?"

"Quiet. Always is when the Ambassador is on vacation."

"As much as he seems to need you, I'm surprised he does not make you go with him on vacation."

"If you met his wife, you'd know why. Sometimes I think she is the real Ambassador and he is just the front guy. Also, she is notorious with her jealousy. I was warned from day one not to even smile when she was around because she would think I was flirting with the Ambassador. You've seen what I have to wear to work. Might as well be a nun's habit."

He smiled and stared at the cleavage she was displaying tonight for his pleasure. "I think she sounds like a smart lady. I know a couple reasons she would have to be jealous." He looked back to her face and she was smiling back at him.

"Well, I wouldn't dress like this at work. I only let the girls out when I'm trying to get your attention."

"Let's order and later, I'll give you all the attention you can handle."

***

After Nate's hijacking of the conversation at dinner the night before, he was going to be buying tonight. They had met on the sidewalk outside their townhouses and walked to a little pizza place a block away. She enjoyed holding his hand as they walked.

"Hey, sorry again about ruining dinner last night with work talk."

"Maybe you'd have behaved better if we didn't make love first," she replied with a smile.

"Ha, you're probably right. This case is just..."

"If you want to discuss it, I'd be happy to help tonight...since you're buying."

"I might make you work a little for your dinner, but first we are just going to enjoy each other for a little while." He held the door to the restaurant open and they went in and grabbed a table. The place was busy, but the waitress was good. In less than two minutes after being seated, she had given them water and taken their drink and pizza order.

"So, what happened on the Hill today? A whole bunch of nothing, like usual, or did they give you something to write about?"

"Actually, you might be interested to know they discussed your priest murders at a Senate hearing today."

"Really?" He resisted the urge to ask her who had said what.

"Yep. They are calling for a full investigation of the church. Seems like they are buying into the theory the killer was abused by the priest when he was younger."

"Probably a safe bet, but it is too early to call that one."

"I thought of you when one Senator asked for the FBI to get involved."

"Yeah, we are expecting that. Pete Marcus is gonna earn his money dealing with all the jurisdictional crap on this case. We are supposed to meet with the Bureau tomorrow."

"Is that what your story will be on?" he asked trying to change the subject.

"No. It wasn't even the reason for the hearing, but it was the only thing anyone wanted to talk about. My story is a bit less exciting...climate change."

"Oh, jeez!"

"I thought you'd like that." She knew the politics of climate change really disgusted him and she braced for the outburst that was getting ready to happen.

"Did the idiots pass some new law to stop us from farting because some politically motivated scientist thinks people cause global warming? Can you quote me in your article?" he asked with a big grin.

"Can I cite you as an unqualified, anonymous source?" she asked with a grin of her own.

"Sure, as long as you don't make me sound like an idiot."

"Now that's going to be tough," she jested and they both laughed loudly enough to turn a few heads in the restaurant.

The pizza arrived and their attention turned to the steaming circle of cheese and sausage. The next ten minutes were dedicated to finding a way to eat pizza without burning their mouths.

"Mmm, that's good stuff," he finally said, after finishing his second piece.

"Yep," she managed to reply with her mouth completely full.

"Can we talk a little business?" he asked.

She paused to swallow. "Sure, but you do remember I'm a sleazy reporter who will take your words and twist them into a juicy story?"

"Yeah? And I'm a cop, with handcuffs, and I'm not afraid to use 'em." He smiled and she knew he was teasing. "Seriously, can we go off the record?"

"Sure, but you got me all distracted thinking about handcuffs," she said, playfully fanning herself.

"Well, we can talk about that later, but I want to get your help before we order a second pitcher of beer."

"You do know there is no such thing as off the record?"

"Too well, but I'm really hoping you'll let me ask all the questions and you'll turn off your reporter curiosity."

"Hmm. I might need to borrow your handcuffs to help restrain my curiosity."

He reached in his pocket to mimic a search for his cuffs. "Oh, sorry, I must have left them in my bedroom. Should we head back there before we can continue?"

"Maybe later. I promise I'll try to behave."

"Okay. I need a little more info on the politicians we talked about last night. Actually, just one guy for right now . . . Stiano."

"Stiano is Catholic and was very close to the Archbishop," Nate responded. "I need to know more about that relationship before I drag him in for questioning."

"Not sure if I know anything that would help," she started. "He's pretty powerful in the Senate Foreign Relations Committee."

"Would that committee have anything to do with the Vatican?"

"Sure, but on a diplomatic level, not religious. Mostly the Vatican is treated like a country."

"I've not found much in this case related to religion. Seems to be more of a matter of perverts and politicians than anything religious. Anything you can think of that ties the Senator to the church?"

"Hmm. Not sure I remember anything specific, but I can look into it. The Pope hasn't been here, but Stiano may have visited the Vatican. It's all public record and easy to find out. I can look it up on my laptop when we get home."

The word "home" felt weird to her. They literally lived at the same place, even if they had two different addresses. The wall that separated their two lofts was thin and without the ground rules, they would be living together in a very real sense.

After an awkward pause in the conversation, Nate broke the silence. "So, you don't even need special reporter powers to find this stuff out?"

"Nope, the Internet is a marvelous tool and the government posts everything, well . . . almost everything. So, you think Stiano is tied to the priest murders?"

"Do I need to get my handcuffs?"

"Oops. Sorry. I withdraw the question, your honor."

"Do we give any funding to the Vatican?" he asked.

"Doubt that. I think the phrase *more money than God* originated in the Vatican."

"Yeah, guess that makes sense, but what about the reverse? Has the Vatican given any money to Stiano?"

"Maybe," she replied. "That's gonna take some reporter superpowers because people are good at hiding contributions. I doubt you can trace any money all the way to the Vatican, but you could find ties to the church."

"So, what's it gonna cost me to find out?"

"Seriously, I'm gonna have to write about this if I dig any deeper. Political contributions are my concern. I'm willing to negotiate with you and hold some information in the name of helping the police, but you're gonna have to let me write something."

He lowered his head and stared at the table. She was not sure if he was mad, or just thinking. Looking up, he said, "I gotta run it by Pete. Can we just put this conversation on hold until tomorrow?"

"Sure."

"One last question…it just occurred to me I should know this . . . are you Catholic?"

"Ha! Not many Catholics in the south," she laughed. "I was raised a Baptist. You?"

"Nah, too much work. I'm a lazy Christian."

The second pitcher of beer arrived and the conversation moved away from religion and politics. She enjoyed the ease of his company and allowed herself to forget about the story for the next 45 minutes.

Chapter 8

The dim glow of Amir's computer screen was the only light on in the small living room of Debbie's apartment. It was 2:00 a.m. and she was fast asleep in the bedroom after a rather active evening of lovemaking. She had added some spice to her normal moves, just as she had suggested at dinner earlier in the evening. He had fallen asleep with her in his arms, but had awakened 30 minutes ago with thoughts of his mission weighing heavily on his mind.

He remotely accessed one of the computers he used to participate in the international chat rooms. He wanted to check to see if the chatter had continued after he had left. People were so easy to manipulate if you just knew the right emotional buttons to push.

Since it was the middle of the night in America, it was daytime in the Middle East. He would not be able to play multiple parts in tonight's chat from this remote computer, but he could still make his IP address appear to come from Iran.

The conversation had turned to hatred of Americans and especially the American President. Both were easy targets for those who wanted to promote extreme Islamic views. Amir marveled at how easy it was to stir up hatred within the Islamic world and fear within America.

Tonight, there were three main posters debating the best way to destroy America. Most of it was hatred-laced dribble, but it provided Amir with the platform he needed to plant another seed. He added to the conversation like he was a fellow American-hater for a few minutes. When the time was right he posted a simple message and then left the chat:

"We will see how strong America is after May 1st."

***

Bishop Charron was in the office early. The Vatican had not been happy the police had been given a search warrant and even more upset he had not found a way to stop them. If they'd known he had actually turned over 200 pages of evidence willingly, he would have been relinquished of his duties. He was not particularly interested in being selected as the new Archbishop, so having the Vatican mad at him was not a big concern.

The small TV in his office was rarely used, but since the murders, he felt it necessary to monitor the news agencies. As he sipped on a cup of English tea, he flipped through the network stations looking for coverage. It wasn't hard to find.

Since neither the police nor the Vatican had released much information, the coverage was mostly expert speculations and rehashing of old stories of Catholic Priests abusing little boys. He had not really paid a lot of attention to the various stories over the years because they had seemed isolated. They had also always been distant from his little part of the Catholic empire.

In his heart he knew the Catholic Church was good and this situation, no matter how awful, did not change a thousand years of great service to God. His faith was even stronger now, even if he was appalled by the reactions of the Vatican. Men are men and not perfect. Faith in God would get him, the Church, and all the victims through this tough time.

His phone rang and startled him from his thoughts. He looked at the phone and saw it was line five. It was late for the Vatican to be calling, but he was sure this had become a twenty-four hour headache for them. "Hello, this is Bishop Charron."

"Good morning, Bishop Charron. This is Senator Stiano."

"Oh, hello Senator," he stumbled as his mind tried to figure out how the Senator had called on the Vatican's private line. "Ah, how can I be of service?"

"Actually, that's why I was calling you. You've had a couple of rough days, we've all had a couple of rough days, and I thought you might need a sympathetic ear."

"That is very kind of you Senator."

"As you know, the Church and especially this Diocese is very special to me. I wanted to offer my services if you needed any strings pulled with the FBI, or even the local police. We don't want anyone making more out of this tragic situation than it is, if you know what I mean."

The Senator's words sounded very similar to those of Cardinal Jespers. That might explain why the Senator had access on line five. He decided not to play along. "No, I'm sorry Senator, I don't know what you mean."

"Well, let's just say that at times like these, you need to stick with your friends and protect the Church from those who want to unjustly tear it down. I wanted to make sure you knew you have a friend in the US Senate who can help. I also want you to know the FBI will be taking over this investigation and I've requested Agent Murphy, another good friend of the church, to take the lead. If the DC police contact you any more, you should refuse to answer their questions or cooperate. If they cause you any trouble, you call me. Agent Murphy and the FBI know how to handle this type of situation much better than some street detective."

"Thank you for this information Senator. I assure you my cooperation with any authority other than God is always guarded to protect the Church. As Jesus said, give to Caesar what is Caesars' and give to God what is God's."

"Ah…yeah." He had successfully confused the Senator. "Okay, well I just wanted you to know you have friends if you need help."

"Thanks, Senator. It is always good to know who your friends are."

"You got that right. Hang in there, Bishop. We'll get through this." With that, the phone went dead.

***

The information Trista had looked up last night on Senator Stiano's trips to the Vatican was another piece of the puzzle. Three trips in ten years was not exactly a smoking gun, but it was noteworthy. Nate put the information in the file he was going to use to update Pete in a few minutes.

The breakfast burrito Nate had eaten on his way to work was not sitting well. He popped a few anti-acid tablets in his mouth, grabbed his cup of coffee and headed down the hall to Pete's office.

"Ready for me?" he asked at the doorway.

"Yep. Am I gonna need some aspirin after this?"

"Why should I be the only one with a headache and queasy stomach?"

"Good point. Give it to me quick, the FBI moved our meeting up to nine, so we only have 30 minutes."

"I heard Congress was calling for the FBI to take over, so maybe we are going to get relieved."

"Seriously, did you really?"

"Yep, my girlfriend is the Post's reporter on the Hill and she said they were calling for an FBI investigation at some committee meeting yesterday."

"Crap. Sounds like this meeting at nine is an ambush."

"Might be. Before I update you, I need to talk to you about my girlfriend and this case."

"She's a reporter? Uh oh, I smell trouble."

"Not really. I actually think she can be a big help. She can give us cover when we go after the politicians."

"First, we have not decided to go after any politicians and second, what the hell are you talking about?"

"So Trista, that's my girlfriend, is well connected on the Hill. She can dig up facts and uncover the story. She prints it and then we have to investigate. Better yet, we let the FBI take that part of the case and we stick to the Church."

"So did you already leak this story to her?" Pete's stare was menacing.

"No, you know better. But, I did ask her a few questions and she's starting to get curious. I think she could help us if we give her a few tips at what rock to look under."

"Hmm. Not sure I like that. Could put her in danger and get our asses handed to us for leaking stuff to the press."

"Yeah I know, but think about it. We're gonna get our asses handed to us no matter what we do when we go after the politicians."

Nate launched into what he had uncovered for the next 20 minutes. After he was finished, Pete didn't say a word. He reached into his top drawer, grabbed a few aspirin, and chased them down with his last sip of coffee. He rose, motioned for Nate to follow and headed down the hall to meet with the FBI.

***

She felt guilty about it, but Trista could not help but dig into Senator Stiano's campaign finance reports. His last election was only two years ago, so the information was easy to find. It was a bit harder to go back eight years to previous elections, and after a couple hours, she had a pile of reports, but no real tie to the Vatican.

She debated giving Nate a copy of the reports to see if he recognized any of the donor's names, but decided she should wait. He'd asked her not to do any fishing just yet, so it was better to lie low and wait for him to ask.

Having spent enough time doing his work, it was time to do hers. She grabbed her purse and notebook and headed to Capitol Hill. She considered herself lucky to work in such a historic and beautiful place, but the grind of the political circuit was starting to get to her. Long hours, editors who would not let her stories run until they were politically friendly, and always having to watch your back were not the type of work conditions anyone could take for long.

It had only been two years, but she was ready to start ruffling some feathers. If pursuing Nate's story led to being re-assigned or a career change, so be it. It was time to see if she was tough enough to make it big in this business. She would either do something spectacular and write a book about it, or go down in a blaze of glory. Either way, the rat race of DC politics was not where she wanted to be in the long-term.

***

It had been a long night. The thin mattress was barely relief from the concrete floor. Kristin had only slept in fits and spurts, worried about her girls. She mentally kicked herself several times for not cooperating with Jake and getting to see her girls. She would not make that mistake again.

Hearing some movement outside the door, she put on her game face. She would execute her plan and get away from this goon. She sat against the back wall and watched as the door slowly swung open. He was standing a few feet outside the door until he was sure she was not ready to attack him.

"Good morning. Hope you slept well," he said in a disarming tone.

"Not bad," she replied, biting her tongue.

"How about a quick visit to the bathroom and then some breakfast?"

"That would be nice, thank you," she said in the most pleasant voice she could muster.

"Do I need these?" he asked holding up a pair of handcuffs.

"No, I'll do whatever you want."

"That would make things a lot easier...on everyone." His smile was a victory sign.

She hid her disgust, but her resolve increased. She was going to make this jerk pay, eventually, but for now, having him believe he was in control was what she wanted.

She felt stronger after eating. That was two meals in a row, if she counted last night's fruit as dinner. Living on the street meant missing more meals than she made. The girls were more important, so often she would give them all the food she had even if she was painfully hungry.

He was leaning against a doorway silently watching her. She had eaten everything he had put out for her: two hardboiled eggs, a muffin and a banana. She looked up as she was swallowing her last bite and noticed he still had his victory smile on his face. She smiled back at him. If she was still capable of flirting, she would, but the street had hardened her.

"You seem to be doing well. Would you like a short visit with the girls?"

She nodded her head instantly. "Yes, please."

"Wait here, I'll be right back." He turned and left the room.

She glanced around quickly to see if there was anything she could take as a weapon, or any possible escape routes, if the opportunity presented itself. Other than a brief thought of removing a leg from the couch, she found nothing to help her cause.

True to his word, Jake was back quickly with the girls right behind him. They squealed "Mommy!" and ran the last few steps into her arms. They stayed locked in a three-way hug for at least a minute before she pulled them back to get a good look at them.

Her quick visual inspection revealed no obvious damage. She hugged them back to her and whispered in Sara's ear, "Stay calm and cooperate. Everything is going to be okay, I promise." Then she pulled away from the embrace and asked, "Are you gals okay? Did you get something to eat? Did Jake give you these pretty clothes?" she asked, looking at their pink dresses.

"Yes, Mommy. We even took a hot shower," Sara replied.

"Mini, you doin' okay?" The young girl only nodded her head. "Everything will be okay, sweetie. Just behave yourself for Jake and Mommy will make sure we are back together soon. Love you gals!" She drew them in close for another hug, sensing her time was almost up. She closed her eyes tight and for the first time in years, she prayed.

***

Agent Anthony "Tony" Murphy had spent his entire career with the FBI and he planned to spend the few years left before retirement with a low profile, not causing any trouble or drawing any attention to himself. He had let his bosses know he was willing to tackle the boring, mundane cases other agents did not want to take. Investigating the Catholic Diocese after a triple murder was not what he had in mind.

It had started with a strange call from Senator Stiano. The conversation had been short, laced with innuendo, and had caused Agent Murphy great concern. The Senator, who Murphy had met a few times at fundraisers for Catholic charities, had told him he was going to be assigned as the lead investigator on the recent Priest murders. The Church, according to the Senator, was counting on him to make sure these horrible crimes were not used to attack the Church and ruin all the good work that was being done.

Thirty minutes later, he had been summoned to his boss's office and assigned the case as the Senator had said. He thought about asking for the case to be assigned to another agent, but it had been made clear he had been selected for reasons that would not be mentioned. He knew the reason and it made him sick to his stomach. At some point in his investigation, he was going to be forced to choose between protecting his Church and his duty as an FBI agent. Either choice was wrong and his allegiance to both institutions was strong.

When Nate and Pete walked into the small conference room, Agent Murphy expected he would have to deal with the petty jurisdictional crap that always revolved around a high-profile case. The local police were generally considered low on the hierarchy, but they often had a chip on their shoulder and the FBI agent was ready to do battle to secure full authority of the case. His church depended on it.

The agent had his back to the door when the local cops entered and intentionally ignored them in an attempt to establish superiority. One of the cops cleared his throat loudly and Murphy turned from the window he had been staring out to face them.

"Thanks for moving this up, I'm Tony Murphy," he said, offering a handshake and a business card.

"Pete Marcus, and this is Nate Romano."

"Again, thanks for moving this meeting up. I know you are very busy, so let's get to it," Murphy said while motioning the two detectives to have a seat at the small conference table. "I was assigned to this case late yesterday afternoon, so I am not up to speed yet. Can you brief me on where we are?"

The agent had intentionally said, "where we are," to indicate this was the opening round of the battle to take over the case.

For the next 30 minutes, Pete shared the basics of the case, but Murphy got the feeling he was holding back a lot of the information. It was not the right time to challenge the detective, so Murphy maintained his poker face.

"What about the Diocese? Did you find anything that backs up Hill's claim of abuse by the priest?" Murphy asked when the briefing was over.

"Nothing concrete yet, but we just started digging."

"Sounds like the guy is delusional to me. The connection to the politicians is probably crazy, too."

"We have not started working the political angle yet. We were hoping we could hand that aspect of the case to the FBI."

"Well, this is your lucky day 'cause I have been told to take over all the conspiracy stuff and let you guys handle the murder case."

"When you say 'all the conspiracy stuff' do you mean the church and the politicians?" Pete asked.

"Yep. My bosses are talking to your bosses this morning and the entire investigation, except the actual murders, will be turned completely over to the FBI."

"Bullshit! You can't do..." The hothead agent was cut off by the senior detective's raised hand before he finished.

"With all due respect . . ." Pete started.

"This has nothing to do with respect," Murphy retorted. "People higher up the food chain than either of us have made this decision. Frankly, I'm two years away from retirement and I have no interest in taking this case from you. It was not my choice."

Pete stood abruptly and Nate followed suit. "Good luck, Agent Murphy. You're gonna need it." With that, Pete turned and left the room and Nate followed without saying a word.

Pete was waiting for the elevator when Nate caught up to him. "This is bullshit, Pete."

"Yep, but I'm not surprised. I'm going upstairs to see if we can get the Captain to stand up to the FBI, but I'm guessing this is coming from way upstairs and there is nothing we can do about it."

"What do you want me to do?"

"Go make a copy of all your files because we are probably going to have to turn everything over to the FBI." Pete turned to face Nate. "Be careful," he whispered in a sarcastic tone, "you wouldn't want to lose any of the information you have before you can get it to the FBI." Pete smiled at the puzzled look on Nate's face.

"Ah, gotcha," Nate replied, understanding Pete's message. "I'll make sure I gather all the case information we just briefed them about." Without another word, Nate turned and headed to his office.

Chapter 9

A plan was starting to formulate in Kristen's mind. She had been very thankful and compliant with Jake on her way back to her cell after seeing her girls. She had realized he was easier to deal with when he thought he was in control. She would give him that illusion until it was time to make her move.

She had even tried turning on her feminine charms to see if he was playable with the thought of sex. It would not have been the first time she had resorted to using sex to get what she needed. It had not seemed to work on Jake. Instead, it seemed like he really wanted to help her.

Could it be this creep had somehow convinced himself he was helping her? She'd have to test that theory and if so, she could use that to her advantage. He had promised to bring her lunch and she would explore this angle when he did. In the meantime, there was nothing to do but wait.

Her plan was simple: earn his trust and then, when the moment was right, knee him in the balls as hard as she possibly could. After that, the plan was vague. She contemplated killing him after disabling him with the blow to the balls, but that was not in her nature…at least not yet.

***

Bishop Charron was at his desk trying to get some work done. The good work of the church still needed to be done, even in this time of crisis. He had mobilized his staff and called upon the priests in the area to help. In an hour, he would be holding a meeting to discuss the need to move forward.

His phone rang and the receptionist announced it was an FBI agent on the line. He thought of his call from Senator Stiano and knew this was both trouble and relief. He debated, for a second, declining the call, but he was never one to put off something just because it was difficult.

"Bishop Charron, this is Agent Tony Murphy with the FBI. I am now the lead on the investigation into the Catholic Church's actions, ah possible actions, related to the recent murders. I'd like to see if you'd be available this afternoon for a meeting."

"I can be. I have already told everything I know to Detective Romano of the DC Police."

"Yes, I know. I met with Detective Romano this morning and he has turned over the investigation to the FBI."

"Do you have the file of information he took?"

"Ah, file? We are still in the process of transferring all the case information to the FBI. I hope to have it this afternoon."

"Well, perhaps you should wait until you review that file before you come see me. It would make for a more productive meeting."

"Sure, Father. I should have that file very soon and will review before we meet. Three o'clock okay with you?"

"Yes, Agent Murphy. I will clear my schedule for you."

"Thanks. And Bishop Charron?"

"Yes."

"From now on, please do not talk to anyone regarding this matter, except me. To do so would be counter-productive."

"I understand your concern, Agent Murphy. See you at three."

The Bishop returned the phone to the cradle while he considered the conversation. Had Detective Romano shared all the contents of the file with Agent Murphy? If he did, the meeting with Agent Murphy would be rather contentious. If not, the truth was more likely to come out. He took in a deep breath and let it exhale slowly. It was in God's hands now and whatever happened was His will.

***

Nate was sorting through the file Father Charron had collected for him and all the other evidence. He had already made a copy of everything and stashed it away in his locked file cabinet. As he went through the various printouts of emails and documents in the file, he was separating them into two piles. One pile was for documents Pete had referred to while briefing Agent Murphy and the other was for items not mentioned in the briefing.

Just as he finished the last document, his phone rang. Instinctually, he reached for the handset and pulled it to his ear. "Detective Romano."

"Detective, this is Agent Murphy's assistant at the FBI. Agent Murphy requests you provide him with all the case information you collected, especially the file of information from your visit with Father Charron. I have already dispatched a currier to pick it up."

"Sure. I'll have it waiting. Anything else?"

"Ah, no. Thank you for the cooperation." The tone of her voice indicated she had not expected him to cooperate. Little did she know how right she was about his intentions.

The entire case file had been over an inch thick. He estimated the file he had deemed ready for the FBI as approximately half that size. He did not like holding information from the FBI, but Nate sensed Agent Murphy was not really planning on solving this case. More precisely, the powers above had decided the FBI would handle this case were likely more intent on making this case fade into the black hole of information that was often the center of Washington, DC.

On a hunch, Nate picked up the phone and called Bishop Charron's personal line.

"This is Bishop Charron, how may I be of service?" His voice was calm and steady and Nate admired the grace the man was able to display under the circumstances.

"Father, it's Detective Romano."

"Hello Detective. I just heard you are no longer working this case."

"I gather you spoke to Agent Murphy."

"Yes, just a few minutes ago. And last night, I had a call from Senator Stiano letting me know this matter would be taken over by the FBI. Seems he thinks they will be more sensitive to the churches privacy than the DC Police."

"You did? Now that is interesting. Father, I think you need to be careful in dealing with the FBI on this. While your cooperation was greatly appreciated by the DC Police, the FBI is a different beast and you should be careful. As we both know, the political element of this case is not something either of us wants to get caught in."

"Seems like you may have already been caught, Detective. I appreciate your concern, but there is no need to worry about me. I serve the church and will continue to do so no matter what the dangers. Detective, may I ask you a question?"

"Sure."

"Will you be turning over the entire file to the FBI?"

"I will turn over all records that I feel have baring on the aspects of the case related to what the FBI is planning to investigate," he said in his best double-speak. "The DC Police will continue to follow aspects of the case the FBI is not interested in. Is that what you wanted to know, Father?"

"Indeed."

As Nate placed the phone back on the cradle, he thought of another person who needed to be contacted. Laurie Ganz was the only other person who knew the entire story. He needed to give her a heads up. He started to pick up the phone, but stopped, smiled at the thought of seeing her, and headed to the lab.

***

Max Pigman was wasting no time. He was waiting at the clerk's office when it opened so he could file a federal lawsuit against the City of Charlottesville for helping a YMCA gym, a tax exempt religious organization, compete against free enterprise. The plaintiff in the case was the Atlantic Coast Athletic Club (ACAC) who did not receive any support from the city, but operated a large gym in Charlottesville.

It had not been hard to convince the owner of ACAC to become the plaintiff. Not only did Max know the owner well, but his services were being funded by an anonymous sponsor. ACAC had a no cost, no risk, and the owner was legitimately upset by the deal the city had given the YMCA to open a major gym that would directly compete with him.

The case outlined the city's agreement to provide the YMCA $400,000 in funding, plus free land in a local public park. In return, the YMCA was supposed to operate some community programs to help the lower income families in the area. The cost of the services to be delivered by the YMCA were going to be subsidized by state and federal funds, so the YMCA was not really providing anything in return for the city's funding.

In addition, the location of the YMCA facility was miles away from the parts of the city that needed the community programs. To access the daycare and other services, disadvantaged citizens would need to take a bus or drive a car. The location was very convenient to the middle and upper class suburban dwellers who would provide the YMCA with the bulk of its members and profits.

The more Max worked on this case, the more agitated he became. By the time he was ready to file the case, he was on a personal mission to take down the city. He also had a personal political axe to grind with the city. Charlottesville was a typical college town, filled with liberal thinkers and politicians. Max was from a part of Richmond where conservative thinking and politics was as dominant as any place in America. He was going to use this case to expose the liberal weenies in Charlottesville.

After filing his case with the federal court in Richmond, Max headed across the street to Capital Square to meet with a few key politicians. He had a large check in his pocket from his sponsor, the Foundation for Religious Freedom. He knew he could not buy a judge, but money talked with politicians. He knew if the political flames were fanned on this issue, the courts would be more likely to support his cause. He knew a half-dozen state politicians who would love to use this issue to stir up their conservative, pro-business voter base.

***

Nate entered the crime lab through the main door and headed to the back section where he knew Laurie usually worked. He found her in front of a large computer screen. "Hey, you working on the priest killings?"

"Oh, hey Nate," she said with a smile, looking up from her work. "Yep, and finding some good stuff. I was just getting ready to call you to fill you in."

"Really? Great minds must think alike," he said, deciding to get her update before telling her about the FBI.

"Yeah, well, maybe, but this case is about all I have been thinking about," she said, lowering her voice and looking around to make sure no one was able to overhear. "I think there is some serious shit going on here. Frankly, it is a little scary how deep this goes."

"I'm with you," he whispered. "Can you show me what you found, or do we need to find a quieter place?" he asked nodding his head toward the conversations going on in the other part of the lab.

She looked at her watch and said, "It's eleven now...let's meet for lunch at Dino's in an hour. I know the owner and she'll save us a quiet booth in the back where we can talk. That'll give me some more time to pull this stuff together."

"Perfect." He turned to leave, but then remembered the need to warn her about the FBI. "One other thing – the FBI is taking over the case. We are giving them the basic case information, but let's not share this heavy duty stuff until we are sure it is legit." He winked at her to let her know there was more to the FBI takeover than he could say.

"Gotcha. See you in an hour."

***

Trista was on Capitol Hill attending a Senate hearing on nuclear power safety standards. The topic and the hearing were both boring her so she whipped out her iPad to do some more digging on Senator Stiano. She checked his record for the bills he had sponsored and found a few interesting ones that might relate to the Catholic Church.

He had sponsored a bill that would have expanded diplomatic immunity to some additional officials in the Catholic Church, including Archbishops stationed in the United States. The bill never made it out of committee, but it was a clear tie to the church.

Next, she searched for the Senator's campaign materials to see if he had run on any issues related to the church. His website made it clear he was anti-abortion and gay rights, two issues near and dear to the Catholic Church, but these issues were also embraced by many others besides Catholics. Another tie, but one that was more circumstantial. She chuckled as she realized she was starting to think of the Senator in terms of a criminal trial.

She put her iPad away and tried to refocus on the hearing. If she was going to have to write a story on this crap, she'd better pay attention. It would be much more interesting to write a story about Stiano and the priest killings than nuclear safety, but that would be getting ahead of things. First, she had to figure out how to share this information with Nate without getting him mad at her.

She pulled out her phone and sent Nate a text asking if they could meet for lunch. He responded back quickly, *No can do. Buy you a drink later?*

I'll need one after this hearing…later.

***

Nate stopped by Pete's office on his way out to lunch, but the office was empty. He dialed Pete's cell and it went immediately into voicemail.

"Hey Pete. It's Nate. Just wanted you to know I turned over the case file to the FBI and wanted to know if you need me to do anything else. Buzz me when you can."

The voicemail was a signal to Pete that he needed to fill him in on some break in the case. Both men planned to continue working on the entire case no matter what the FBI and their own bosses told them. They'd have to be careful and a bit sneaky, but they were not about to let this case get shoved under the rug.

He turned his thought to lunch with Laurie and realized he had a few nervous butterflies in his stomach. Was this the excitement of learning some good stuff on the case, or something more personal? He dismissed the thought and tried to refocus on his next step in the case. They would need this case, or at least certain parts of it, to go public to give them some cover. Otherwise, it would be tough to keep investigating either the church or the politicians.

As he walked through the office on his way to lunch, he passed a TV in the lobby set to CNN. He heard the talking head on the screen say, "The Catholic Church is no different than our own government." He stopped to listen and noticed the caption under the image that identified Senator Terry McDermott. "The recent priest killings," the Senator continued, "are a perfect example of the oppression citizens feel when they are governed by religion. In this tragic case, a citizen took drastic action to break free of the tyranny of Catholic Church."

Nate stood there a few more seconds as the Senator droned on. What he said did not make any sense, but CNN had still given his airtime. The crap that passed for news these days never ceased to amaze him.

Dino's was only a block away and he arrived before she did. He mentioned to the hostess that he was meeting Laurie Ganz and she gave him a knowing smile and led him to a booth in the back of the restaurant. From there he could see the entire restaurant and the entrance to the bistro. A few minutes later, he watched Laurie enter, nod to the hostess and head to the booth.

"Hey," she said with a friendly smile and a slightly haggard tone. "Sorry I'm a few minutes late. I wanted to make a copy of everything for you and the damn printer jammed."

"Thanks," he said taking the half-inch thick folder from her. "Are you going to give me a guided tour, or should I just dig in?"

"I'll walk you through it, but first, let's order. I'm starved." Like magic, the waiter was there right on cue. "Did you look at the menu yet?" she asked.

"Yep. I'll have Pesto Chicken Salad and an iced tea." The waiter nodded, made a note on his pad and looked to Laurie for her order. She ordered a Monte Cristo and a side salad without looking at the menu.

"You come here often?" he asked in a mocking flirtatious tone.

"Yeah," she laughed. "The owner and I were roommates in college."

He touched the folder she had given him. "What's in here?"

"Two sets of evidence. First, I dug up all the financial transactions between the church and the families of the victims. Turns out there was a lot more money to this than we thought. In many cases, the totals were well into the hundreds of thousands of dollars."

"No wonder no one complained. That kind of change will buy you a lot of silence."

"Yep. And the rest of the file is another topic I am still working on. I've watched the killer's video three times now. He implicated three politicians, two senators and a representative. The ringleader is Stiano and the other two seem to be his gang. Tracing the political contribution from the church to the politicians is still a work in progress, but tracing the money the other way – from politician to church is easy."

"That makes sense. One is a charitable deduction and one is a political bribe. Sorry, I'm a bit cynical."

"With you on that. So all three of our politicians have given in excess of $50,000 to the church in the past year. I'm not sure yet, but it seems ten times that amount has come back to the politicians from sources connected to the church. Most notable, Archbishop Reilly gave $20,000 to each of the three in the last campaign. It has to be fleshed out a bit still, but it appears the financial ties between the church and the three stooges is large."

"Wow! What about ties between the victims and the politicians?"

"Huh. I had not thought of that. I'll look into it. That would be a smoking gun."

"Yep. Hey, you need to know what you are dealing with here. This is not a normal case."

"No shit! Oh, sorry, excuse my French," she said with a smile.

"We think the FBI has been brought in to the case to protect the church."

"Yeah. Wish I could say that was a surprise."

"Me too. Father Charron got a call from Senator Stiano telling him he was having the case assigned to the FBI, essentially to protect the church."

"Did you give the feds all the stuff Father Charron gave you?

Nate looked around to make sure no one was able to hear him. "No, but I don't want to mix you up in this. It may get dicey."

"Look Nate, I'm a big girl. I know how the politics work in this type of thing. I'm in with you as long as we keep everything legal."

"Ha! Legal is the least of my worries. This could get dangerous. I don't want you to be put at risk."

"Look, I'm Catholic, or at least I was raised Catholic. I'm not much on it now, but I can't stand the thought my church could cover this crap up. Why didn't they turn these perverted priests in? I feel betrayed and want to make it right. The church is a great institution, but this crap needs to be dealt with. If they are going to try and hide it, and I know about it, I'm just as guilty. Don't try to protect me."

He looked at her with a mix of admiration and inspiration. She was right and he knew it. "Look, this could get dangerous. This is not a few local gang members mixing it up. This is international and religious. Lots of money and power at stake. We are worried about this playing out in a bad way. I cannot ask you to help."

"You also can't stop me. I'm in and understand the dangers. Us lab rats don't get to experience the dangerous side like you do. Maybe I'm naïve, but this makes my job seem worthwhile. I'm in, all in."

He looked at her in the eyes. She was serious and probably not as naïve as he thought. She stayed silent watching him look at her. The silence was long and pregnant. "Okay," he finally said. But you can back out at any point. This is probably gonna get nasty."

Looking him directly in the eye, she said, "I'm in. I trust you, Nate."

Chapter 10

Agent Murphy was a few minutes late for his three o'clock meeting with Bishop Charron thanks to the heavy DC traffic. There were still a few news trucks parked across the street from the Diocese and he was thankful he had worn a suit instead of a FBI windbreaker. The camera crews quickly jumped to life as he pulled in, hopeful to get some meaningful pictures for the evening news.

The guard at the gatehouse quickly checked his ID and waived him inside the walled compound. He parked next to a Police car and got concerned Detective Marcus had not called off his investigation. As he approached the large ornate entrance to the Diocese, a uniformed officer stepped out from behind a pillar and blocked his way. The two men stared at each other for a few seconds, both attempting to intimidate the other.

"Agent Murphy, FBI. That your car?" he asked nodding his head toward the squad car.

"Yep," the officer replied flatly.

"Have you been told the FBI has taken over the case?"

"Yep. But not the security of the Diocese."

"Correct. You the only officer here?"

"Yep."

"Well, this has been a fun chat, but I have an appointment with Bishop Charron and I'm a little late." He attempted to walk around the officer, but the young officer moved to block his way.

"Need to see your ID," the officer said, with a smirk on his face.

Murphy, realizing the officer was just trying to piss him off, decided not to take the bait. He took a half step back before reaching into his jacket to withdraw his ID. Without saying a word, he handed it to the officer. After several long seconds, he was given his ID back and allowed to pass.

"Thank you for your excellent security procedures," he said in a mocking tone as he went through the door.

Waiting inside was Sister Mary Elizabeth. "Agent Murphy, please follow me," she said as she turned and quickly headed towards the back of the building. He had to hustle to catch up and she was already knocking softly on a large wooden door when he finally did. She opened the door, announced his name and motioned for him to enter.

"Hello, Agent Murphy. I'm Bishop Charron."

"Hello, Bishop. First, let me say how sorry I am for the church's loss. This must be a very difficult time around here."

"Indeed, but this too shall pass." He motioned for him to be seated on a couch and the Bishop took to a large armchair.

"Have you read the file yet?" he said, referring to the inch-thick folder he had provided Detective Romano.

"Yes and I have a few questions for you." Murphy shifted on the couch and unzipped his leather portfolio. He withdrew a rather thin folder.

"Did the police search the Archbishop's office?"

"Yes, and his computer," answered the Bishop.

"Did the Archbishop use email?"

"Yes, we all do. Even the Catholic Church has embraced the wonders of the Internet."

"I did not see any email communications from him in the file."

"Archbishop Reilly regularly deleted his email. We all do. If we need to keep a record, we print and file it."

"I see. And is there a file for the Archbishop's emails?"

"Not that I know of."

"I'll need to take his computer with me," Murphy said matter of factly. "We have some scary smart nerds who can find stuff that has been deleted."

"The police have already taken his computer."

"Did they take anything else?"

"No, except the folder of documents."

"Can you show me his office? I'd like to poke around and see if I can find anything they missed."

"Sure." Bishop Charron stood and the agent rose to follow. "His office is down the hall."

***

Nate spent the rest of the afternoon reading through the documents Laurie had printed for him. She was right; this was clear documentation there was a tie between the church and the three politicians. Money was the language that translated between industries, between countries and between religions. Nate had always said, follow the money and you will find the truth. Clearly that theory applied to this situation.

The day was drawing to an end and Nate was ready to call it a day. As a cop, he did not always get to decide when his day was done, but today was a good day. He decided to text Trista to meet him at Sloan's Pub for a drink. It was right around the corner from their place, or places, to be more accurate, so it was a great way to end a workday. They could have a few drinks and walk home.

She quickly replied back she would be there around 5:30. He wrapped up a few loose ends to his day and set off for home. He found a great parking space on the street near his townhouse and was feeling good about things when he saw the black man dressed in jeans and a green t-shirt. He was large, six foot six inches and probably 300 pounds of muscle. His dark sunglasses did not hide the fact he was staring right at Nate.

Acting like he was putting his car keys in his pocket, Nate subtly clicked the safety off his revolver. He trusted his cop instincts for trouble and was ready. He shut the door to his car, clicked the key fob to lock it and turned to find the man facing him. His hand went to his gun, but the man did not attack.

They stared at each other for a few seconds before Nate said, "Can I help you?"

"Maybe. You Detective Romano?"

"Yep. Who are you?"

"Name's George. You don't need to know more. I understand you are looking into the priest murders."

"Yeah, so?"

"I know some shit that might help you." Nate just eyed the big man and shrugged his shoulders. "I was also abused by the three dead priests."

"Really?" Nate watched George's body language and concluded he was telling the truth. "Okay, what can I do for you George?"

"Not sure. I just don't want the bastards to get turned into some saint like Pope Paul did. Those priests deserved to die. This Hill guy did the world a favor."

"Yeah. Did you know Hill?"

"Nah. Just saw the news. Wish I had been there to watch the bastards suffer."

"So, George. Why haven't you come forward before?"

"Couldn't. They paid a lot of money to my parents to keep us quiet. Most of it went to therapy for me, but I was not allowed to tell my story. Now that they're dead, guess I'm free to talk."

"George, I'd like your help, but this is a very dangerous situation. Frankly, I'm not sure you are safe. The church is pretty scared this is gonna come out and I'm not sure what they will do to protect themselves."

"Thanks for your concern, Detective, but I can take care of myself. I'm really glad this is over, or at least it is ready to be over. For years I've lived with a nasty secret and I'm ready for the lie I've been living to come to an end. I will not be happy until the truth is out."

"So, can I get a statement from you and count on you to testify?"

"Yes."

"Give me your name and number and I'll give you a call tomorrow."

George reached into his pocket, withdrew a business card and handed it to Nate.

"George Knowles, Landscape Architect," he read from the card. "I'll give you a call tomorrow. By the way, how did you find me?"

"Bishop Charron."

"Good man. Thanks, George. I want to get the bastards as bad as you. Please be cautious, this is some deep shit and I don't want anyone to get taken down who shouldn't be. Oh, by the way, don't talk to anyone else about this. Not sure who we can trust just yet."

"Gotcha, Detective. I'll be careful."

Nate walked the half block to Sloan's Pub. Trista was already there waiting for him and greeted him with a great kiss and hug that washed away all the problems of the day.

She was looking good in her tight jeans and scoop neck shirt and Nate was sure she had not gone to work dressed like this. "Looks like you had time to go home and change?"

"Worked from home all afternoon. Great thing about my job is I can do it from anywhere. If I didn't have to attend boring Senate Committee meetings and interview stuffy politicians, I could live anywhere."

"Where else would you want to live? In your line of business, this is like fishin' in a barrel. Plenty of misbehaving politicians to write about," he added with a sarcastic smirk.

"My job is pretty easy, but I'm not sure how much longer I can take working this beat." Her suddenly serious tone caught his attention.

"Bad day?"

"Not really. Just want to do more with my career than write about new nuclear power safety regulations."

"Can you get transferred to the crime beat? I could feed you lots of juicy stories," he added with a smile.

"Speaking of that, I did find out one interesting thing about your pal, Stiano."

"I thought we agreed that you'd hold off at looking into him. What have you done?" His voice was sterner than he intended and he could tell by her body language he may have over-reacted. "Sorry. Didn't mean to sound so angry. I'm just worried about you."

"Worried?"

"Yeah, these folks aren't the type to mess with."

"I'm used to corrupt politicians."

"Yeah, but combine that with the most powerful church in the world. These guys haven't survived for thousands of years by letting reporters or cops take them down. I'm telling you, you'd better be careful."

"Okay, okay, I will. Do you wanna hear what I found or not?"

"Yes, sorry. I'd just rather you write stories on nuclear safety than international conspiracies."

"I'm not writing any story, yet," she smiled, teasing him playfully.

"Okay super-reporter. What did you find out?"

"Oh, so now you are back to being the good cop," she teased. "I was a little bored, so I started looking into the Senator's record. One thing jumped out. He sponsored a bill a few years ago that would have given diplomatic immunity to Bishops living in America. Just like ambassadors and other reps from other countries."

"Really," he said with eyebrows raised.

"Yep, never made it out of committee, but certainly puts him on record as a supporter of the church."

"Thanks, that helps some. Appreciate the research, but for now, please stop your research. You'll get me in trouble if it looks like I'm leaking stuff to the press."

A coy smile came to her face. "So, basically what you are saying is your butt is in my hands?"

He smiled, "Hey, I kinda like the sound of that, but before you decide how to handle this power, remember, I still have handcuffs."

Their laughter gave him a brief reprise from the stress the case. His plan had been to use a little alcohol and flirting to take her mind off the wedge this case was driving between their relationship. Based on the smile on her face, it was working.

***

It had been another long day locked in this room, but Kristen spent it getting mentally prepared to enact her plan. There was a noise outside her door and her spirits lifted. She rose to her feet and waited against the wall opposite the door. The door slowly opened and Jake stood there looking at her. She smiled at him to let him know he had tamed her.

"Hi, Jake. How are the girls?"

"Doing well. They just had dinner and I got them some new clothes."

"Thank you. I appreciate you taking good care of them. Not sure what your plan is, but I trust you. You seem to be a good guy."

"No worries, Kristen. Everything is going to be okay. You hungry?"

"I guess so. I'm not used to eating regularly. This will be the third meal I've had today. Not used to that."

"Those days of living on the street and scrounging for food are over. Your new life is going to be great."

As they talked, she slowly moved towards the door and he stepped aside to let her exit. She faked a little dizziness and fell against the doorframe as she left the room. He instinctively reached out and grabbed her arm. She let her weight be held up by his strong grip.

"Thanks. I must have stood up too quick," she said, as she softly touched the hand he held her with in an affectionate manner. "I think I'm okay now."

"Good. We need to get you strong and ready to go."

"Yeah, where are we going?"

"I've found a great place for you and the girls to live. You'll be leaving in a couple days."

"Are you coming with us?"

"No, I've got to help others like you. Let's get you something to eat and I'll tell you all about it."

She was very curious about where he was sending them, but knew it was not all good. She'd play along with this guy until the time was right, but then she'd attack. First, she needed to build his trust and get some more information. She'd play this guy with the street smarts she'd learned in the past year and then... She couldn't finish the thought with anything good. She had no place to go that was better than this. She quickly pushed that thought into the deep recess of her mind and refocused on the task at hand.

After a dinner of a sub from a local deli, she started up the conversation. "So, can you tell me more about your plans for us?"

He paused for a few moments, apparently searching her for sincerity. He must have decided she was ready to move forward because he continued to explain. "There is a man who needs someone to help. He wants you to come work for him and live on his ranch."

"You got me a job and a place for us to live? Jake, that's great. Where does this man live? What kinda work will I be doing?" So many questions were in her mind that she couldn't ask, so she kept it to these simply ones, hoping it would not tip him off.

"Calm down. It is a complicated situation that will only work with someone like you." The puzzled look on her face encouraged him to continue. "Kristen, you and this gentleman have a lot in common. Most importantly, neither of you are living high-profile lives. Neither of you have any family that can help and both of you are survivors."

"The difference between the two of you is what makes this work. You need a place to live and a new start to your life. He needs someone to help him maintain his privacy. More precisely, he needs someone to help him stay in hiding."

"Hiding? What is he hiding from?"

"Best you don't know. Let's just say a lot of people could be hurt if anyone finds him. That's why he needs you. He's offering you a good life in return for helping him stay private."

"And what exactly do I have to do?"

"Nothing illegal. Easiest way to say it is he needs someone to keep him company. Do light chores and stuff like that."

"And my girls?"

"They will be able to join you eventually. First, you have to prove yourself trustworthy."

"That's a lot of news to take in." She thought about asking him if she had a choice in this deal, but decided she did not, so why ask?

"Yes, I understand this is quite a lot to process, but I promise you your new life will be much better than living on the street."

***

Amir had been working his computer magic all day and into the evening. He had stirred up quite a lot of American hatred in a couple well-known Islamic chat rooms. He had to restrain himself and let his imaginary chatter unfold slowly. He had one primary goal – give the NSA enough hints to put them on alert about May 1st.

When the full plan was carried out, the NSA would easily jump to conclusions about who had initiated the attack. He was certain the people he was chatting with were a combination of real Islamic extremist and NSA agents. The ones he could trace to an actual location were the real terrorists and the ones that were harder to trace were likely to be NSA agents trying to infiltrate the chat rooms by pretending to be radical Islamic sympathizers.

After a few days, he had figured out who was who and was in the process of playing them all. It was easy for Amir to use his computer skills and human behavior knowledge to manipulate the system. It was already early April, so he had less than a month to plant all the seeds needed to accomplish his part of the mission.

He knew very little about the main mission. As a security measure, he had not been given the location or nature of the attack. All he knew was it was going to be of massive scale and the death toll would make 911 look like a picnic. He doubted it would live up to that type of scale, unless they used nuclear weapons and he was really hoping that was not the case. He did not know where the attack would happen, but figured it would be at a venue with a lot of people present.

Curious, he started to do a little research. He searched for large sporting events and concerts to see if he could figure out where the attack might happen. He knew he shouldn't, but he had to find out. If they were going to use nuclear weapons, he wanted to make sure Debbie was safe, not to mention his own safety.

May 1st was a Saturday, but there were surprisingly few sporting events or concerts being held in the entire country. There was a regular schedule of baseball games, but the most likely teams to inspire an attack – the Mets, Yankees and Nationals – were either on the road, or had the day off.

Searching by cities found a few possibilities. Denver had a large rock 'n roll concert at Mile High Stadium and Pittsburgh had a major country concert. Neither seemed like the high-profile target that would attract the attention desired. A few more searches and a little luck led him to a possible target, a religious rally at the old JFK Stadium in DC.

The rally was sponsored by a group called United in Christ and was a non-denominational protestant organization that boasted almost four million members. Over 50,000 attendees were expected on May 1st at JFK.

Amir admired the brilliance of this target selection, a Christian group in the capital city of America. With any luck there would be a few politicians present, or better yet, their kids. All he had to do was provide the NSA with enough evidence Muslim extremists were behind the attacks and a religious war would follow. America would have to attack Syria, Iraq, and Iran and the sleepy little religious war that had been around for almost two decades would be ready to erupt.

Chapter 11

As best she could tell, it had been two days since she and her girls had gotten into the Mission's van and been taken hostage by the man she now knew as Jake. This was the day he had told her she would be moving to her new home and her new life. She had gained a lot of trust with him, but she had not been able to execute her escape plan.

She had not been told how she would be traveling, but Kristen knew he was not going to let her just walk out the door and catch a bus. A tearful meeting with her girls this morning had allowed her to say goodbye and assure them they would be together again soon. The girls had believed her, and she was determined to make it happen.

The noise outside her door told her it was time to go. As the door opened, the anxiety of the unknown got to her. The tears were rolling down her cheeks by the time he opened the door and stood there silently looking at her.

"It's gonna be okay, Kristen. You'll see, this is going to be way better than living on the street."

"I know," she said, wiping her eyes with the back of her hand. "I just hate being away from my girls."

"We just need to get you settled and make sure you are happy before the girls can join you."

"But, what if I'm not. What if this place is horrible and this man is evil?"

"Now, now. That's not gonna happen. You are going to be living in a beautiful home and have everything you ever wanted. Once you realize how good you have it, I'll bring the girls to join you."

She did not trust him for a minute. If this was such a good deal, why had he kidnapped them? There was more to this story than he had told her and she needed to seize any opportunity to escape with the girls now, before they were separated.

"It's time to go. We have to do this secretly and safely. I'm gonna have to put this over your head," he said holding up a black cloth sack. "And sorry, but I have to handcuff your hands behind you."

"Why?"

"Well, Mr. Williams needs to guard his secrecy. No one can know where he lives. You will not be allowed to leave, but it is a wonderful place to live."

"I won't be able to leave? Ever?"

"Well, Mr. Williams is 85 years old and in failing health. You will be compensated well, but you will only get the money if you stick with him until he dies."

"Money? How much?"

"Hundred grand a year, in cash. No taxes."

"Whoa. No shit?"

"There's more if you treat Mr. Williams well. He is very rich and does not have family."

"So, can I ask? What's the catch? This sounds too good to be true."

"Fair enough. There's a catch. First, you are not allowed to have any contact with anyone outside the compound. Second, there is a certain expectation Mr. Williams has." He paused and tried to read her puzzled expression. "Mr. Williams is a lonely man. He needs a companion."

"Companion? You mean sex?"

"He's 85. Taking care of his needs should be pretty easy."

She wanted to ask him if she had a choice in the situation, but she already knew the answer. He was pimping her out and if she did not play along, she'd never see the girls again. Once he put the handcuffs on and the bag over her head, there would be no turning back.

***

Nate had spent the last few days organizing his case and formulating a strategy. He checked his watch and noted his meeting with Pete Marcus was still 30 minutes away. Laurie had helped him form his plan and would be here any minute to review things one final time.

Working on the case together over the past few days had actually been enjoyable. He was not sure why they had made such a strong connection, but they were a good team. Maybe it was because they had a secret that could not be shared with others, maybe it was the magnitude of the case, or maybe the bond was more personal. All he knew was he enjoyed her company and she was a very good lab tech.

Before he could analyze the situation more, she knocked on his door. He looked up and her smile caused him to smile back. She entered the tiny office without waiting to be invited and sat in the lone guest chair. "Are we ready?"

"Think so," he replied. "I would like to run through the plan one more time before we take it to Pete."

"Let's do it. We were going to start with reviewing the evidence, right?"

"Yep. Then we should paint the ugly picture for him. He knows most of it, but we need to remind him of all the political crap, the power of the Vatican, and the corruption of the FBI investigation. He'll never buy this crazy-ass plan if he isn't reminded this is not an ordinary case."

"Yeah. This whole thing sounds more like some novel written by a nut-case than real life."

"Maybe we'll write a book after this is all over…assuming we don't get ourselves killed. You sure you want in on this? These people scare me more than the gangs of DC."

"Hey, I told you not to worry about me," she said, mockingly waggling her finger at him. "This plan is good and will work."

"It sounds more like something a politician would think up than the DC police. Are we in over our heads?"

"Probably, but we can't trust anyone. The church's reach is too deep. If this is going to get done, we have to do it. Now, let's review the plan."

Twenty minutes later they headed down the hall to Pete's office. It took them a full hour to convince Pete the plan might work, but they finally got a nod. Pete did not have the authority to approve what they wanted to do, but no one else did either. Nothing in the plan was illegal, but it was so far outside standard protocol it was not covered in any police manual.

Pete had not really approved the plan as much as he had agreed to keep it secret. It was his case and out of respect, Nate had insisted they let him in on it. Normally, such approval would cover his ass if something went wrong, but this was more of a case of professional courtesy. The plan would put them all at risk and Nate wanted to make sure everyone was willing to play this game to the end…no matter how it ended.

***

It was a beautiful spring day in the nation's capitol and Senator Stiano looked like any other businessman taking a break on a park bench to enjoy the weather. He sat in the middle of the bench in order to discourage anyone from joining him. Casually scanning the park, he found what he was looking for, or rather who. Agent Murphy was approaching from the far end of the small park. His pace was slow and casual and as he approached the bench, the Senator moved to one end. Agent Murphy took a seat at the opposite end.

The two men did not greet each other or look at each other. Cameras were everywhere and they were treating this rendezvous like it was a clandestine meeting…and it was. Both men fully realized they were breaking a number of laws, but if it was for the good of the Church, they were more than willing.

The Senator pulled out his phone and pretended to check email before he started the conversation. "Thanks for coming," he said in a quiet mumble, being careful not to speak clearly enough to have his lips read. "How's the investigation going?"

"As planned. It was a little tricky getting the Archbishop's computer from the police lab and to the evidence room without having our lab geeks look at it. I removed the hard drive, so if anyone ever notices it was never properly processed, there will be nothing left to find."

"I appreciate your efforts, Agent Murphy, but the less detail you tell me the better. For both of us."

"Gotcha."

"Have the police stayed out of the case?"

"Yes. They know better than to mess with the FBI," he said with enough arrogance that it made the Senator smile. "In fact, we have found them to be very cooperative. Sometimes a case handoff like this can get territorial. I think they knew they were in over their heads."

"Good. Your efforts are appreciated and our nation's security will benefit greatly from your work. This is a very sensitive diplomatic issue and secrecy is essential. This must be kept between you and me, understood?"

"Of course."

"Good. After I leave, you can find a little thank you gift taped under the bench. Keep up the good work." With that the Senator stood and headed slowly down the sidewalk towards the quiet backstreet where his car was parked.

***

Debbie's workday at the German Embassy was going smoothly. She had made several travel arrangements for the Ambassador and his aids, written several thank you letters to dignitaries and completed her research of the special guests attending an embassy dinner later in the week.

During her short lunch break, she had texted Amir to check-in and do a little flirting. He was not available this evening, but plans were made to get together on hump day. She smiled just thinking about how appropriate it was to have a day in the middle of the week dedicated to humping.

Their relationship had grown beyond what she had ever intended. The natural compatibility of a Middle Eastern man and a German woman was both surprising and unexplainable. The bottom line was, they enjoyed each other's company and fed off of each other's preferences in the bedroom. In everyday life, he was the leader, but in the bedroom, she was in charge. Their relationship had evolved that way, not on purpose, but naturally.

When she returned to the Embassy after lunch, the receptionist told her the Ambassador wanted to see her as soon as she returned. She took the steps to the third floor, where both her office and the Ambassador's office were located. As she approached the secretary sitting outside the Ambassador's office, she felt a cold mood waffling around the anti-room.

"Gilda, is everything okay? I was told the Ambassador wants to see me."

Without looking her in the eye or responding to the question, Gilda simply said, "I'll let him know you are here."

After a few seconds, the door opened and she was motioned to enter by the Chief of Security at the Embassy. Two other men in dark suits were in the room. She did not recognize them, but sensed they had some sort of authority.

"You wanted to see me, sir," she said to the Ambassador.

"Debbie, these men are with the United States Government. Mr. Simons and Mr. Farcas," he said introducing the two with a nod of his head. "They have made me aware of an issue that concerns you?"

"Me? What is it?"

"It concerns your boyfriend," said the man introduced as Mr. Simons.

"Amir? What about him?" She was starting to shake a bit and decided to wait for an explanation before freaking out completely.

"Ms. Neuberger, we have evidence that links Mr. Assad to some extreme Muslim groups. Frankly, we think he is a terrorist."

"What?"

"Yes ma'am. Have you noticed anything suspicious about him, or seen or heard him having any suspicious meetings or phone calls?"

"Sorry, I don't know what you are talking about. What has he done?"

"Debbie," interrupted the Chief of Security in a stern voice. "Just answer Mr. Simon's questions. You are in enough trouble already."

"Trouble? I have done nothing wrong. And neither has Amir, as far as I know. I'll be more than happy to help, but I do not know what you are talking about. As far as I know, Amir is a great guy. What has he done that makes you think he is a terrorist?" She wanted to accuse them of profiling him simply because he was of Middle Eastern decent, but she decided to hold off until she knew more.

"Relax, Ms. Neuberger. Let me explain," Simons added in a calm voice. "How long have you known Mr. Assad?"

"Ah, I'm not sure, but probably 6 months or so."

"What do you know about him?" Everyone was staring at her now and her mind was spinning a million miles per hour.

"Well, not too much. Before we went out, I searched the web to see what I could find on him. His name is very common, so it was a bit overwhelming. On our first date, I asked him what he did, where he was from, and stuff like that. Then I came back and had security do a background check on him. He checked out."

"Is this true?" asked the Ambassador looking at the Chief of Security.

"I'll check it out," he answered on his way out of the door.

"Have a seat," the Ambassador gently commanded, as he pointed her to the leather guest chair across from his desk. "We need to know everything about Mr. Assad. A lot of people's lives are depending on your help.

"Of course, Ambassador, I will be happy to share whatever I know. This is a bit confusing. What has he done? Is Amir his real name? Is he a spy?"

"Ms. Neuberger," answered Mr. Farcas, the other man in the suit from the United States Government. "We can only give you certain details at this time. This information is highly sensitive. Let's start with what you know about Mr. Assad."

She looked at the seriousness in the man's face and then over to her Ambassador, who nodded his approval. "He told me he worked for some big oil alliance in the Middle East. He is in America to represent their interests with the American Government. He was born in Saudi Arabia and has lived here for several years . . . maybe ten?"

"Do you know any of his acquaintances?"

"No. Now that you ask, I guess he doesn't seem to have any friends. I never really thought about that before. It was always just the two of us."

"How often do you see him?"

"Recently, three or four nights a week. He travels some. Frankly, lately we've been spending as much time as possible together. I think we are falling in love." With that statement, reality set in. Her little dream relationship was now all but over. She felt betrayed and confused. Her eyes watered and tears started to roll down her cheeks.

"I know this is tough, but we need your help," the Ambassador said, while offering her a tissue.

"You said he traveled," Simons chimed in. "Where and how often?"

"Um, maybe twice a month. Boston most recently. Chicago a few times and Pittsburgh once."

The door to the office opened and everyone turned to look at the Chief of Security. Without being asked, he announced, "We did do a security check on him six months ago and we found nothing of concern. He is here on a legitimate visa and his employer checks out. We saw no reason for Ms. Neuberger to be concerned or avoid Mr. Assad."

The interrogation went on for another thirty minutes before she was dismissed to her office with strict instruction not to have any contact with Amir. She left the Ambassador's office looking haggard and feeling very confused.

Chapter 12

Washington works differently than any other city. The International news media, led by the New York Times, was what drove the agenda in this town. Even in this day and age, when the Internet empowers individuals to have a voice in public conversation, it is the media that decides which issues are important. If the Times published an article, everyone else had to weigh in on the topic with his or her own spin.

A single blogger or small news outlet could write a great post or story, but until the Times weighed in on the matter, the issue would not go viral. No one, not the media nor the politicians, would admit that Washington's agenda was generally run out of New York, but everyone knew it.

Politicians, at least the ones who wanted to get re-elected, had to worry about and react to the issues that the media was telling their constituents were important. If the media said a balanced budget was important, you better be ready to address the issue with your voters. Even if you did not really care about an issue, you had to act like you did, or the voters would think you were out of touch.

Many politicians and special interest groups attempted to influence the media by planting stories, providing "leaks" of insider information or staging a political stunt. Often times this worked, but not always. The media exercised enough discretion when selecting stories that it gave the system a plausible sense of credibility.

There was no member of Congress who understood better than Senator Terry McDermott how the media in Washington worked. For the past few years, he had been attempting to get the media's attention on his issue, but the media had seldom been interested in his rants about the need to separate church and state. Until now. Thanks to the murder of the three high-ranking Catholic Bishops and the allegations of a cover-up, his issue was ripe for the press.

The days since the killings had been very busy. The Senator had appeared on a half-dozen talk shows and was being quoted widely in the media. His main point was to spin his issue as a parallel to the corruption of the Vatican. The Vatican, he argued, was a church-state and provided a perfect example of the corruption that resulted when there was not complete separation of church and state.

He was completely energized. His message was finally being heard and he had renewed hope for his legislation to remove "In God We Trust" from US currency. He also wanted to use the court case from Charlottesville to show how America was a church state, but he had promised Max Pigman he would not tie himself to the case.

***

The past few days had seemed to fly by for Nate. Other than a few text messages, he had not connected with Trista. He had spent a lot of time working with Laurie and he had enjoyed getting to know her better in a professional setting. She was very competent and a lot of fun. The plan they had devised together was simple, yet well thought out. Now, it was time to start to put things in motion.

Congress was on a short recess, so Trista had been working on some related stories to the new regulations on nuclear power plants. She had traveled to Three Mile Island outside Harrisburg, PA to interview a plant manager and corporate executive and was not due back until 8:00 p.m. He had agreed to make dinner and have it ready when she got home.

Cooking was not his best skill, so he had kept it simple; he'd picked up Chinese on the way home. Chicken and Broccoli and a couple of egg rolls would do the trick. She was about 10 minutes away and he had the table set and the cold beers waiting. After dinner, he would need to talk business with her, so he did not light candles or dim the lights. Not that the evening had to be all business, but he did not want to send her mix messages.

The knock at the door was his signal to spring into action. He heard her enter the unlocked door and bolt it behind her. He quickly popped the cap off a cold beer and met her at the top of the stairs with a kiss and a cold beer. Her smile and deep sigh was all the reassurance he needed to know he had hit her sweet spot.

"Hungry?"

"Starved, but first I need to visit the little girls' room." She took a sip, handed the bottle back to him and headed down the narrow hall to the bathroom.

The whole scene was both comfortable and awkward for their relationship. This was his bathroom, his townhouse, and his private space, but it was essentially a mirror image of her space.

It was nice to have her come "home" for dinner and companionship, but he also liked his own private space. Was he ready to give that up? Was he falling in love with her, or was this simply a romantic episode in their lives . . . too many questions for right now.

When she returned he noticed she had untied her blonde ponytail so her hair could hang freely. In addition, he took note of the extra button she had released and knew both changes were done for his benefit.

Dinner hit the spot and the beer eased the stress of a long day for them both. They made small talk as they woofed down the Chinese take-out. As she took the last mouthful of chicken and broccoli, he handed her a fortune cookie and took one for himself. "Let's play a game."

"Yeah, what?"

"When you read your fortune, you have to add *in bed* to the end. I'll go first," he said ripping the plastic wrapper off and breaking the cookie open. *"Expect a new experience...in bed"* He smiled at her laughter. "Okay, you go."

She extracted the small piece of paper and read it to herself before playing his game. The look on her face was hard to read. She was not laughing or even smiling, but there was a look of surprise as if she had just found a long-lost treasured object. After a few seconds she took a deep breath and gave him a smile. "Well, this is interesting. Mine says *You can't hide from your future...in bed."*

"Interesting. Not sure what that means for tonight, but I think it hit a little too close to home for you somehow. What's running through that pretty little head of yours?"

"Nothing. Well, I don't know. Spent a lot of time driving today and did a lot of thinking. I want to move my career along. The Post is not willing to let me write the stories I want to write. They only want to write non-controversial stuff that doesn't ruffle any feathers. I want a bit more excitement."

"Huh, funny you should say that. I have an idea that might just take care of that."

"I'm not talking about your cute little *in bed* game. I'm talking about a career change."

He smiled at her. "I'm not talking about getting you in bed either. I have an idea that could change your career.

"In what way?"

"I'm talking about the dead priest story. How'd you like to have a *deep throat* informant that gave you the inside scoop on the case?"

"I thought you'd get in trouble if you leaked stuff to me. They'll know it is you."

"Not if they don't know it is you."

"What?"

"You'll do the writing, but under an alias, and for a different publication."

"How is writing under an alias going to help my career?

"Once the case is uncovered, you'll be able to take credit. Probably a book deal, speakers circuit… you probably won't have time for us little people anymore."

"Oh, stop. I can't write for another paper. That would not be ethical. Why can't I write it for the Post?"

"You said yourself, they lack the guts. This is gonna take down several politicians and maybe the Pope. Besides, if it comes from the Post, it won't take long to link me to you," he added.

"What publication?"

"The Times. Not as big of a circulation, but with the web, this thing will be worldwide."

"So, let me get this straight, you want me to compromise my professional ethics, jeopardize my job, not take any professional credit until I'm ready to cash in on a book deal . . . all so you won't get in trouble for leaking stuff to the press."

"When you put it like that, it doesn't sound so good, I guess."

"No, it doesn't," she replied sharply.

"But you are missing the big picture."

"No, you are. I cannot write for another publication."

"Do you think you could find someone at the Post you could trust with this? Some editor who can keep this under cover?"

"Yes. Joel Serby over at the City Department. He used to be the Political Editor, but got moved over because he wouldn't toe the party line. I've shared my frustration with him and he felt the same way. He's kinda near retirement, so he might not want to mess with the pressure he'd get, but then again, maybe he wants to go out in a blaze of glory."

"Will you talk to him?"

She thought for a few moments as he watched her silently.

"So, here's the deal," she started. "You have to give me something. Something big so I can show Joel what I'm talking about. Then we'll see if this could work."

"That's fair, but you also gotta know this is very dangerous. If you don't want to do it, that's okay. I really don't want you to do it, frankly. That's why I want you to write under an alias."

"You have not told me enough yet. I don't really know what I'm getting into."

"Okay, fair enough. Here's the scoop…"

***

It was getting late and it had been a long day for Debbie. They had taken over her office computer and her cell phone had been taken. She was only told they were doing some checks to see if Amir had compromised her in any way. She knew they were also seeing if she had accessed any files she was not supposed to be in or done anything else out of the norm.

She had been allowed to send Amir a short text to tell him she had to go out of town unexpectedly with the Ambassador. She had convinced them he would be suspicious if she didn't check-in with him. They had actually typed the message for her.

This was all a bit scary and very sad. Had he been playing her to get to some state secrets? She had a hard time believing this since she could think of nothing she'd told him of importance. Upon questioning she had revealed their conversation about the Ambassador's wife being jealous, but otherwise, she had told Amir very little insider information.

At this point, she believed this was all some sort of mix-up, or if he was a terrorist, she was just part of his cover. They had been good together, but that was over now whether she wanted it to be or not. She only hoped this would not cost her the job. It probably meant she would be re-assigned back to Germany, at least. The thought of leaving DC was not appealing and added to her sadness.

The door opened and in walked the director of security followed by a female under-secretary named Joyce. "Ms. Neuberger, you are under house arrest until further notice. We should be finished with our investigation in a few days and we'll see where you are going from there. For now, you are not to leave this building and you are to have no contact with the outside. Is that clear?"

"Yes, I understand." She did not try to defend herself. There was no telling what Amir might have done to compromise her. For now, it was best to stay as quiet as possible.

"Joyce will show you to your room. It's best if you just stay put. We'll bring you some food in the morning. You can call the security office if you need anything."

The middle-aged Chief of Security turned and left without a further word. Joyce motioned for her to follow and took her to a beautiful guest room in the Embassy that was normally used by visiting officials from Germany. It was a very nice prison cell, but it was still a cell. She kicked off her shoes and, without even removing her clothes, curled up in the large bed and cried herself to sleep.

***

The night agent in the NSA lab had been told to monitor Amir's online activity. With Debbie out of town, he should be free to work in the chat rooms. Amir had no idea the NSA was using very sophisticated tracking devices to watch what he was doing. They could not break through his firewalls, but they were listening to everything he said, which wasn't much, and could even track the keystrokes of his computers.

Under the Patriot Act, they could arrest him and hold him without filing charges for as long as they wanted, but it was a better idea to monitor him and hope he led them to others. They were watching the chat rooms where extreme Islamic dialog was generally found. By syncing up his rhythmic keyboard strokes with the posts that appeared on the sites, they could tell which ones were his comments.

His encryption software was impressive to the NSA geeks, but there was more than one way to track his activity. It was his momentary lapse of security had led them to him. He had used a common off-the-shelf texting program to communicate with his girlfriend from the German Embassy at the same time he had engaged in this emulated terrorist chatter. Somehow, the two software systems had crossed and his identity was matched on both sites by the NSA threat computer.

Alerted by the computer system that possible terrorist activity had occurred, the NSA agents had quickly found Amir and then connected him to Debbie. He had even provided them his current cell number in his brief on-line chat with her. They had gotten lucky, but now they needed to figure out how lucky.

Chapter 13

Very few people knew more about the issue of separation of church and state than Senator McDermott. In fact the only person he could think of, was John Keagan, Chair of the Department of Political Studies at Princeton University. Few politicians could even participate in a conversation on the concept of separating religion from government. The general public was helplessly confused by the political and religious rhetoric that surrounded the debate.

Professor Keagan had appeared on many talk shows alongside Senator McDermott, supposedly to offer a different point of view. While the Professor was much less extreme in his views, he often backed up McDermott's points with scholarly research. Over a beer, the Senator believed they could agree on almost every aspect of the topic.

Professor Keagan was supposed to appear on CNN this evening and McDermott was impatiently sitting through a less than riveting story about some Hollywood starlet who was accused of shoplifting a $75 pair of gloves. Finally the segment he was waiting for was up next . . . after a short commercial break.

The CNN talking head came back on and introduced Professor Keagan and started the discussion. "Professor, let's start with the big question on this topic," the attractive, middle-aged anchorwoman began. "Does the Constitution call for a separation of church and state?"

"Yes, and no," the Professor stated flatly. "The words 'separation of church and state' do not appear in the Constitution, despite what many people, including many in Congress think. But, there is a call in the Bill of Rights, the very first Amendment, that the *Congress will make no law respecting an establishment of religion*. That does not exactly say the Founding Fathers were calling for a separation of church and State."

"What does it say, then?"

"To know what was intended when these founding documents were created, you have to take a look at what was going on at that point in history. We had just fought a war to free ourselves from England. Most scholars would agree the two most significant reasons we wanted to break from England were taxes and religion. The Church of England was a significant player in how England governed its colonies. In addition, many of our early colonists came here specifically because of religious tyranny. That is, they wanted the freedom to practice their religion without having to sneak around in back alleys."

"So, are you saying the Revolutionary War was a religious war?"

"In some respects. If you look at all of history, the most common reason wars have been waged is, by far, religion. Even many of the wars that have supposedly been fought over land disputes had a religious base to them. Just look at the Middle East for an example and that dispute has been going on for thousands of years. The Revolutionary War was really a war over freedom from tyranny, but a large part of that was the treat of religious tyranny."

"Why is it important to have a separation of church and state?"

"In all the research I've done on this issue, it all comes down to a fairly simple concept, *freedom*. When you decide to follow a particular religion, you are agreeing to give up some freedom. You are deciding that the ethical and moral guidelines of that religion are within an acceptable parameter you can stay within. While you don't typically choose to join a government, it is much the same. If you do not agree with the freedom restrictions of a government, you can decide to leave the country.

"So, both government and religion have a role in deciding what is right and wrong, or what is a sin or a violation. Obviously government is more concerned with what you might call civil sins, and religion covers moral sins. When the two are mixed, the lines are blurred between what is a moral sin and what is considered a civil sin."

"Interesting. So you are saying by keeping religion apart from government, we are separating what is considered a civil sin and what is considered a moral sin?"

"Exactly. It is that separation of sins that allows us to be a free society. By mixing the two, we require citizens to give up more freedom. In some cultures that is okay, but in the United States, freedom is the foundation of the Union. To mix the two would require us to give up a lot of freedom and there is no indication the majority of Americans are willing to do that."

"I would agree," she interrupted. "Does the Catholic Church and the recent allegations of an internal cover-up of the sexual molestation of children teach us anything about the need to separate church and State?"

"Yes and no. The Catholic Church is a country, but unlike any other country, you don't have to live within the Vatican walls to be a citizen. Also, people voluntarily join the Catholic Church, so the issue of separation is not really appropriate. But, what I think this recent trouble shows is the possible corruption that can result when we merge civil and moral laws together.

"While the Catholic religion deals mainly with moral sins, the Catholic Church is a hierarchy that is really a lot like a civil government. In some cases, such as divorce, the Catholic religion has stricter laws than most countries. That's okay because the Church's laws are not in conflict with civil laws. But when the Church ignores civil law because they feel they are on some kind of moral high ground, we get a glimpse of how combining church and State can be a problem. Religious beliefs, in most cases, are stronger than political beliefs, so when the two are combined, civil freedoms are often trampled upon."

"That makes sense. Thank you, Professor for bringing some context to this issue. Based on recent events, I think this discussion is just getting started. We'll be right back..."

"You're damn right," McDermott muttered to himself. "We are just getting started."

***

American television had always baffled Amir. He did like the plethora of news shows on, but the hundreds of channels featuring an endless array of worthless dribble did not make sense. Did Americans really watch this stuff? Most of all, so called "Reality TV" was really confusing. He had observed enough Americans to know these shows were anything but reality.

Mostly, Amir kept his TV on CNN and MSNBC. It was laughable how easy it was to gather intel in America. The only challenge was trying to decide what was fact and what was opinion, but after watching for a few months, it was easy to tell which shows were spewing rhetoric and which were reporting the news.

CNN was a mix of both, but mostly they tried to cover the news. Tonight was no exception. CNN was playing in the background as Amir worked the chat rooms. The drone of the news anchor occupied his subconscious so he could devote his full focus on the multiple personalities he was working in the chat rooms tonight.

He had not even realized his attention had shifted from the chat rooms to the TV until the guest on the show mentioned religion and war in the same sentence. The title under the speaker's picture said John Keagan, Professor, Princeton University.

The concept of a religious war was nothing new, but few Americans understood their own revolution and the current war were both religious wars. They preferred to think of them as justified in civil or human rights, but the reality was religion was at the heart of most wars. This professor was brilliant and Amir took in his every word. Maybe he could use this to help enflame the masses. Better yet, maybe he could use the good professor to help advance his mission.

***

Typically, they didn't sleep together on a work night, but tonight was different. Nate had dropped a very big story in her lap, but she could not just write a story and be done with it. It would consume her, probably for months and maybe longer. It was not a night to be apart, so she had not even argued when he suggested she stay over. She did not have any meetings tomorrow until the afternoon, so the normal chaos of getting to work in DC would not be an issue. Besides, she needed to be with him tonight.

They had made love, but it was not up to their normal standards. She had hoped it would relax her and help her sleep, but she was now lying in his arms listening to him breathe softly. Her eyes were wide open and she was willing herself to relax, but her mind was still racing with thoughts of the story he had shared.

Wanting to have your career be more exciting and actually having that happen are two different things. Was she cut out for this? Was she willing to make this story her defining moment? More importantly, was she will to risk her life?

***

The ride had taken hours. Normally that would not have been bad enough, but with a bag over her head and her hands handcuffed behind her back, it had been miserable. The last hours of the trip had been particularly rough. She had broken down into tears and become an emotional wreck. He had attempted to talk to her and calm her down, but after the first few hours, she was so disoriented, nothing he could say would help.

"We're here," he announced with a hopeful cheer in his voice. She tried to pull herself together, but her sobs were heavy and out of her control.

He lifted the bag from her head and she blinked her eyes to try to focus. "We cannot let Mr. Williams see you looking like this. Wait here," he told her as he removed the cuffs on her hands.

She looked around through her bleary eyes and saw him talking to a man who was standing under a spotlight that illuminated the night in an eerie glow. She could not hear the conversation, but was sure this was not the 85-year-old man to which he had sold her.

She willed herself to gain some self-control. Not having the bag on her head helped a lot. She ran her hands through her hair and tried to brush away the tears. Her eyes were almost swollen shut and her throat was dry. She noticed the bottle of water he had left for her and she guzzled it down. It almost made her feel human.

She watched him walk back to the car and open the back door. "Okay, let's go," he announced like he was a tour guide getting ready to show her around. Her legs were wobbly as she stood and he held her arm to keep her from falling. "Mr. Williams has gone to bed and you should do the same. Tomorrow we'll show you around the place and introduce you to your new best friend."

Too exhausted to argue, she resisted the urge to tell Jake to go fuck himself. Instead, she just remained quiet and let him lead her into a nearby building looked like a nice cottage. As they entered the door, Jake flipped the light switch and revealed a beautiful great room that opened to a kitchen with marble counter-tops and dark wood cabinetry.

Kristen had not realized she was standing there gaping at the place until she noticed Jake smiling at her. "See, I told you you'd be living well here. This is your place," he said, waving his arm wide.

"This is where I'm gonna live?"

"Yep, and there is even a nice room already set up for the girls when they join you," he added pointing to an open door a few steps away. "You will not want for anything ever again. Go ahead, look around."

If she had not spent the last few hours sobbing her eyes dry, she was quite certain she would be crying right now. Maybe this would be okay after all. The will to resist this deal was difficult to find. Maybe he had broken her, or maybe she was just completely exhausted, but either way, she could not resist the vision of living in such a nice place.

"I know this is a lot to take in right now. It's been a long day, you should call it a night and we'll look things over in the morning." He paused to wait for her nod of consent. "Just so you know, the security around here is very tight. Cameras everywhere, dogs, electric fences and stuff like that. No one comes or goes without permission."

"Is that my room?" she asked pointing to a door on the other side of the large room.

"Yep. You have your own bathroom and the dresser and closet are filled with new clothes. Anything else you need, just ask. You go on to bed, we'll talk more in the morning."

The bedroom was beautiful. Before she could finish taking it in, she heard the door shut as Jake left. Fighting the urge to continue to look around, she went to the window to see what type of escape might be hatched. There were metal bars on the outside of the window, so she would not be climbing out here. There was not much she could see with the only light coming from the streetlamp on the other side of the house.

Turning back to the room, she decided to wait until daylight to plan her next move. An enormous feeling of exhaustion overcame her and the large bed with a fancy green and light blue comforter and matching pillow shams was very inviting. This would be a much better arrangement than the mattress on the floor of her cell at Jake's place.

Chapter 14

It was still dark outside when Debbie awoke with a start. At first she didn't remembered where she was and that jerked her to attention. The dark room was not familiar to her and by the time she remembered where she was, her heart was racing and a sick feeling was turning flip-flops in her stomach.

Turning on the light confirmed yesterday had not just been a bad dream. Lying back down she had to resist the urge to scream. She was angry. Angry at Amir, angry with herself, and angry at the circumstance. She had felt herself falling for Amir the past few weeks, and now the world seemed to have come unglued.

His image appeared as she closed her eyes trying to hide from her feelings. For a moment the images were joyful, he was laughing and teasing her as he chased her into the bedroom of her apartment. Suddenly the image turned evil and came at her with evil intent. Her eyes flew open and an audible gasp escaped her.

Launching herself out of bed, she headed for the bathroom to splash some water on her face. The mirror revealed a rather scary picture. Her clothes were wrinkled and askew from sleeping in them and her hair and face were horrid.

It was going to be a long day of interrogation and she was not going to start the process looking like a homeless person. She quickly removed her clothes and laid them out as neatly as she could. Then she jumped in the shower and let the hot water revitalize her.

The room was well equipped with a hair dryer and ironing board. There was no make-up, but she generally didn't wear much. Her clothes were fixed with a good ironing and other than having the same outfit on as yesterday, she looked just like she would on any other day at work.

The clock said 7:00 a.m. and her body craved some caffeine to shake off the fog of a rough night. She picked up the phone and it automatically starting ringing on the other end. Debbie recognized the cheerful voice of the daytime receptionist who probably had just started her shift. "Please connect me to the security office," she said flatly, hoping her voice was not recognized.

"Yes, Ms. Neuberger. How may we help you?" answered the security officer on duty.

"Could I get some tea? I'd be happy to come down to the kitchen and get it," she added hopefully. Coffee had been her preferred caffeine fix until Amir had got her hooked on tea.

"Certainly, Ms. Neuberger. I'll have some sent up to you shortly. I'll send a little breakfast along as well. We will not need you for a few hours, so make yourself comfortable and let us know if you need anything.

"A toothbrush and toothpaste would be nice."

"Why, of course. Not a problem."

The Embassy may not have been a real hotel, but it was very accustom to having overnight guest. For a jail, she thought, this wasn't so bad. She only hoped this was the closest she got to jail thanks to Amir.

***

As Senator McDermott entered his office in the Russell Building, a CCN report on the office television caught his attention. There was a banner that read BREAKING NEWS on the bottom of the screen and a subtitle that said *Muslim Extremists attack Catholics at Mass*. The office was still empty so he grabbed the remote and turned up the volume.

The Catholic Church that had been attacked was in Florence, Italy. Gunmen had come in right in the middle of Mass with automatic weapons and fired hundreds of rounds at the crowd before fleeing. 23 dead and over 100 injured. The terrorists had left a manifesto behind declaring this a war on Americans, Christians and other infidels who failed to recognize Islamic law.

When the reporter used the term "religious war," McDermott's attention spiked. This was the second reference to a religious war he had heard in the past 12 hours. As a US Senator, he would have thought he'd know about a possible flare up in a terrorist network, but then again, he was a dead man walking in the halls of Congress. He was not going to get briefed on anything he did not need to know, especially if it might help him in his own personal war on religion.

He was not cold-hearted enough to be happy about such a senseless slaughter, but he did realize he could use this incident to beat his drum again. Not only were the Muslim extremists a good example of why religion and government needed to be kept separate, but also the Catholic Church provided him some talking points.

The simple fact the terrorist manifesto had listed Americans and Christians in the same sentence meant the terrorist saw the United States as a religious entity. He had been trying to convince the public 911 had been a religious attack and the start of a widespread religious war. Maybe they would listen now.

***

They both felt like they had a hangover. Lack of sleep has that effect on the human body. The alarm was not a welcomed sound, but both of them were already awake when it went off. Nate slid out of bed and headed to the kitchen to make them some coffee.

While Nate was in the other room she pulled back the covers and swung her feet to floor. After a few seconds of sitting on the side of the bed, her head cleared enough for her to command her eyes to focus. She rubbed them with the back of her hand and yawned. She did not feel refreshed from a good night's sleep, but she was energized.

Sometime in the middle of the night she had wrestled herself to a clear decision. The clarity of knowing what she was going to do was energizing, but, admittedly, a little sleep would have helped. She rolled over in her mind the words she would use to tell Nate. The gentle smile on her face meant she was sure of her plan. Nate was going to have to play things her way, like it or not.

Pausing in front of the bathroom mirror to look herself in the eye and assess her true determination, she almost laughed at her appearance. It was hard to be seen as strong and determined when your hair looked like a rat's nest and you were wearing your boyfriend's extra large Washington football jersey. It was easy to decide to wait until after coffee and a shower, or even longer, before telling Nate her plan.

Nate walked back into the bedroom and announced "room service" loud enough for her to hear behind the partially open bathroom door. She smiled and shook her head at his silly antics. He was a goofball, but that kept things fun in the relationship. She was going to miss that . . .

He was turning on the TV when she exited the bathroom. "Thanks for the coffee," she said as she passed by him with a playful swat on his butt.

"Hey! Watch it, now. You shouldn't poke a bear, especially before his first cup of coffee."

"Oh yeah," she replied with a playful smile.

"Well, didn't think you'd be in such a good mood after such a rough night. I figured you'd be pissed off at . . ." He never finished the thought. The morning news on his television distracted them both and changed the subject rather quickly.

***

It was one of the best night's sleep Kristen had had in years. Perhaps it was her complete exhaustion, or maybe the first comfortable bed she'd slept in, but the results were rejuvenating. The sun piecing the sheer drapes made her squint as she tried to focus her eyes.

There was an assertive knock on the front door she could hear through the closed door to her bedroom. "Her bedroom" had a nice ring to it. She quickly rose and slipped on the fluffy robe she had found in the closet last night.

Jake and an Asian man were at the door with a tray that appeared to be breakfast. "Good morning, Kristen," said the man who had kidnapped her. "This is Thon," he said motioning to the Asian man. "You'll need to know Thon, he runs the kitchen. Thon, this is Kristen. I want you to look out for her."

"Good to meet you," he said with a heavy accent. "I make you some breakfast." Thon pushed himself by Jake and her and headed to her kitchen with something that smelled delicious.

"After you get some breakfast and get yourself ready, come over to the main house," Jake said, pointing to the large structure on the other side of the driveway. "I'll be waiting for you there. Take your time, but not too long. Mr. Williams wants to meet you."

"Got it. See you soon," she said with a smile as Thon walked out of the door.

Breakfast was amazing. Eggs Benedict with fresh cut fruit on the side. Even the coffee was better than any coffee she had ever tasted. She polished it all off quickly and then slipped out onto her small back porch to sip a second cup of coffee. She could get used to this.

After a luxurious shower, she found some very nice clothes in the closet to wear. She felt compelled to dress nice and make a good first impression on Mr. Williams. One last glance in the mirror and she headed across the small courtyard to the main house.

She knocked as she opened the door and was relieved to see Jake waiting for her in a large armchair. He looked at her approvingly. She looked very good in the skirt and blouse she had selected. Even the shoes she had found in the closet had fit her perfectly.

"Nice! You look perfect. Mr. Williams will be very pleased."

"Thanks, I'm tryin'. I want my girls back and I'll do whatever to make that happen."

"Good. I told you you'd like it here. You keep that attitude and we'll get the girls here to join you. And don't worry, I'll take good care of them meanwhile."

"Will I be able to talk to them?"

"We'll see. Now, let's go meet Mr. Williams. He's having breakfast out by the pool."

"Wait, what do I say? Should I flirt with him?"

"Ha! Just be yourself, at least the nice Kristen I've gotten to know. Just ask him about this place, and his hobbies."

"His hobbies? What hobbies?"

"You'll have to ask him. Just don't ask him why you can't leave, or why he is hiding here. He doesn't like to talk about that."

She took a deep breath to try to relax. "Okay, let's go."

He led her out through a large kitchen to the backdoor and then through a small garden to the pool. She saw him on the other side sitting under an umbrella guarded from the sun. He was old and a little fat, but way better than the image she had conjured up in her mind.

"Mr. Williams, this is Kristen," Jake said as they approached.

The old man rose and they waited for him to make the next step in the meet and greet. He looked at her from head to toe, obviously sizing her up. He didn't say anything for a few seconds, but it seemed like minutes to Kristen. Finally, he smiled and said, "Welcome to the family, Kristen. I hope you find happiness here."

"Thank you, Mr. Williams. That's a very nice thing to say."

"Everyone should find happiness. Some people just don't know where to look for it or how to accept it when they find it."

"Well, I'm off to a good start," she replied. "That was the best night's sleep I've had in years. And a fabulous breakfast."

"Good. Now sit down and tell me about yourself. I think I'm gonna really enjoy getting to know you," he added with a smile that seemed rather mischievous to her.

***

Agent Murphy was waiting outside Bishop Charron's office. He had been told Bishop Charron was on the phone with the Vatican, but he had heard no evidence of any discussion going on behind the closed door. That was either a very thick door, or the conversation was a whisper.

Finally the door opened and Bishop Charron walked out. "Sorry to keep you waiting, Agent Murphy. The Vatican is very interested in what is going on here. Please come in," he said waving his hand to motion the FBI agent into his private chamber.

"Thanks, Bishop Charron," he said somewhat awkwardly. "I wanted to give you an update on the case."

"Really," Bishop Charron started slyly. "I'll be most interested in hearing your progress report."

"Well, not much progress to report. We are looking at wrapping this investigation up pretty quickly. It is a real help when the killer confesses and does not try to hide what he's done. We are listing this as a cut and dry case."

"What about the allegations of sexual abuse?"

"We have no concrete evidence to go on for that. Seems to us this is just some nut job who went berserk and killed some fine followers of God. Very sad loss of life."

"Indeed."

"Bishop Charron, has anyone else been in contact with you about this case since the FBI took over? Specifically the DC Police?"

"No. Just you and the Vatican. I've not even discussed it with my staff."

"Good to hear. What about the press?"

"I've not been taking their calls. The Vatican has directed us to leave any response up to them. We are hoping this will all quiet down soon."

"Let's hope so." With that, Agent Murphy stood to signify the end of the meeting. "Please let me know if you are contacted by anyone else on this case. It is critical to the investigation that the FBI maintain full control of the situation."

"Of course," Bishop Charron replied, rising from his chair. "Thank you for keeping me updated."

Chapter 15

By mid-morning, Jake was on the road headed back to DC. Now he had delivered his package to Mr. Williams, there was real work to do. He felt good about helping Kristen get off the street and into a great living arrangement, but the bag full of cash he had earned for supplying his client with a companion was going to be put to good use. He was doing God's work and whatever laws he needed to break were just the laws of men. He answered to a higher calling.

The 200,000 dollars in the bag would give him the resources he needed to carry out the operation he had been planning for six months. Kristen was the third and final companion he would deliver to Mr. Williams. He had not asked what happened to the first two young ladies the old man had purchased, but his greater cause allowed his conscious to be clear. The costs Kristen and the other women had to pay was worth the benefit to man.

He had no plan for what to do with Kristen's two daughters, but that was a low priority right now. First, he had some souls to save and a life he would need to end. It was all in God's plan.

It was almost mid-day when he pulled into the dirt driveway of the farmhouse in rural Virginia just outside the tiny town of Washington. The streets of the little town had actually been designed by George Washington and it looked like nothing had changed in the past 200 years.

The farmhouse was modest, yet well-kept, and the barn out back was old, but in good condition. As he exited his car, a large German Sheppard came charging out of the barn barking rather ferociously at the intruder. He held his ground but did not close the door to his car. If he needed to jump back in, he was ready.

The dog circled the car baring his teeth and growling between barks. Jake did not even notice the man depart the barn with a 12-gauge shotgun until he was 15 yards away. Their eyes met and the man seemed to relax at the recognition. "Kuno," he yelled at the dog. "Down," he commanded. The dog obeyed immediately, but did not take his eyes off of Jake.

"Thanks, I'm Jake."

"Any trouble finding the place?"

"Nope."

"Follow me." The man turned and headed back to the barn without waiting to see if Jake followed. The dog gave him one bark and followed his master toward the old barn.

The inside of the barn was rustic, but much cleaner than normal barns. It had not been used to store crops or shelter animals in quite some time and did not, Jake guessed, smell like most barns. Several tables were set up that appeared to be a variety of different worktables. Unusual metal parts and plastic bins were spread out on the tables and Jake assumed this was some sort of assembly line.

"Let me see the money," the man said in an all business tone as he eyed the bag.

Jake placed the small duffle bag on a nearby table and unzipped it. Pulling it open wide, he tilted it toward the man to show the wads of 100-dollar bills inside. Jake could care less about the money. He was on a mission from God and money was not important.

"Leave it on the table and follow me," the man said, heading toward the back of the barn. "Hey, how's old man Williams doing?"

"He's doing well."

"You're part of a very small club that knows he's even alive. Frankly, that's the only reason I'm helping you. Otherwise, I'd never trust a stranger."

"Likewise," Jake retorted.

The man lifted a tubular device out of an open box. It was made of white PVC pipe and appeared to be two tubes and a small box held together by grey duct tape. He held it in front of him for a few seconds appearing to admire his work before turning and handing it to Jake.

"Relax," he added sensing Jakes uneasiness with holding the device. "It is not armed. What you are holding is a powerful incendiary device. In one tube is a small amount of plastic explosives and in the other is my secret blend of chemicals I call Hellfire. Separately, the two are not enough to cause much trouble, but together they can do a lot of damage.

"The trigger device," he said, pointing to the small box attached to the tubes, "can be programmed to go off at a certain time or triggered by a cell phone. Just like you ordered. The trigger makes the plastics go boom and provides enough heat and energy to ignite the Hellfire. Like the name implies, instant hell for anything within 20-30 yards."

"Perfect. Tell me about the trigger."

"Simple," he said, taking the device back from Jake. "Flip open the lid, turn the power on and set it like you would an alarm clock. It is on military time to make sure you don't mix up a.m. and p.m. You can't set it to blow for longer than 24 hours. That'd cost more. If you want to trigger it with a cell phone, just call this number," he said pointing to a label on the side of the trigger. "And on the third ring it blows."

"Perfect."

"One last thing," he said grabbing a cloth off the table and wiping the device. "This is all free of finger prints. Even after the explosion and fire, the cops can possibly get a print, so I'd suggest gloves while you are handling it. I put a couple pairs in the top box for you."

***

With the news of the terrorist attack in Italy, the topic of exposing the Church and their friends in Congress had fallen by the wayside. Trista and Nate had agreed to meet for lunch and continue the discussion. She had only let him know she had developed a plan.

He sat patiently in the booth at a small sandwich shop across the street from the main office of the Washington Post. He'd checked his emails, sent a few texts, and even made a phone call while he waited. Finally, he heard the door to the restaurant open and looked up to see her smiling face. With her, to Nate's surprise, was a man in a crumpled grey suit.

"Nate, this is Joel, hope it is okay, but I needed to bring him with me."

"Sure, but I only ordered two sandwiches."

She could see the confusion on his face. "I can share my sandwich with him. Joel's part of my plan, a big part. You guys eat and I'll explain." There was a keen excitement in her voice and body language.

"Sorry we are late. I'd have sent you a text, but my phone was dead. I spent most of last night thinking this through and finally came up with a plan I think works for everyone. Some of it you're not gonna like, but I think it makes sense."

"All right. How much have you told Joel? I'm guessing too much." His voice was irritated.

"Joel's onboard with my plan. I trust him and needed to make sure he was good before I could move forward. I explained enough to him to get his attention, but he does not know names. Hell, you haven't really told me too much, so I couldn't give him but so much." She sounded defensive, but Nate would just have to deal with it.

"I'm only worried for your safety," he said in an intentionally calming voice. "This is some scary shit, not a game. You could both be in danger if we move on this."

"I'm good," replied Joel, flatly. "I've covered wars and mobs in my career. I know how to take precautions. Just listen to the plan and you'll see. This will work. We can take these crooks down and maybe she'll win a Pulitzer along the way."

Nate stared at the two journalist for a few seconds, looking into their eyes for any sign of weakness. "Okay, let's hear it."

For the next 30 minutes the three discussed, tweaked and developed her plan while sneaking in a bite of a sandwich every now and then. In the end, they formed a pact to keep this between the four of them, including Laurie Ganz from the crime lab. Nate was nervous, not because the plan wouldn't work, but because people he cared about would be in harm's way.

"Wait," he said just as they were starting to leave. "Which part of this did you think I was not gonna like?"

"Uh, Joel, I need to talk to Nate. Do you mind giving us a minute?"

"No problem. I need to head back to the office. Deadlines are awaiting."

She watched him leave the restaurant before turning to face Nate. "I didn't want to tell you in front of Joel."

"Shit. I don't like the sound of that."

"Look Nate. This story is big and I decided if I was gonna do this, I was gonna do it right. You know how I feel about you. The past six months have been great. To be blunt, I think I'm falling in love with you. But, this set up, this story, it complicates things. All kinds of things."

"Are you breaking up with me?

"I'm not sure. We cannot do this and still sleep together. When this story breaks, if I'm sleeping with my main informant, it doesn't look very professional. We can't have our cake and eat it too."

He looked down at his half-eaten sandwich. She reached out and put her hand on top of his. "Do you think someday, after this is all over, we might be able to start over?" he asked.

"I don't know, but I hope so. If what we have is real, this will be a good test."

***

It was just after 1:00 p.m. when Debbie's room phone rang. She had been watching CNN's coverage of the terrorist attack in Florence. Such a senseless waste of life and all in the name of religious beliefs. Her religious beliefs may not be strong, but she was pretty certain God did not sanction people killing each other for any reason.

"Hello," she said into the embassy phone.

"Ms. Neuberger, we are ready for you. Please come to the security office." The phone went dead before she could even reply.

It felt good to leave the room. Even a luxurious room could feel like a prison if you were told when you could come and go. She took the stairs down to the security office. She was trying to convince herself not to be nervous, but it was not working. The uncertainty of what she was involved in was probably more stressful than whatever trouble her relationship with Amir had caused.

Upon entering the small anteroom, she was warmly greeted by Gilda, the secretary for the department. She had met Gilda several times and the warm welcome calmed her nerves considerably. Maybe she had been cleared of any wrongdoing already and she could return home.

"They are ready for you, go on in," the middle-aged woman said in a heavily accented English. Despite the fact everyone who worked at the embassy was a native of Germany, they had all been instructed to speak English while assigned to America.

Debbie turned the knob of the heavy wood door and entered with more confidence than she really felt. Three men in suits were in the room. Two she recognized as the FBI agents Farcas and Simons. The third man also looked like FBI, but sat in the corner chair and was not introduced.

"Ms. Neuberger, may I call you Debbie?" asked the one she remembered to be Farcas.

"Of course," she replied with as much confidence as possible.

"We have completed our investigation into your involvement with Mr. Asad. You'll be happy to know you have been cleared of any wrongdoing. It appears you are completely unrelated to Amir's plot and simply part of his cover as a normal male looking for female companionship."

She was both relieved and offended by Farcas's statement. "Frankly, I think you have misjudged our relationship. Amir may or may not be a terrorist, but what we have . . . or had," she corrected herself, "was more than simple companionship. I am quite certain we were falling in love."

"Or so you were supposed to think," chimed in Agent Simons. Based on his nasty tone, he was playing the part of the bad cop.

"Think what you want, but I know what we had," she snarled back at him.

"Take it easy, Debbie. It is entirely possible he was really in love with you. You do not seem to be part of his plans and there is nothing we know of you could provide him based on your position here at the Embassy."

"Thank you," she said as she shot a nasty look at Agent Simons.

"Unfortunately Debbie, your relationship with Amir has put you in a rough situation."

"You mean other than breaking my heart," she replied as a tear rolled down her cheek despite her best efforts to hold it back.

"Yes, I'm afraid so. Your relationship puts you in a prime position to help us save many lives." He paused to see if she was going to respond, but she just looked at him with a blank stare. "We have talked to the Ambassador and asked for cooperation, your cooperation."

"Of course. I've told you everything I know."

"Yes, but we need your help getting more information. Specifically, we need you to resume your relationship with Amir and act like nothing has changed."

"Should be easy since you are in love," Simons added in a snarky tone. Both Farcas and Debbie shot him a nasty glance and he looked away in defeat.

"You mean act like none of this has happened?" she asked incredulously.

"Yes, exactly. We need you to see Amir again, and ask him a few questions."

"What type of questions?"

"Have you ever heard him talk about May first?"

"May first? No, why?"

"We can't tell you everything, but we believe Amir is part of a terrorist plot that is set for May first."

"Sorry, I don't remember him ever saying anything like that."

"So, what we want you to do is see him again and ask him to go away with you on a romantic trip on May first. If he refuses, then we can confirm the date of the attack."

"Attack? What kind of attack?"

"We can't say," Simons chimed in but quickly shut up when they both shot him a nasty look.

"We are not sure," added Farcas in a calm tone. "We just know it could be big and Amir is involved somehow."

"I'm not sure I can face him again after all this."

"I certainly understand your reluctance, but the Ambassador is expecting you to help as part of your duty to your country. You will not be in any danger and we will be monitoring the situation to make sure you are completely safe. This is NSA Agent Brown," he said nodding at the man in the corner. "He's an expert in electronic surveillance. If we sense any danger, we'll pull you out. Worse case is he figures out his cover is blown and we storm in and arrest him."

"Frankly, I can think of some worse things," she replied with a reluctant sigh of agreement.

***

It was a warm day for early spring. Not really hot enough for a swim, but warm enough to sunbathe around the pool. Mr. Williams had suggested she slip into a bathing suit and spend the afternoon around the pool with him. She correctly interpreted his "suggestion" as a command and returned to the pool in a tasteful once-piece suit and flowered cover-up.

She knew she was being pimped out to the old man, but at least he did not have sleazy tastes. She shuttered to think what kind of suit a younger man might have expected her to wear. She was no stranger to selling her body. She had done what she had to do to feed her children, but she had avoided becoming a full-fledged prostitute. A few favors every now and then in return for food or money was just something you did when you lived on the street.

This was different . . . worse in some ways because she had the ability to actually think about what she was doing instead of simply relying on her survival instincts. The perks were way better here, but the moral dilemma was harder for her to overcome. She was not surviving; she was caving in to evil in return for a life on easy street.

Standing in front of the mirror in her cottage was a test to her resolve. She examined herself in the bathing suit and liked what she saw. She still had a youthful appeal despite two children and a year on the streets. Thinking about how her life on the street had been a great diet plan made her chuckle. Cleaned up and dressed up, she looked pretty good.

While the mirror did not lie about how good she still looked, it also told the truth about how she felt deep inside. She looked at herself in the eyes and saw a determination that had grown within her over the last year. This was not the life she wanted to live, no matter how splendid, for her or her girls. This was yet another temporary stop on her road to living a real life off the streets.

His eyes looked her over good as she peeled off her cover-up and settled into the lounge chair next to him. She glanced at him and gave him a quick smile. It was obvious she pleased him in this tastefully cut suit, which made her feel strangely good about herself.

"Kristen, that is a nice suit and it fits you well."

"Thanks. How did you know my size? All the clothes seem to fit perfectly."

"If you know the right people, you can know whatever you want . . . or at least what you are willing to pay for."

"I suppose. Aren't you going to put a suit on?" she asked looking at his slacks and button-up shirt.

"Ha, I suppose I should, but I'm not gonna look as good as you in mine."

"Aren't you sweet," she said in a flirty tone. "I'll bet you still look pretty good."

"You mean for a man my age?"

"I mean for a man." She smiled at him and watched as he left the pool deck without another word.

She used the time alone to look around the pool and plot possible escape routes. Not much to see as the hedges around the pool blocked most of her view. This placed seemed to have no more opportunities than Jake's prison.

Out of nowhere an older Hispanic woman appeared. "Miss Kristen, I am Regina. Would you like a cocktail or a glass of tea?"

"Oh, hello." She took Regina for a house servant. "Yes, please. How about a Margarita?" If she was going to have to have sex with Mr. Williams, a little tequila would help make it tolerable.

"Yes ma'am," she said and turned for the house.

"Regina!" She waited for the older woman to turn around. "How long have you been here?"

"22 years."

"Really?" Kristen did not know what else to say. Without a further word Regina turned and went back into the house.

***

The Vatican had stopped calling. Bishop Charron guessed that was because the case against the church had basically been closed. More exactly, it had been shoved under the rug. The only way this matter would get back in front of the press or even the authorities was if Detective Romano found some way to make it happen. Bishop Charron wanted both the case to go away and he wanted justice to be served.

He had returned to his normal routine, or at least what would be the normal routine had he been the official head of the Diocese. Nothing could be described as normal since the murder of the three priests. At least he was working on church business, serving the Church and God instead of doing damage control.

There were communications to write, priests to counsel, and parishioners to serve. The Vatican had sent word the Pope was considering who would fulfill the Archbishop spot and he had all but been told he was the most likely candidate. Normally, the Church would not consider promoting from within for such a high post, but this was a special situation.

Either way, he did not really care. If it was God's wish for him to be the Archbishop, then it would be so; if not, he would see what God and the Church needed from him. His only wish was to get back to serving the Church and glorifying God. Politics, either within the Church or the real politics of DC, were not what he considered his calling. In that sense, he doubted he would be called to serve as the Archbishop.

The ringing of his private line startled him. Only three people were likely to be calling on this line: the Vatican, Senator Stiano, or Detective Romano. He stared at the phone and wished it had caller ID. At last he lifted the handset and said, "Hello?"

"Bishop Charron, it's Senator Stiano."

"Hello, Senator."

"I understand Agent Murphy has closed the books on the case. I'm glad that is behind us. It would have been tragic to drag the Church though the mud because of the accusations of a very disturbed man. I'm sure you are feeling relieved."

"Indeed, Senator. The Church is much better off with all of this behind us," he said, truthfully. "We will get by the tragic loss of our three leaders with God's help in due time."

"Yes, we will. Bishop, I did want to make sure you understand it is also in the Church's best interest to not link me to this investigation. I was helping out as a loyal member of the Catholic Church and not as a Senator. I did nothing any member of the Church wouldn't have done to help, but some might think it inappropriate for a Senator to help the Church. Not a big deal, but best if we keep me out of this. Understand?"

"Of course."

"Good. Well, always feel free to call if you need anything else. By the way, I'm pulling for you to be named Archbishop. You'd make a fine leader of the Diocese."

"Thank you, Senator. You are very kind."

Chapter 16

Trista had spent the entire afternoon poring over the files Nate had given her. There were a few smoking guns, but nothing worthy of an indictment. That was not really her goal. She was more concerned with getting the truth out and making all the politicians involved squirm a little.

More to the point, she was looking to break some real news that would make a difference. In her mind, this had the potential to be as big of a story as the original "gate" scandal, Watergate. That story had served notice to all politicians they would no longer be able to get away with lying to the press and the American people. If she had her way, this story would let politicians know they could not use their power to serve personal causes and beliefs. She might win awards along the way, but that was not really what she was after…she wanted to make a difference.

The angle of her first story was taking shape. It would be a shot over the bow of the Senate and designed to get the attention of Senator Stiano. After the first article, the story would evolve based on her anonymous source and the reaction of the Senator and his pals.

Joel would provide support for her, moral and editorial. She knew her political editors were going to be hesitant to rock the boat with a story like this. Joel would go to bat for her and said he would even threaten to publish it in his City Section if Trista's editors balked. They both knew that would cause an internal war at the *Post* would likely draw the publisher in to settle the dispute. They were ready for battle, energized by the magnitude of the story.

The plan was to publish the story in Friday morning's edition. The Senate would not be in session and many of the Senators, including Stiano, would be heading back to their home states for a four-day weekend. Publishing the story when the full Senate spin machine would not be assembled in DC would help the story get legs before the Sunday morning political talk shows.

She had told her editor she was working on a big story they might want to save space for on the front page of the Political Section. When pressed about the story, she simply said, "I may have found a Senator with some inappropriate religious views." Surprisingly, that had been enough to avoid further questions.

She sat down in front of her laptop at her small kitchen table. This is what she called her home office. She took a deep breath and let it out slowly trying to settle her nerves. This was going to be the start of a story that could change not just her career, but also her life. Nate crossed her mind before she began to let the story pour out of her. If they were meant to be together, he'd still be there on the other side of this adventure. There was a feeling once she touched the keyboard, fate would be in control.

***

The afternoon at the pool had been delightful. Mr. Williams had been charming and he had actually looked pretty good in a bathing suit. The two margaritas had gone straight to Kristen's head. She had never been much of a drinker, but had not even had a drink since she started living on the street.

Although she had flirted with him all afternoon, he had not seemed interested in her sexually. He had been very curious of her life and asked her many questions. She had asked a few questions about his past, but his vague responses gave her the signal she needed to take it easy on delving into areas that might be forbidden.

As she headed back to her cottage to shower and change for dinner, her mind was racing to evaluate what would be expected of her. Was the old man just looking for companionship? If all she had to do was flirt with him and treat him nicely, why would she want to escape? But she knew there was more to it than that. She would just have to wait to find out what the catch was that would require such drastic action to get her here. If it was such a good deal, why had Jake kidnapped her and held her girls hostage?

***

Amir had spent the afternoon re-establishing his spider network that would make his activity on the terrorist chat rooms impossible to track.

The ring of his latest burner phone startled him. He had set up a special ring tone for Debbie to call, but the default ringtone meant it was someone else. He glanced at the number on the screen and saw it was a local DC number and debated whether to answer it or not. She was the only one who had this number, so it was either her calling from her office phone, a sales call, or a wrong number. He decided to take a chance.

"Hello?"

"Hey there," she replied.

"Hey, where are you calling me from? I don't recognize the number," he added to try and sound less paranoid.

"My office. My cell is dead. I wasn't planning to be traveling and didn't bring my charger cord."

"So you are back in town?"

"Yes and I was hoping to get to see you. Tonight," she added somewhat awkwardly.

"Sure, you okay? You seem a bit strange."

"Sorry. You know me too well. I can't hide anything from you."

"What's wrong?"

"They might be transferring me back to Germany."

There was a tense silence on the line. He had known this relationship was going to need to end soon, one way or the other, but he was not ready to end it yet.

"I don't like the sound of that."

"Me either. Can I grab some takeout and come over for dinner tonight. Are you busy?"

"That sounds great. Is seven okay? I have some work to take care of, but can be finished by then."

"Perfect. Can't wait to see you."

"Me too."

***

It was late in the afternoon and Nate was starting to think about ending his day. Unfortunately, his evening plans would not include any time with Trista. She had really surprised him with her plan to write the story without him in her life. He was worried about her and her safety. If he could not be there to protect her, then he was even more concerned.

The fact that she had essentially broken up with him had not fully set in to his conscious brain. In his mind, they were just taking a break until after this story had run its course. A few months and then they could get back together, or at least that's the way he saw it.

The ringing of his mobile phone brought him back to reality. The sight of Laurie's name on his screen made him smile, although he was not really aware of it. "Hey Laurie," he answered with more energy than he should.

"Hey. You sound like you're in a good mood. Or did you start cocktail hour early?"

"Ha, funny. No, but it won't be long. Wanna join me? I need to brief you on some progress."

"That sounds good. Where?"

"Barney's at 5:30?"

"Perfect. I have some stuff to tell you, too. I found some smoking guns that should blow this whole thing up."

"Really? What?"

"Best if we talk later."

"Gotcha. See you at Barney's." He checked his watch. It was already 5:00 p.m., so he might as well head over to the bar and save them a table.

Thirty minutes later Laurie came bouncing in the bar with an extra spring in her step. Her shoulder length dirty blond hair was bouncing and rocking as she strode into the bar looking for him. Nate had chosen a booth that was tucked into the corner and she walked beyond him without noticing his private spot. She was wearing jeans, which was standard for a lab rat, but Nate was pretty sure most lab rats did not fit into their jeans this well.

"Laurie," he called over the dim background music of the bar.

She spun at the sound of his voice and flashed a big smile. She slid in across from him and caught him staring a little too much. "What?" she asked with a flirty grin.

"Nothin'. You look happy," he said, hoping to change the subject.

"Some people, like me, are just lucky to have a job they love to do."

"Yeah. Maybe I should ask you if you've already been drinking," he jested.

"Oh yeah. Well maybe you should buy me a drink instead of questioning my mojo."

He raised his hand and got the waitresses attention. He ordered her a beer and made small talk until her drink arrived. "Cheers," he said, raising his bottle in salute. "To loving your job and taking down bad guys."

"I'll drink to that."

"So, what'd ya find that has you so excited?" he asked.

"First, it's not hard to get this girl excited," she said with a raised eyebrow. "After all, I love my job." Her smile confused him. Was she really talking about her job?

"Are you going to make me beg or are you gonna tell me?"

"Okay, okay." She took a long pull off her beer and then started. "So, like the saying goes, follow the money. That's what I did. Didn't take me anywhere at first, but I'm like a dog with a bone sometimes . . . I'm gonna gnaw on it until I get to the meaty center."

"Yeah? I'm not sure what to make of that visual. Might ruin my dinner."

"Well, the meat in the center is Arkin Industries. Ring any bells?"

"Ah, nope."

"Didn't work for me either. But it was obvious the trail to Arkin had been well hidden by a few transfers to offshore accounts and other cyber tricks. So, I knew I was on to something . . . remember the dog with a bone thing?"

"Yeah, so?"

"Arkin is a real company, sort of anyway. Not much of a company really, but it is a wholly owned subsidiary of Meade International. Allegedly, Arkin is an import/export company, but the only thing they seem to move is money."

"So, how does that link to our case?"

"Are you always this impatient? Let a girl enjoy the moment, why don't you?"

"Sorry, sorry. I'm all ears," he said making a motion like he was locking his mouth with a key.

"Arkin is really unimportant. Their parent company, Meade, is where the trail gets warm. So Meade is a real company, estimated sales over two billion last year and still privately owned. They make airport stuff like jet-bridges, baggage movers, de-icing machinery and a bunch of other crap. Since there was not much to go on with Arkin, I decided to dig into Meade. Not much there since they are privately held, but woof, woof," she said, acting like a dog.

"So, next I read every newspaper fluff article on Meade, drilled into their website and so on. Nothing, but I now know all about the equipment it takes to run an airport. Finally, I did a deep Internet search and stumbled onto a court case in Indiana that named Meade as the defendant. Not much there except a name. The name of who was the face of Meade in court. One Joseph Sorosee. Recognize that name?"

"Nope, should I?"

"No, it was a trick question."

Her smile kept him from being impatient. He was enjoying watching her. This was one smart lady and the confidence was oozing out of her. He silently nodded to her to keep going.

"Okay, this is where it gets good. Stay with me. Sorosee was a mystery to me, so I dug deep into him. Not much to him, rich guy, President of Meade since 2002. Since this is DC, I decided to check his political connections. Guess who Sorosee gives lots of money to?"

"Is this another trick question?"

"No," she replied with a cute giggle.

"Okay, I'm going with Senator Stiano."

"Ding, ding, ding, we have a winner! And that is the gun. You ready for the smoke?"

"Ha, I think I'm enjoying this as much as you. Go for it."

"Okay, so if you are keeping score, Sorosee, who is president of Meade is giving big bucks to Stiano, who serves on the Armed Services Committee. Meade sells stuff to airports and the Armed Services Committee is responsible for funding numerous Air Force bases. You smelling any smoke now?"

"Let me guess, Meade sells a lot of stuff to the Air Force."

"Twelve billion dollars worth since Sorosee took over in 2002 . . . nothing before that."

"So we have a crooked politician selling contracts for contributions. That type of case is hard to prove. They are good at covering those tracks."

"True, and besides where's the sport in finding corrupt politicians. That's like fishing in a barrel. You are looking in the wrong direction. Remember I said I followed the money to Arkin and Meade?" She waited for his nod. "Well, I never said where it started." She paused long enough to build suspense. "I followed the money backwards from the victims of the Priest abuse to Arkin. So Stiano is tied to Meade, Arkin, the Church, and now the victims."

"That's some serious smoke. No shit. You're amazing," he said, lifting his glass in toast. "I'm gonna buy you dinner and another beer."

"Damn right you are."

Chapter 17

Kristen had anguished over what she was wearing like a schoolgirl on the first day of class. The final choice was a red and white flowered skirt with a white blouse. The mirror did not lie; she looked pretty good. As a final touch, she unfastened one extra button to hopefully give the old man a little thrill.

It was not that long ago she had used this same technique to catch the attention of the man she would marry. That hadn't work out so well, but the technique had proven effective.

Dinner was at seven and she did not want to be late. It was now 6:45 and she was ready to go. The little bit of sun on her face felt good and the lingering buzz of the margaritas was making her mellow. Another drink would keep her from losing her buzz and tonight she might need a buzz. There was a bottle of wine in the fridge and she decided that would do the trick. One quick glass here and probably more at dinner and she would be able to face whatever the old man wanted to do.

A few minutes later, she walked across the small yard that separated her cottage from the main house and entered the door. Regina met her at the door and motioned her towards the dining room. The table was formally set for two. It had been a long time since she had seen that many forks at a place setting. Actually, she corrected herself, it had been a long time since she had the luxury of sitting at a table to eat.

When he entered the room, she was admiring a painting on the wall of a beautiful field of flowers. "That's a Hawthorne. Picked it up in England many years ago. Always been one of my favorite."

"Oh, Mr. Williams. I didn't hear you come in. It's a beautiful painting."

"Yes it is, and so are you, my dear. Shall we?" he asked pulling out her chair.

The table was large, but they only used one end of it. He sat at the head of the table and she was to his right. Regina appeared and poured wine without asking and soon followed with the first course, a beefsteak tomato and mozzarella salad.

"A toast," he said raising his glass towards her. "To a very lovely lady and a great dinner."

"Well, thank you. That's very kind. I'm starving and looking forward to a great dinner. What, may I ask, is for dinner after this lovely salad?"

"I asked Thon to make stuffed veal chops. I'm not supposed to eat a lot of meat, but this seemed like a special occasion. Wouldn't you agree?"

"Yes. This is a special occasion. I'm happy to share it with you."

Dinner, all four courses, was fabulous. The wine had also been good, but she was having trouble remembering how many glasses had been poured for her. Her subtle buzz from the afternoon margaritas was nothing compared to how drunk she was now. If she had not eaten such a large meal, she probably would have passed out.

It seemed like Mr. Williams was pretty drunk as well. She had seen mean drunks and funny drunks, but she had never experienced a charming drunk. The drunker he got, the more he flirted and teased with her.

After dessert he took her hand and raised it to his lips and kissed it. She waited to see what would happen next. "Shall we have some coffee and then continue the evening in my room?" he asked with a charming and expectant smile.

"Why Mr. Williams," she started in a fake southern bell accent, "what kind of girl do you think I am?"

His eyes locked on hers and let the silence linger between them as he simply smiled at her. "I hope," he started and raised her hand to his lips for a gentle kiss, "you are the type of lady who likes to have a man bring you great pleasure. With age comes experience and I have experience in sexually satisfying ladies."

"You do? Pretty bold statement. I might just be drunk enough to call your bluff on that claim."

"I'm counting on it."

***

The takeout food was from a little Greek restaurant down the street from Amir's apartment. Debbie had gotten to know him well enough that it was easy to order food for him. He was not a strict Muslim, at least with his diet and prayers, but he did have particular likes and dislikes.

As she approached the steps that led up to the old converted row house, she glanced across the street at the black van parked along the curb of the narrow street. She could see no activity inside, but she had been told that was where Agent Brown would be stationed with his listening devices. She was assured he would be able to hear everything and they had arranged a safe word, "panda," for her to use if she needed to signal them to save her.

The emotions she was feeling were a mix of fear and anger. She also held onto a tiny bit of hope this was all a huge mistake. This was not going to be easy for her and she had better do a good job of acting or Amir would figure her out. Who knew what would happen then. She knocked on the door and it opened to a smiling man who two days ago she would have said she was falling in love with. It was that feeling that leaped forward when she saw him. The door wasn't even shut before they were locked in a loving embrace.

Dinner went well. He opened a bottle of wine and they consumed the gyros while making small talk about the possibility of being transferred back to Germany. After dinner they retired to the couch and he leaned in and kissed her with passionate intent. It was not hard for her to fake her returned passion, but the knowledge that Agent Brown was listening in was awkward. She wondered if he'd keep listening if they moved to the bedroom and got into it.

"Hey, I have a surprise for you," she started, hoping to keep him from asking more about her potential transfer.

"Oh really? Does it require me to be naked?"

"Yes. Yes it does in fact."

"Okay," he said as he stood up and started acting like he was going to strip.

"But, not right now." The look of feigned disappointment on his face made her giggle. He was good at that. "The surprise is I have been asked to house sit for the Senior Consulate at his beach house in Cape May. It is supposed to be a beautiful place and if you agree to come with me, being naked quite often is required." Her flirtatious smile was not hard to fake.

"Really! That sounds wonderful. When?"

"It is a Friday thru Sunday the end of April and the beginning of May. Friday is the 30th and Sunday is the 2nd." She had intentionally avoided saying the 1st for fear of blowing her cover. "We'll have the entire place to ourselves and there is some big festival in town."

"Hmm," he said looking off to the ceiling as he considered the dates. She watched him hoping the agents were wrong and he was not involved in whatever was being planned for May 1st. "I think I can do that. Sounds like a great time."

She was very happy when he agreed to go and she gave him a kissed filled with promise. She considered this proof the FBI was wrong about Amir and they did have a future together. She stood up and almost commanded him to follow her into the bedroom. He was more than willing to oblige and she was more than willing to give Agent Brown the most X rated surveillance he'd ever conducted.

***

Jake found a parking place by the curb just across the street from Senator McDermott's house. It was not a fancy house and the Senator did not own it, but by DC standards it was a quiet and safe neighborhood. Jake had followed the Senator home the week before and was doing more reconnaissance on his target. His plan was simple; executing it would be hard. The Senator had a driver/security guard and it was not his intent to harm an innocent man. The Senator was a friend of the devil and whatever harm came to him was just part of the damnation he had brought on himself.

It was beyond Jake's imagination how this Senator thought he could single handedly take down the religious principles of this country. He seemed to think everyone should be forced into atheism and burn in hell along with him. Jake would not let that happen.

He was a cultural warrior and according to some conservative talk show hosts, he was supposed to stand up and defend his country against those who wanted to morally corrupt the United States and take away its divine right to lead the world. The best way he knew how to do that was to cut the head off the snake. McDermott had to die to save the country.

Every time Jake heard McDermott speak he had referenced Thomas Jefferson's *wall of separation between church and state*. Jake had another Jefferson quote he would share with the media after he had eliminated this threat. He was going to send the following simple message to Fox News:

"The tree of liberty must be refreshed from time to time with the blood of patriots and tyrants."

Thomas Jefferson.

Senator McDermott had to die.

Sincerely,

A Patriot

If you watch a house long enough at night, you can get a good feel for the interior layout based on the way the lights go on and off. After 30 minutes, Jake had figured out the Senator's bedroom was in the front of the house on the second floor. The room seemed to have heavy curtains, but still light leaked out around the edges. There were few streetlights in this area of town, which allowed him to easily see lights go on and off in the house.

The simple plan was to plant the hellfire bomb under the Senator's bed and then use his cell phone to set it off when he was sure the Senator was sleeping. The explosion would be enough to wake the Senator, but because of the thick mattress, it probably would not kill him. Jake hope the Senator would live long enough to realize he had gone to hell before the fire engulfed him.

The difficulty was getting inside to plant the bomb. There would be a security system and probably window jams to keep the lower windows from being pried open with a crowbar. Jake was not a talented burglar, but he wasn't planning on taking anything. He only needed 30 seconds to plant the bomb. After that, he did not care if the alarm went off.

He'd simply break in the same door the Senator used when he came home. The alarm would not go off for 30 seconds after the door opened. He'd make a mad dash to the upstairs bedroom, plant the bomb under the bed and then leave. The alarm would then go off, but he'd be long gone before the police arrived. The police, after determining nothing was missing, would just assume the alarm had scared off the intruder. Case closed.

He would come back when the Senator was home and wait until the Senator was in bed. The plan sounded simple, but Jake knew it would be tough to execute. The big mystery was the possibility that video cameras were present. That might show the police his true reason for entering the home. His mask would keep him from being caught, but they would likely find the bomb.

Tomorrow the Senator would be leaving town to give a speech to some crazy anti-religious group at a meeting in New York City. Public figures were so easy to track thanks to the web. He spent the next hour plotting his escape routes and canvassing the neighborhood for a good place to stash his car during the break-in. Satisfied he was ready to go, Jake went back to the mission to get some sleep. The past 24 hours had been exhausting.

***

Trista's story was about half finished. She had forgotten to eat dinner because she was so focused on her work. Finally hunger got the best of her and she took a short break. A banana with peanut butter, her old standby meal, would have to do tonight. Thoughts of Nate invaded her conscious mind. It sure would be good to have him here tonight to cook her dinner and take care of her while she worked. A good man was hard to find and she had just pushed one away.

Forcing herself to forget him, she headed back to her laptop. The story did not need to be submitted until 5:00 p.m. tomorrow, but she wanted to finish it by noon. The Political Editor at the Post was going to be a tough sell. Joel would be with her and vouch for the facts of the story. Her editor would be furious about Joel being involved, but they would explain this story was not just political because it also involved the Church.

Since the first part of the story would focus on politics, it should run in the Politics section, but if her editors balked, Joel would just threaten to run it in his City section. One way or another, Friday's edition would launch a story likely to change her career.

The clock on her computer said 9:30 p.m. She decided to write until 11:00 p.m. and then call it a night. A fresh mind in the morning would be needed to finish the story and meet with her boss. The next time she looked at the time, it was just after midnight. She closed her laptop and headed to bed, a smile on her face.

Chapter 18

The sunlight peaking around the edges of the curtains woke her. At first, Kristen did not know where she was and the light hurt her eyes and kept her from focusing on the room. A dull headache did not help her think, but memories of the previous evening came flooding back. She had been drunk, but not so drunk she did not remember the rather remarkable events of last night.

After several blinks, her eyes finally were able to focus. She was alone in a large bed in a spacious bedroom. Her clothes were strewn across the chair beside the bed except for her bra and underwear, which were on the floor. She smiled as she recalled her striptease act as he watched from the bed. The wine had broken away any inhabitations she had about sleeping with the old man, but the sobriety of the morning would soon allowed regret and common sense to take over.

Sitting up with her feet on the floor was all she could muster for a few minutes. When her head had cleared enough to stand, she made her way to the bathroom to pee and clean up. Despite feeling compelled to leave his bedroom as fast as she could, she had to admit the old man was an impressive lover, certainly the best she had ever had as far as being focused on her needs. If she was going to be forced to have sex, at least it was not some sort of kinky, violent stuff.

Dressing quickly and heading downstairs, she hoped to slip out and back to her cottage without seeing Mr. Williams. No such luck. He was having coffee and reading a newspaper at the bottom of the steps.

"Ah, good morning. I trust you slept well. How's your hangover?"

"Not too bad," she lied.

"Come sit and have coffee." It was more of a command than a request.

She poured a cup from the silver pot and curled up in a chair next to his. As she silently sipped the hot brew she could feel his eyes on her. Taking her time to express what little control she had, she focused on her coffee and refused to look at him. Ten minutes later, without saying a word or looking at him, she finished the last drop and looked up at him. He was staring at her with a huge smile on his face.

"What?" she asked with her own involuntary smile.

"Nothing. Just like watching you, that's all."

She stared back at him for a few seconds before deciding to play along. "And what's that grin on your face all about?" she asked, knowingly.

"Ha," he chuckled. "Beautiful women make me smile, especially the day after a night of passion. I trust you really did enjoy last night and that was not just an Academy Award-worthy acting job?"

"I'm not much of an actress."

The smile on his face broadened from ear to ear. Clearly he was proud of himself. "Are you hungry?"

"Not yet," she replied as she poured herself another cup of coffee.

"When you are, just see Regina or Thon and they'll fix you up. I've got some work to do this morning, but will be by the pool this afternoon. I hope to see you there."

She understood his gentle command. "Sounds fun, but this time I'm gonna watch what I drink."

"Ha, where's the fun in that?"

She stood and faced him as he sat in his large armchair. Smiling coyly, she leaned over towards him with one hand anchored on each of the chair's arms. Her low cut dressed fell gently away from her chest revealing her bra-covered breast just inches from his face. She knew he could not resist the view. "I guess you'll have to try to charm me out of my dress tonight instead of getting me drunk."

It was a risky play. She knew men could be manipulated with sex. Actually, it often only took a flash of cleavage, but either way, it was the only card she held. If the old man took her bait, she would be on her way to getting what she wanted . . . to be united with her girls.

"Very nice," he said staring down her dress, "but I need to warn you."

"Oh yeah? About what?" she asked playfully.

"Despite my performance last night, I am unfortunately an old man. Let's just say I'm more about quality than quantity. Tonight, I will want to enjoy your charming company instead of your delicious body. But, thanks for the view."

"Okay," she said trying to hide her relief she would not have to sleep with the old man too often. "See you this afternoon." She flashed him another smile and headed back to her cottage.

***

Trista woke up just after 6:00 a.m. She would have liked to sleep another hour or so, but the story would not leave her mind at rest. She fought her brain to relax, but gave up after a few minutes and got up. In 15 minutes she was busy at work on the story with a hot cup of coffee in hand.

Her concentration was interrupted by the sound of the door to Nate's apartment shutting. She looked at the clock: just before 7:00 a.m. That would be Nate coming home after a morning run. Until today, she would have been asked to join him. She decided she would call him later and discuss the story and see what other leads he could give her. She forced herself to forget about him and get back to work.

The next two hours passed in what felt like a minute. A quick click on the save button and she was done with the first draft. Undoubtedly her editor would want changes, but she was used to that. The story had turned out well and a wonderful feeling of accomplishment washed over her. This was just the start, but she still felt like celebrating an achievement.

She thought about calling Nate, but decided to wait a bit. She decided to hit the showers and put on a power suit to do battle with her editor. She had arranged to meet Joel for lunch to review the draft. For internal security, she emailed the article to Joel using his gmail account instead of the Post's email system.

After her shower she checked her email and saw Joel's one-word response, "wow!" Her hand was shaking slightly as she typed her short reply. "See you at lunch."

***

It had been a long night for Agent Brown. The stakeout of Amir and Debbie had been entertaining, but unproductive. She was not supposed to have spent the night, but it was obvious she had determined the FBI was wrong about Amir being a terrorist. It was not the first time he had spent the night in his car on a stakeout, but it was never a pleasant experience. He would have left after she went to sleep, but he had to make sure she did not tip him off about the FBI's suspicions.

The loud and animated love-making had lasted for over an hour and then she fell silent, probably asleep. Amir had gotten back up after a while and, based on the clicking of keyboards picked up on the listening equipment, he was very active doing something. He had called into the lab monitoring the Internet to see if they could mirror Amir's keystrokes with the posts on the terrorist sites. He patched the sound of the keyboards into the listening lab to see if the computer software could match the distinct sound of his keyboard with what was being posted. This would provide proof of which post could be attributed to Amir.

Thirty minutes later, he received a call from the lab. "Brown, whatcha find?" he said answering his phone.

"How many people are in the apartment?"

"Two. One's asleep."

"You sure? We have sounds from three keyboards."

"Pretty sure. She could be awake, but I'm only picking up sounds consistent with one person."

"Maybe he's using three computers."

"Three? Why would he do that? Have you matched his posts yet?"

"Not yet, but we are seeing some tracks on a few different posts that are possible."

"Huh. You think he is posting as multiple people in the same chat room?"

"Maybe. That would explain the three keyboard sounds."

"Interesting. Why the hell would he do that? Keep me posted." With that he disconnected the call and went back to listening. His mind drifted back to the passion he had overheard earlier. She knew he was listening, so she must have wanted him to get an ear full. Was it just her way of saying 'screw you' to him? It wasn't the first time he'd had to monitor that type of thing, and it wouldn't be the last.

About 3:00 a.m. Amir called it quits and went to bed. By then, the keystroke recognition program had tracked his activity under three different screen names participating in the chat. They had scientific evidence to prove he was inciting violence, but other than deporting him, this was not what they needed. They needed to know what the big plan was for May 1st.

Debbie left the apartment at 7:00 a.m. and jumped in a waiting taxi. Agent Brown was expecting his relief any minute and decided to just let her go. She was supposed to be back at work by 9:00 a.m. and he would debrief the other agents by phone and then get some sleep.

Amir was still asleep when the next agent showed up to relieve Agent Brown. He decided to hit the nearest pancake house for some breakfast before calling his report in to Agents Simons and Farcas. He figured Debbie would be headed home to shower and get ready for work. It was not going to be a good day for her. He guessed she was convinced more than ever her boyfriend was not a terrorist, but the evidence he had gathered while she slept proved otherwise.

***

The weather had been delightful for Nate's morning run and it had helped clear his head. Upon his arrival at work, reality hit him and pulled him back into the weeds. Pete met him in the hall on his way to his office and handed him two new cases to cover. "I know you might be busy," Pete whispered in a knowing tone, "but business is hot and we can't do without you."

Nate simply nodded, took the files and headed to his office. Since he was not officially working the priest case, he needed to work other cases to make sure no one suspected what he was up to. He'd have to work in some time to dig into the politicians.

He typed out a quick email to Laurie down in the lab, *Got a couple new cases that are gonna keep me busy. Might need your help. Keep you posted.*

Checking the rest of his messages he noticed one from a name he did not recognize. It wasn't really a name as much as a random email address: adgjl13579@gmail.com. The subject line was "tip." After 15 years on the force, he had received his fair share of anonymous tips, so he opened the message with a bit of skepticism. Normally it was some pissed off lover or rival gang member trying to get the police to settle a score.

The first sentence grabbed his attention: *Senator Stiano's hands are as dirty as the perverted priest.* He read the entire message three times to make sure he was understanding the somewhat cryptic meaning of the anonymous source. Next he wrestled with whom to call first – Trista, or Laurie. He opted for Laurie so he could get an objective opinion before making this a news story. Besides, he was going to have to verify this tip before slipping it to Trista to print.

On a whim, he clicked the print button and then closed the message and moved it out of his inbox. By the time the one-page document was finished printing, he had locked his computer and was ready to run down to the lab. Pausing for just a second, he picked up the two case files Pete had given him and tucked them in his small briefcase with the email printout.

As he entered the lab, Laurie looked up from her small cubicle and flashed him a killer smile. "Hey, Detective Romano, can I help you?"

At first he was taken aback by her rather formal greeting, but then realized the lab was crowded with other lab techs. "Ah, yes, I need some technical help with this new case. Gotta minute?"

"Sure, show me what you have," she said with a nod to the paperwork he was extracting from his briefcase.

He lowered his voice. "These are my two new cases, but this," he said, handing her the printed email, "is from another case. Can you do your magic thing and find out who sent this email?"

She looked at the gmail address and frowned. "Probably not, but I might be able to figure out where it was sent from. Gmail accounts don't require any sort of ID verification, so anyone could have made up this address. Do you have the message still on your computer?"

"Yes."

"Good, forward it to me when you can and I'll see what I can find." Before she handed the message back to him, she took a second to read it. Halfway through she paused and looked up with her mouth gapping open in amazement. "Well," she said after letting out a long sigh, "that's interesting."

While she had been reading, Nate had used his phone to forward the message to her. "You should have it now. Text me if you find out anything," he said as he started towards the door.

"Will do."

***

The state senator was a great orator and loved the spotlight of a dramatic press conference. Max Pigman stood under a tree 30 yards away from the capitol steps where the senator stood behind a temporary lectern. Although he had engineered the entire show, Max did not want to be linked to the senator.

"Churches serve a vital role in our society as a spiritual anchor and it is critical we make sure government is not punishing them or controlling them with taxes and regulations, but when a church ventures outside its religious mission to blatantly compete with private enterprise, we must treat them as we would any business. Recently there was a lawsuit filed that brought this injustice to my attention. The city of Charlottesville, which has been controlled by liberal Democrats for decades, has stepped across the line that was first drawn in their own backyard by Thomas Jefferson. Indeed, it was Jefferson who first wrote about the need to have a wall of separation between church and state, but in Charlottesville that wall has been re-built between free enterprise and freedom.

"The liberals in Charlottesville have provided funding to subsidize the YMCA, a liberal religious-based group, and create a situation where small businesses cannot compete. I've seen the plans for the Y in Charlottesville. This is not a facility designed to serve the underprivileged in the city. This is a top-notch facility located on prime real estate that will sell gym memberships to consumers in Charlottesville.

"Since the Y is a religious organization, it is exempt from paying taxes. So, to summarize, the liberals on Charlottesville City Council are funding a liberal, quasi-religious, tax-exempt organization to compete against hard-working citizens who drive our economy and pay a lot of taxes. This is wrong and that's why I will be introducing legislation that prohibits tax dollars from being given to an organization that directly competes with private businesses."

Max smiled at the rhetoric the senator was slinging around, like campaign brochures on Election Day. Several news agency were represented and based on the questions that followed the senator's comments, this was going to be a big story. Within the hour, the Internet would start the firestorm that should set the stage for a favorable ruling in his complaint. Pulling out his cell phone, he called Senator McDermott to report the success.

Chapter 19

Joel was late for lunch, but Joel was generally late for everything. It always amazed Trista that a man whose career revolved around deadlines could never seem to be on time for anything else. While she waited, she decided to text Nate.

Hey. First story done. Miss you, but hope you understand.

A few seconds later he responded, *Congrats, yes I do, but hate it.*

Thanks, me too.

I need to see you soon. When can we meet?

She re-read the message a few times to make sure he was not meaning he needed to see her on a personal level. Finally she decided he sounded like he wanted to give her some more information on the story and replied, *I have to submit the story by 5, so after that I am available.*

Let's wait till morning, probably not good to get together at night. Not sure I can be trusted ☺

Okay. How about I make you some breakfast? Pop over at 7:30?

Perfect

Joel walked in and spotted her right away. He slipped in the booth opposite her and didn't bother to apologize for being late. He was a little more haggard looking than normal, but that was not a surprise. She suspected the gravity of the moment was showing on her as well.

"Hey. Nice work on the piece. I have a few changes, but it might be the biggest story I've been in on. Not sure if I'm just nervous, excited, or coming down with something," he said rubbing his temples like his head hurt. "You sure you want to do this? It is gonna get dicey. It is either gonna define your career, or end it."

"Slow down, now. Let's try to get through this story. I'm not sure they will agree to print it," she said, referring to her editors. "I need you to focus on getting that done. After that, we can assess my career issues."

"Yeah, sorry. I'm supposed to be the calm rationale one here." He took a deep breath and let it out slowly. "Okay, I'm back. Let's start over."

"Okay, so tell me what you thought about the story. Too dramatic or balanced?"

"Balanced. Frankly, if it were about the different bird species in the park, it would still be a well-written article. You've always been good at the writing, this is just a different league."

"Yeah. I know. But this is the type of story I've been craving. For the first time in a while, I feel completely energized by my work. Articles about nuclear power are boring. You know?"

"Yeah, but you need to go into this with eyes wide open, if you know what I mean."

"I do. Now let's get to it. You hungry, or do you want to tell me your changes?"

"Food first, I get grumpy when I'm hungry."

"You really need to eat more often," she replied with a playful grin.

"Yeah, whatever."

Thirty minutes later, Joel was licking the spicy residue from his seasoned fries off his fingers. His mood and his energy level had both improved. She wiped her mouth politely and waited for him to begin.

"Okay, I gotta head back soon, so let's get to it." He opened his portfolio and handed her a copy of her article with his red pen marks all over it. "Just a few suggestions. Like I said, good work. Only question I have is with the tie to the church. The only thing we have is the killer's ramblings. The proof is really hearsay and you didn't contact the Senator to get his side of the story."

"I tried, but he was unavailable for comment," she said, while making air-quotes with her fingers. "I'm hoping he is gonna want to talk to me after this is published."

"Okay, good. You should add he was unavailable for comment. Otherwise, I think you are good to go."

"Good. Thanks. Do you think I'm in over my head?"

"Sure, but that's the only way to learn to swim with the sharks. You'll be okay, but this is not going to be easy."

"Nothing worthwhile ever is." They sat in silence letting it all sink in.

"Okay, see you at four." With that, he stood up and left her to pay the check. She figured she probably owed him that.

***

Based on the professional-looking driver, Jake assumed the Society for Religious Freedom had arranged for a car to pick up McDermott and bring him to their event in New York City. According to the official program posted online, he was to be the after dinner speaker. Jake just wanted the Senator to stop talking, but this group saw him as a hero.

Jake watched from across the street as the driver loaded the Senator's suitcase into the car. The Senator walked out of the house, locked the deadbolt and slipped into the car. Jake pulled out a few seconds after the Senator's black Town car, but made the first turn so as not to be noticed or suspected.

He did not need to follow the Senator, but wanted to confirm that he had indeed left. After dark he would return and place the bomb. This Senator needed to pay for attacking Christians and what better way to kill a devil than with a bomb called hellfire.

***

It had been a long day for Debbie. By mid-morning the FBI had contacted the German Embassy and let them know of her defiance from the night before, without the unnecessary intimate details. She had not stayed with the plan and the Embassy was told she was a "possible conspirator" in a terrorist plot of mass destruction. The Embassy had been instructed to hold her until Homeland Security arrived.

Embassy security had locked her in the same room she had spent the night in before. Her smartphone had been taken and even the television in the room had been disconnected from the outside world.

She had only mildly protested because she knew she had defied orders to cooperate. She figured this would likely get her fired and sent back to Germany. She knew she had acted hastily in exonerating Amir of any wrongdoing.

The joy of him not falling for the trap of traveling with her on May 1st had overridden any objective evaluation. Now, locked in a cell, she had plenty of time to realize the errors in her judgment. If he was part of a terrorist plot, it would be a perfect cover story to distract her from his true plans. Had she used her head instead of her heart, she would have been less blind to the situation.

It was mid-afternoon when they came for her. Two armed men from Embassy security escorted her to the conference room inside the security office. Waiting there was Agent Brown, sipping a cup of coffee. The two men left and closed the door behind her.

"So, why didn't you stick with the plan?" asked Agent Brown.

"I'm sorry. I was just so happy when he agreed to leave town I lost my head."

"Do you know how much trouble you are in?"

"I guess I'll get fired."

His sarcastic laugh caught her attention. "That's the least of your worries."

"What do you mean?"

"Debbie, you are dangerously close to a charge of aiding a suspected terrorist and failure to cooperate with the United States Government. At the very least, you will be deported, but I would not rule out a few years in jail."

"Jail! I have not helped a terrorist. Even if Amir is a terrorist, I have not helped him."

He just smiled with confidence until she looked away from him and stared at the floor. "So, let me tell you what your boyfriend did last night after you went to sleep. He got up and used three different computers to participate in a known terrorist chat room. He used three different screen names and all three spewed jihadist rhetoric. He's not only a terrorist, he's three terrorists. And based on the sounds coming out of the bedroom last night, you let all three of them fuck your brains out."

"It was a mistake," she said as the tears started to roll down her face. "I just have a hard time believing all this. I'm sorry. I'm sorry." The sobs overcame her.

He abruptly left the room and returned in a few minutes with a box of tissues and a glass of water. Without saying a word, he placed them on the table in front of her.

"Thank you," she said, trying to pull herself together. They did not speak another word for the next five minutes. She gradually pulled herself together and he just sat there and watched. Finally she looked up at him, took a deep breath and exhaled loudly. "All right. Where do we go from here?"

"That's up to you."

"I'm willing to do whatever you want. No more bullshit. I understand he is a terrorist, or at least up to something no good, and I'm willing to help."

"How do I know I can trust you? It would be easier if I just arrest you and be done with it."

"Can we cut a deal?"

"Ha. Why should I cut you a deal?"

"Because I can search his place without him knowing it."

"You underestimate the powers of Homeland Security. We don't need you for that."

"What, then? What can I do? I don't want to go to jail."

"We have a plan, but if you screw us again, I can promise you'll be arrested immediately."

"I won't. I promise."

Over the next hour, she listened to him explain what she was going to do. Only once did she interrupt him to ask why, but he shut her down quickly. In the end, she was escorted back to her room, broken by Agent Brown and ready to fully cooperate. All hope of Amir being innocent had vanished.

***

"Hey, you find anything?" Nate said, answering his cell phone.

"Yep," Laurie answered. "Like I said, not going to find out a who, at least not without a court order, but I got a location."

"That's a start. Where?"

"Starbucks near Wisconsin and M. Probably not much help. Could have been anyone who visited during that time frame."

"Can you pull credit card receipts around the time of the email?"

"Done, and waiting in your inbox."

"Man, you're good."

"You only know the half of it," she replied with a chuckle before she hung up.

Nate stared at his phone, trying to figure out what she meant by only knowing the half of it.

The document with the credit card records would be hard to read on his old smart phone, but he opened her message up to try. He noticed she had sent it through a random sounding gmail account. Probably smart to cover her tracks.

He read her message and realized what she meant by only knowing the "half of it." The other half was she had already cross referenced the list against government employees and found seven who had visited that Starbucks within an hour of the timestamp on the email. In this town, seven out of the total 15 visitors was about the right amount of government employees per capita.

Of the seven, according to her message, only one worked in the Senate and she included the name with a smiley face icon next to it. Nate guessed that was Laurie's way of saying "got'em." Bertram Godfrey worked for none other than Senator Stiano.

Now the ball was in Nate's court. What should he do, quietly contact the source himself, or turn it over to Trista? He was old enough to have heard of Deep Throat from the Watergate scandal. Was this Trista's Deep Throat, or his star witness? He decided to discuss it with her when they met for breakfast tomorrow.

***

It had been a tougher battle with her editors than Trista expected. If Joel had not been there to advocate for the story, she was sure the political editors would have wimped out and not published. As it was, they only agreed to run it by the Publisher for approval.

"Spineless bastards," Joel mumbled as they left the editors' office. "The two of them," he said referring to the Editor and Assistant Editor for the Politics and Opinion section, "don't even have a set of balls between them."

"Thanks, Joel. They'd have killed it if it weren't for you. I owe you."

"Just break this story and give me a small acknowledgement in the book and movie and we'll call it even."

"Ha! Deal. Do you think Malcolm Potter will make them run it?"

"Yes. He's old school and didn't get to be Publisher by keeping his head down. Besides, I already talked to him."

"What?"

"I figured these two would go running to him with their tails between their legs, so I decided to beat them to it. He's pumped and I only told him half of it."

"Joel, you." She stumbled for words. "I love you," she said as she rose on her tiptoes to kiss him on the cheek. "I'm going to make you the leading man in the book."

"Stiano better be the leading man, or the books not gonna have a happy ending." He turned to her and his face turned serious. "Listen, you watch yourself from here on. I guarantee the Senator will have a copy before the presses are rolling. Stay true to your professional ethics, your journalistic integrity, and to common sense for your safety. You mess one thing up, and they will rip you apart and try to discredit you."

"Gotcha."

Without another word, he nodded his head and turned to walk away. She watched him walk away and smiled. For the first time, she realized it was him, his professionalism and skill that had caused her to want to do more than cover boring nuclear power hearings. He was and had been her mentor for the past several years. She would make him proud if it was the last thing she did.

***

It was a delightful day around the pool. Kristen had no idea what state she was in, but she did know it must be south of DC to have an 80-degree day this time of year. Even Mr. Williams had his shirt off enjoying the warm sun.

Despite her pledge to not drink too much today, he had convinced her to have a Bloody Mary to help with her hangover. One led to two and two led to being a bit tipsy. With her inhibitions suppressed by alcohol, she became rather chatty with the old man.

She asked him about Jake, the man who brought her here, but the old man was tight-lipped. She approached the topic from a couple different angles until she finally scored a good response. She had questioned Jake's faith, saying his fake religious ties made true religions look bad.

"Oh no. There is nothing fake about his religious ties. He is a true believer and dedicated to his cause."

"Really? What cause?"

The old man had hesitated before responding, but finally asked her, "You know that idiot Senator who is doing his best to make this a godless country?"

"No. I've gotten behind in current affairs over the last year," she said, leaving out the part about being homeless.

"Well, there's this Senator, got his family killed in a tornado out west somewhere and is now convinced there is no God. He's made it is life's mission to stop prayer in schools, posting of the Ten Commandments at the courthouse and other such moral traditions in America. Basically, he's the devil and Jake's gonna send him to hell."

"Really. That Senator sounds like a real nut job. Good for Jake," she said, without really meaning it. Her hope was the old man would keep going if she baited him a bit.

"Jake's a good man and I have you in the deal," he said, raising his glass in cheers. "And you get a fantastic new life. Everyone wins, except the devil Senator."

"Indeed," she said raising her glass back at him. "I think I'm gonna love this new life, but I didn't realize I was part of a bigger deal."

"Yep, a little horse trading. I needed a new companion, you needed a new life, and Jake needed a bomb to take care of the Senator. I called the deal a bomb for a bombshell, get it?"

"Are you calling me a bombshell? You old sweet talker."

"Who you calling old. Showed you a few things last night, didn't I?"

"Yes, you did. Now, if you'll excuse me, I need to run back to my room and hit the little girls' room."

Twenty minutes later when she returned, the old man was fast asleep. She decided it was a perfect time to explore the house. Regina was out in the small garden in the back of the house and Thon had driven off earlier. She quickly made her way through the house and peaked in every room she could find. She wasn't sure what she was looking for – maybe a gun, or telephone – but she had to get out of this place. Some wacko planning to blow up a Senator had her little girls and she had to save them.

A heavy wooden door was locked when she tried it. Living on the streets had taught her a few tricks about locked doors. More than once she had jimmied a lock to get in out of the cold night. She quickly headed back to the kitchen and grabbed a butter knife. The standard lock could be opened with just some gentle pressure. She eased the door open, not sure what to expect and slid quietly inside.

The room was only lit by a small window up near the ceiling. It was an office with a large desk a telephone and a computer. She went straight to the phone and dialed 911. The phone made a strange tone and then an automated voice said, "invalid number." What in the hell? Where was she that even 911 did not work?

She quickly tried to think of someone to call, but after living on the street for a year, she couldn't remember anyone's number. She dialed zero, but got the same response as before. Frustrated, she started poking numbers madly. Suddenly, the phone made a different noise and she got a new sounding dial tone. The only number she could think of was from an infomercial she had watched that morning, 888-888-1888.

The nice lady on the other end of the phone probably thought she was some nutcase at first. It took a few minutes and a very panicked voice to convince the lady she was, indeed, in trouble.

"Can you hold the line while I get the police?"

"I don't think I can. I'm gonna get caught if I stay in here much longer. I'll lay the phone down so maybe they can trace the call and find me, but I gotta go."

"Okay. Good luck."

With that, Kristen laid the phone on the desk and left the room. She stopped by the kitchen and grabbed a glass of water. The old man was still asleep when she returned to the pool, so she quietly slipped into the chair next to him and prayed for the first time in a long time. She had to get out of here, for her girls and to stop Jake the nut job before he blew up a Senator.

Chapter 20

The phone line had gone dead before the telephone sales agent could convince the police that Kristen was really in trouble. Right before it went dead, she thought she heard someone pick up the phone and listen. She had wisely muted the phone while she called the police on her cell phone. Her hope was anyone discovering the call would not hear anything and think it was a dead line.

The police had come storming in five minutes too late and she had been grilled for two hours before she was allowed to leave. The police seemed particularly interested in the threat to the Senator's life and had no trouble identifying him. Evidently Senator McDermott was well known and there had been other threats.

When asked if they would be able to trace the call, the officers were not sure, but promised to do whatever they could to find the lady named Kristen Carr.

***

Trista enjoyed an evening run, followed by a salad and a beer, before sitting back down to write. She wanted to outline the follow-up story that would be needed before the shit hit the fan with the publishing of the Friday *Post*. She suspected the Senator would agree to talk to her after that. That thought made her smile.

The follow-up story would not be much because it would be printed in the Saturday edition. Even with the Internet, most Americans were too busy with life on the weekend to read a paper on Saturday. The bigger story was plotted out for Sunday, the biggest day for readership.

She heard a little bit of noise coming from Nate's side of the wall as she set up her computer to get to work. She'd love to discuss the story over a beer, but they had set a new boundary, or rather, she had. Boundaries had always been important in their relationship, but she really hoped this one would be temporary.

The chirping of her cell phone startled her. The caller ID was a DC number she did not recognize. Her curiosity got the best of her and she decided to answer.

"Good evening, Trista. This is Malcolm Potter."

"Hello, Mr. Potter. Good evening," she stumbled at what to say. Her publisher had never even spoken to her, much less called her.

"Please, call me Malcolm. I don't think we've had the opportunity to meet, but based on your inflection, I see you know who I am."

"Of course," she replied with a more confident tone. "I wasn't expecting you to call."

"Well, I suppose this visit is long overdue. You've been doing good work for us and I should have come to see you sooner."

"When you say come see me, ah…"

"I'm on my way there now. I should be there in five minutes."

"Oh, well I'm not really suitable for a visit. I just got back from a run and I'm pretty grubby."

"Isn't that a coincidence, I'm on my way home from the gym myself. Sorry to barge in, but I need to talk to you on a rather pressing matter."

Five minutes later there was a knock at her door and she descended the steps, looked out the peephole and opened it for her boss. "Hello, Mr., ah Malcolm. Please come in."

He was dressed in a suit with no tie and she resisted the urge to ask him if this was the attire he worked out in, or had he just pretended to have been at the gym. It didn't really matter, but she was feeling self-conscious about looking and smelling bad when she first met him.

Once inside, he eyed her computer setup with her notes strewed all around. "So, this is where the magic happens?"

"Yes, sir."

"This story, the one you are running Friday."

"Yes?"

"I'm worried about it. A lot."

"I have good sources. It is a solid story and I think it is just the tip of the iceberg."

"Calm down, Trista," he said holding up his hand as if to stop her from running away. "I'm not worried about the story. I'm worried about you. Do you know the kind of people you are going to piss off? Technically, WE are going to piss off?" She stared at him blankly, so he continued. "These people have everything to lose if this story gets legs. Everything! That means they will be desperate, crazy desperate. People can do some really nasty stuff when they are desperate."

"Yes, sir, I know, but I'm tougher than I look."

"Look, I don't mean to patronize you, Trista, but I'm not worried how tough you are. I'm worried how dead you might be."

She looked at his face for a few seconds before she could respond. "Are you threatening me?"

"Good God, no. I'm on your side. I will back you the whole way on this story. I'll catch hell from some very powerful people, but I don't give a damn. I'm 62 years old and ready to retire early anytime. You, you're young and have a lot ahead of you and I don't want something to keep you from living that dream."

"What are you suggesting, then?"

"We need to take some precautions. I've hired a security detail to watch you," he said, motioning her to come look out the window. "They will be with you 24/7 until further notice."

"Is that really necessary?"

"Yes. In fact, it is not optional. If you want to continue to develop this story, you will have to cooperate with this."

"Who do you think I should be more worried about, the church, or the politicians?"

"Not sure. It depends on where the story is going to lead. I hear this story might lead to some pretty big names. If that happens, you may have them both after you. Where is this heading?"

Her mind suddenly sounded an alarm. She was not ready to trust anyone with the details and expectations. "Not really sure," she lied. "I suppose a Senator or two is going to have a lot of explaining to do." She knew this was a vague and rather dodgy answer, but she hoped it was enough to satisfy him.

The Publisher looked at her for what felt like a long time. She stared back at him with a quiet confidence in herself and in the story. She could tell he was sizing her up and this was a critical moment in her career.

He looked away and reached into the breast pocket of his jacket and pulled out an odd looking phone. "I want you to use this. It has been modified to provide you extra security. The GPS has been disabled and the number is untraceable to you. My private number is programmed into it for you.

"People are going to be watching you, listening to you and following you. If you make a call on your phone, expect someone to be listening. They will also be tracking your phone's GPS to know where you are. Don't use this phone in your home. Word of this story has probably already leaked out and by tomorrow, every word spoken in this apartment will be monitored by someone."

"How do you know?"

"Experience. I've been working this city for a while and know stories less serious than this have caused a big fuss. This town is filled with powerful people and amazing surveillance experts. I'm hoping my visit tonight beat them to the punch, but you need to be paranoid starting right now."

"This feels like some spy movie."

"Maybe someday it will be a spy movie. I just want it to have a happy ending for you and the paper."

"Thanks. Me too."

***

Senator McDermott's speech had been well received by the small crowd. The Society of Religious Freedom was not a large group, but at least they agreed with him. He lingered briefly after his speech to chat with the attendees and then headed to his hotel. The plan was to grab a few hours of sleep and then head back early to DC. Traffic would be bad, but it almost always was in the corridor from DC to NYC.

Since he had a driver, he could get some work done during the trip. Work, for a Senator, generally meant reading a ton of information. Reports, draft legislation and sometimes intelligence information. He had not been given much top-level information since he had taken up the fight against religion, but there was still plenty of information for him to digest.

Before hitting the pillow, he clicked on the TV to check-in on the world. As expected nothing on his speech, but CNN had a brief story of the court case in Richmond against the city of Charlottesville for supporting the YMCA with tax dollars.

He fell asleep with a smile on his face knowing Max Pigman was making great progress.

***

Nate heard some commotion next door at Trista's place rather late at night. He immediately went into defense mode, worried about her safety. He pressed his ear up against the wall that separated their townhomes, but all he could hear was muted talking. It did not sound like a dangerous discussion, but he was still worried.

Checking the perimeter, he noticed two strange cars out front. Both had drivers behind the wheel and both looked like high-level government issued or serious private security vehicles. Nate went back to trying to listen to the garbled voices, ready to take action at the slightest hint of trouble.

After a few minutes, the voices stopped and he could hear footsteps heading down to the front door. Quickly returning to the window, he saw a well-dressed man get into the back of the one car and drive off. The other car remained in place.

Everything okay? he texted Trista.

Yep. Visit from the boss. He is worried about me.

Is that security parked out front?

Yep. 24/7 until further notice.

Good. Call if you need me. Still on for bfast? 7:30?

Yes. Goodnight.

Chapter 21

Trista woke up early. The excitement of the day had pulled her from a deep sleep. Oddly, her first conscious thought was about having breakfast with Nate. She smiled, got out of bed and her mind started racing. She peaked out the window and eyed the newspaper box on the corner. She half expected a crowd to have lined up to purchase a copy of her big story. Instead, a few pigeons were the only sign of life on the street.

Oh, wait. That black car had someone in it. Must be her security detail. Mr. Potter's warnings had not kept her up last night, but they were suddenly causing a knot in the pit of her stomach. She had a sense that her life had already changed dramatically and today everyone else in the world would know it.

Sitting upright in bed, she looked at her phone. Mr. Potter's warnings last night made her phone seem toxic. They would track her every move based on the GPS chip in her phone. She needed to see a few key people before she could allow them to follow her. For their safety, she reached over and powered off her phone. She needed to go dark for a few more hours.

After a long shower and a brief review of her notes, she packed up her stuff and headed over to Nate's for breakfast. First, she went to the paper box and deposited a few coins. She smiled at the fact she was buying her own paper, but she had to have a copy. She gave a quick wave to the security guard before turning towards Nate's door.

Using the key he had given her, she unlocked the door and announced herself before walking up the steps to his kitchen. He met her at the top of the steps and gave her a long hug. She made no attempt to break it.

"Hey, great story," he said motioning to the paper spread out on the kitchen counter. "I almost forgot to cook breakfast I was so engrossed."

"Glad you didn't, 'cause I'm starving."

They made small talk about nothing important knowing they should get breakfast out of the way before turning to business. He had made pancakes with chocolate and peanut butter chips and some sausage links.

"So, did you have something in particular you wanted to discuss?" she asked, putting the last bite from her stack in her mouth.

"Yes, but I also want to hear what you've discovered. Sounds like you found a few things," he said, motioning towards the front page of the paper. "Congrats, by the way. First cover story for you?"

"First above the fold. You go first and then I'll fill you in," she added, pulling out her laptop to take notes.

"Okay. We got a significant lead. I received an anonymous email saying some juicy stuff about Stiano."

"Really. Any way to prove any of it?"

"Maybe, but it would be easier if we could talk to the guy. We did a little digging and think we know who he is. I was thinking this could be your deep throat."

"That would be fantastic, but hope you don't mind if I call him something different. How'd he get your name, by the way? You're not even officially working the case."

"Not sure. Maybe Father Charron. His name is Bertram Godfrey. Works in Stiano's office. He sent the message from a Starbucks using a made-up gmail account, but Laurie did some magic and found him. We don't have 100% proof it's him, so you are going to have to be careful approaching him."

"That'll be tricky. Do you have a home address?"

"Yep, and a cell phone."

"Yeah, about our phones, she replied. "The visit I got from Mr. Potter, the friggin' publisher himself last night, is going to make our communications rough. He thinks they will have me completely bugged by the end of the day. My phone, even conversations like this, will be listened to by very powerful people. We will not be able to do this again for a while."

"He also gave me a special cell phone to call him," she continued. "Said it was untraceable and had the GPS disconnected."

"Makes sense, unfortunately. Let's work out a system to alert each other when we need to talk. Probably okay to talk while we run together. Hard to listen to a moving target, especially with all the street noise. Also, music can be a good cover," he said, as he got up to turn on his stereo.

"Tomorrow we run a follow-up story with not much earth shattering stuff, but Sunday I'm hoping to drop the next shoe. I'd love to connect with Bertram before then. Wow, Bertram, what an unfortunate name. Think he goes by Bert?"

"I'll leave the tough answers up to you," he said with a smile.

"Thanks, for everything." She added her own smile.

***

A junior member of the Embassy security staff woke Debbie up with a knock on her door. She was groggy and only partially dressed and asked him to wait before he entered the room. She quickly slipped on a robe and glanced in the mirror. Her hair looked like a rat's nest and her face was puffy with dark rings under her eye. Surprisingly, she didn't really care. It was hard to care about little things when she had such big problems.

"Come in," she announced.

"Good morning," said the young man in a dark suit. He was carrying a tray with tea and he sat it on the table. "I thought you might like some tea."

"Yes, thank you. What time is it?"

"Just before eight o'clock. They'd like you downstairs at nine. Someone, probably me, will be here to get you just before then. There's a muffin and some juice on the tray as well, do you need anything else?"

She figured him as the good cop. Young, good looking and charming. He was going to try to be her friend while the others played bad cop. "No, I'm fine. Thanks." With that, he turned and left the room. She heard the door lock behind him.

She was really not sure why they were treating her so harshly. She was telling them everything she knew and cooperating completely. Still they had yelled at her and held her for hours without letting her go to the bathroom. She was not looking forward to another day of interrogation and intimidation.

At this point, she was convinced Amir was indeed a terrorist working with Muslim extremists to forge some sort of attack on the United States. Maybe it was a good thing for her to be sent back to her country; at least she would be safer there.

As the hot shower water rained on her head, she suddenly recalled something Amir had said to her several months ago. It hadn't really made sense at the time, but now she knew he was a terrorist, it fit. She stood still letting the water hit her, afraid to move and disturb the thought.

About six months ago, they were lying in bed on a Sunday morning reading the newspaper. Personally, she did not really enjoy reading the paper, but Amir seemed obsessed with *The Washington Post*, especially the Political and Opinion sections. She had grown tired of him reading and ignoring her, so she snuggled up and started to fondle him hoping to convince him to stop reading.

Instead, he became angry with her and pushed her away, one of the few times he resisted her advances. She asked him why he cared so much about reading *The Post* and he said it was a great way to learn how to manipulate the masses. He believed the American media was always being manipulated by politics. Anyone who could learn to play the media could put fear in the hearts and minds of Americans.

His answer had not really made sense, but she let the conversation drop and had not thought of it since. Maybe this had something to do with his May 1st attack plan. She quickly finished her shower and was waiting when the young security guard came for her.

Before Agent Brown, her interrogator, even spoke a word she told him what she had remembered. He politely thanked her and left the room. A few minutes later, the young security guard was there and escorted her back to her room.

***

Despite computers and massive databases dedicated to crime fighting, information did not travel quickly from one police force to another. Kristen's call to the phone center located in Scottsdale, Arizona had taken almost a full day to be transferred by the local police to the FBI and Secret Service.

The Senator was almost back to DC before he received a call from the Secret Service informing him of the threat on his life. He had also been informed by his private security agency that someone had broken into his house last night. Nothing had been taken, as the alarm seemed to have scared the intruder away.

The Senator was smart enough not to believe in coincidences and alerted the Secret Service. Within the hour, bomb dogs were in the Senator's home and quickly found the Hellfire Explosive.

Senator McDermott had been told to go to his office and wait for more information. Just before noon, the Secret Service arrived and gave him the full story, including the details of Kristen's phone call.

"Did you find Miss Carr? She is in great danger and I kinda owe her my life."

"No, sir, the FBI's on the case."

"Get me someone at the FBI. I want this to be a high priority case." Even a political outcast like McDermott still carried around the considerable clout of a United States Senator. If he said the FBI needed to make this a high priority case, the FBI would listen.

"Yes sir, Senator, we'll get in touch with them right away."

"And, what am I supposed to do? Can I go home tonight?"

"Yes, sir. In fact, there is a real possibility we may be able to snag the guy tonight. He probably does not know we have found the bomb. It had a remote detonator that is triggered by a cell phone. The likely plan was to watch your house tonight, wait for you to go to bed and then trigger the bomb. If you go home as if nothing is wrong, then we may be able to grab they guy while he's waiting for you to go to bed."

"You think he could tell us where Miss Carr is being held?"

"Yes, I do."

"Okay then. I'll be heading home around 6 p.m."

"Perfect, we'll make sure the FBI has their people in place. Just act natural and don't look around when you get home."

***

It was after ten when she finally woke. The sun was streaming in the windows of her cheery little cottage. Kristen felt a little groggy, but well rested after a 10 hour sleep. After making a cup of coffee in her small kitchen, she decided to take a stroll while she enjoyed her morning brew.

She had not really been behind the house, so she decided to head that direction first. Her slow pace was to protect her coffee and to make sure no one thought she was trying to escape. The grounds around the house were beautiful and she saw a man and a woman working on the landscaping. She had not met them, so she figured now was a good time.

Neither of the gardeners was very tall and both looked Hispanic. Their backs were turned and they were too busy at work to even notice her. Before she got too close, she cleared her throat loudly and the pair turned to face her.

"Hello, I'm Kristen. I'm new here."

The gardeners looked at each other and then the man turned back to her. "No hablo Ingles."

"Sorry, no hablo Español." With that, she waived and then turned to continue her walk. How many slaves worked here? Were these gardeners also prisoners? Maybe they were illegal immigrants who were just glad to have the work. This place was a mystery and she knew she had to escape despite the luxurious trappings. She had to save her girls.

She continued her stroll around the grounds, casually looking for security cameras. It was not hard to locate the cameras, but she could not figure out where they were being monitored. The compound included several buildings that could be the security center. She decided to push the issue and try to flush out her captures.

She took a sudden turn away from the house and headed toward the tree line. The distance to the edge of the woods was around 50 yards and she moved at a moderate pace. After covering half the distance, she heard some commotion in the distance behind her. A motor roared to life and some sort of vehicle started towards her.

Casually looking over her shoulder, she saw a man in a golf cart-looking ATV headed her way. She slowed her pace to make sure they did not think she was trying to escape. As the ATV came closer, she stopped and turned to face the man. The man pulled up next to her and killed the engine.

"Good morning, ma'am," said the middle-aged man in a heavy southern accent.

"Good morning. I'm Kristen, what's your name?"

"TJ, ma'am. You don't want to go out there," he said with a nod toward the woods. "We have some nasty dogs that patrol the perimeter that don't like strangers."

"Well TJ, maybe you should introduce them to me since I live here now."

He looked at her, obviously considering her suggestion. "Okay, get in."

They headed left parallel to the tree line until they came to a small dirt road that cut through the woods. Several hundred yards ahead, the woods suddenly opened up and the ATV slowed. There was a fifty-yard clearing with a 12-foot fence running down the middle. Shinny razor wire lined the top of the fence.

The ATV stopped and TJ jumped out and gave a loud whistle. She stepped out and looked quickly for security cameras. She found one with little effort and also saw large floodlights mounted in the trees. This was a seriously well-defended perimeter.

"Ma'am, you need to get back in," he said motioning to the ATV. At that moment, a dog appeared from the woods and dashed towards them growling viciously. She quickly obeyed TJ's command and he stepped between her and the charging dog. He raised his hand to signal the dog to stop.

"Sit," he commanded, as the attack dog came to a stop. The dog obeyed. "There are some dog biscuits in the cart. Grab one and get out of the cart slowly." She did as he said. The dog watched her with what appeared to be a cross between anger and delight.

"Rufus, this is Kristen. Ma'am, hold out the cookie and approach him slowly."

"Hello, Rufus," she said holding out her hand showing the large dog the cookie. She approached slowly, as instructed, and offered the cookie. Rufus opened his mouth in a surprisingly gentle manner and took the cookie.

"Peanut butter flavored. He loves peanut butter."

"May I pet him?"

"Let him sniff your hand first and don't make any sudden moves."

She did as he said and in a few minutes, she was scratching the dog behind both ears and he was wagging his tail in gratitude. "You're not such a mean guy are you? Where are the others?" she asked looking back at TJ.

"Spread out around the perimeter. Over a mile of fence to watch. Eight dogs in total."

"Can I meet the rest?"

"Not today. Let's get you back to the house. Mr. Williams is gonna want to see you, I'm sure."

Chapter 22

Bertram Godfrey was a bit of a political mystery. He was one of the few Senate staff members Trista had ever heard of who had worked for both a Democratic Senator and now a Republican. He was not the top staff person for Senator Stiano, but he was probably number two. His title, Senior Political Analysis, was a common one in DC. Like most jobs in the Senate, he did whatever was necessary to move the Senator's political agenda forward.

She needed to be careful how she approached him since she was, or soon would be, watched and listened to whenever possible. She needed an intermediary. She needed Joel. She would need to make the first contact, but then the two could never have direct contact. First, she needed to do her homework and make sure she knew everything about him before contacting him.

She decided to look into the personal side of this potential informant first. Facebook often provided a good first glance at someone's personal side, but like many involved in the dubious political realm, Bertram's profile was largely hidden from public view. She did have ten friends in common with him, so she decided to see if there were any backdoors she could get in. It would not be a good idea to send him a Friend Request, but if she were lucky, one of her friends was close to him.

The first seven common connections yielded no information on *Seagull*, the code name she had decided to give him. On the eighth, she had a little luck. She found a status update that tagged Seagull in a photo of a softball team. Checking the Internet, she found the schedule of the softball league and when they would be playing. As luck would have it, there were games this weekend.

Next, she decided the best tactic was to be bold. The Senator's office would be open today and although the Senator was not likely to be in, she could stop by to see if he wanted to talk to her now. With any luck, she'd run into Seagull. Maybe she could slip him a note.

To help make her visit to the Senator's office look legit, she requested a photographer to join her. Nothing made a politician more nervous than a camera. There really wasn't much to photograph, but the effect would work for her.

As predicted, Senator Stiano was not in the office, but she had instructed the cameraman to take pictures of everything. If she was lucky, she'd get some good intel on Seagull. There were only three staffers in the office and she made it a point to introduce herself to each of them. Fortunately the Chief of Staff was not around, so the go-to person in charge was not clear.

When all the commotion had calmed down, she was left talking to Bertram who was doing his best to get her out of the office as soon as possible. He was checking the Senator's schedule and getting her contact information while the other two staffers went back to work. She handed him her business card and also slipped him a note. He looked up at her, not understanding the extra piece of paper. She smiled and nodded at the piece of paper. He seemed to get the picture and casually slipped it into his pocket.

The note said:

You can trust me to protect you. I know you have some information about the Senator's involvement in the cover up of the Catholic Priest abuse cases. Real people, kids in fact, have been harmed by his actions and I need you to help me make sure he does not get away with this.

I will protect your identity at all costs if you will help me. To keep you safe, please follow these procedures:
- *Do not contact me directly. People are watching me and have my phone bugged. You should assume they are listening to all my conversations.*
- *Instead, Contact Joel Serby, my colleague at the Post. Use his private email at jserby@gmail.com or his private cell at 202-367-1324.*
- *Your name for all communications is Seagull. Mine is Crow and Joel's is Eagle.*
- *DO NOT discuss this with anyone, for your safety and mine.*
- *Do not use any government issued devices to communicate.*

•   *Only use payphones and library computers to communicate and never the same one twice. We will get you a secure phone, but for now, do not use any device that can be connected to you.*

Thanks! You are a real hero!

Crow

***

It was noon when Trista made it into the office. There were lots of friendly smiles, a bunch of "congratulations," and even a few high-fives as she made her way to her cubicle. In the newspaper business, getting a lead story was a big deal anytime, but your first time was something to be celebrated.

She did not even bother to sit down at her desk, but did notice the red flashing light on her phone that indicated she had voicemail. That would have to wait; she needed to see Joel. The trip to his office, normally a two-minute trip, took twenty minutes. Everyone wanted to talk to her about the story. She forced herself to stay calm and be polite, while at the same time being vague when asked specific questions about the story.

When she made it to Joel's office, she found him standing up in front of the small TV mounted on his wall. Mid-day had become a significant time-slot in the news with all the networks having live shows. Generally, these shows just re-hashed the morning news, but sometimes they used the time-slot to allow subject matter experts to speculate on breaking news. If you didn't have facts, opinions were a valid way of keeping a story alive until more facts were known.

"There you are. Everyone seems to think I'm your personal assistant today."

"What?"

"Got calls from your editors and even Mr. Potter. Frankly, I was worried. Said you weren't answering your cell."

"Yeah, I left it at home by mistake." They both heard the CNN talking head say her name and their attention switched to the TV. "Are they covering the story?"

"Everyone is. That's why folks are looking for you. All the networks want you to come on and tell your story. Oh, and the big boys might be a little pissed that you weren't around to get the paper some free publicity."

"Publicity? I thought that's what we do here? Aren't we competing with the networks on this? Why give them the story?"

"Spoken like a true reporter. Yes, of course, but management likes the credibility we get when other news agencies mention us as the source."

She raised her finger to her lips to let Joel know he needed to not question her. She took the TV remote from his hand and turned the volume up. "Potter visited me last night," she said leaning in close. "Said people would be watching me and listening to my every word."

"Makes sense."

"So, from now on, we need to be very careful. In fact, we need to not be seen together. Our only communications should be in writing, not digital, old school handwriting. There is a large flowerpot outside the bathrooms on the 4th floor. That will be our drop point. Just slip a note under the pot if you have anything for me."

"Gotcha, but I doubt I'll have much to help you."

"Well, that's the other thing and the reason we cannot even be seen together. I have a mole in the Senator's office. It would be too dangerous for him to contact me, so . . ."

"You told him to contact me?"

"Yep. Sorry, but I couldn't trust anyone else. His code name is Seagull and yours is Eagle."

"Code name? Shit. Well, at least I got a decent name. What's yours?"

"Crow."

"Ha, I get it. How's he gonna communicate with me?"

"Gave him your cell and private gmail. One other thing, we need a signal to let each other know we've dropped a note under the pot. I know you hate Twitter, but it is perfect for this. Just tweet something with the word 'sunshine' in it and I'll know you have something. I'll tweet something with the word 'water' in it to signal you."

"So, you want me to actually read Twitter? Crap. First you want me to put my life and career in jeopardy and now you want me to tweet? Next you're gonna make me do Facebook."

"Well, you figured me out. This whole thing is just a ruse to make you pay attention to Twitter." They enjoyed a good chuckle before turning serious. "Joel, please be careful."

"You too."

***

It was already noon and Kristen had not heard or seen the old man all day. The expectations of her had not been made clear. Was she supposed to wait for him to beckon, or go looking for him? She decided a little of both might be the best idea.

It was lunchtime, so she would go to the house and see about lunch. Maybe she would run into the old man, or at least others could let him know she was available. As she entered the main house, she thought about the phone call. Had he found the phone off the hook? After seeing the perimeter defenses, she wondered if the interior of the house had the same camera security.

Trying to be subtle, she looked around for cameras. She saw one guarding the entrance, but after turning left into the kitchen area, there were no more to be found. Hopefully there were no cameras in the office where she had made the call. It was not looking good for rescuing her, but hopefully she saved the Senator. Getting rescued looked more and more like something she would have to do herself.

Regina was in the kitchen preparing something, probably tonight's dinner. "Hello, Miss Kristen," she said, looking up from her work.

"Hello, Regina. Any chance I could get some lunch?"

"Yes, Miss Kristen," she said putting down the knife she was using to cut vegetables. "I have some chicken salad in the refrigerator. Would you like some?"

"Yes, that sounds delicious. I'll get it, you're busy," she said hoping to stop the woman from waiting on her hand and foot.

"Don't be silly. Mr. Williams said I am to treat you like the queen of the castle."

"Ha, did he now? Well, this is a nice house, but it's not a castle and I sure as heck am no queen. But, thank you. It is very kind of you to treat me so special."

"My mother always said it was easy to treat nice people well, and you are nice people."

"Ah, thank you Regina. You are nice people too. Speaking of nice people, where's Mr. Williams today?"

"He is out in the big barn playing with his antique cars. He has six old clunkers he likes to work on. After you eat, you should take him a glass of iced tea and get him to show you. He is very proud."

"That sounds like a great idea."

A few minutes later she left the kitchen with two tall glasses of iced tea and headed for the larger of the two barns on the compound. The large sliding door was closed and she struggled to open it with the two glasses in her hand. She stuck her head in as she used her shoulder to push the door open.

"Hello," she announced not seeing the old man. "Mr. Williams?"

"Over here," came a muffled reply. She worked her way past a perfectly restored Mustang from the 60's and an old black pickup truck. "Under here." She noticed a pair of legs hanging out from under a car. "Give me a second and I'll be done. There, that does it. Can you pull me out?"

"Sure," she replied putting down the glasses of tea and grabbing his shins. The old man rolled out easily and he smiled up at her and laughed at the disgusted look on her face.

"Just a little grease. Nothing to get grossed out about," he said referring to his filthy t-shirt, hands and face. "Well, I have to say, I may look disgusting, but you look quite nice from this angle." She was wearing a blue jean skirt and a light green sleeveless blouse. From his vantage point, she was guessing he could see most of the way up her skirt.

"I brought you some tea. I'd help you up, but I really don't want to touch you right now."

"Ha, can't blame you, but hope you'll feel differently after I'm cleaned up," he said as he struggled to his feet. For an old man, he was pretty agile, but getting up from the floor was still a chore. "Thanks," he said, taking the tea from her.

For the next hour he showed her around his prize collection of classic autos. He started each one up so she could hear the engine purr. It was a great collection, but her mind was racing as to how she could use one of these classics to escape.

"Which one is your favorite?" she asked hoping to get the old man to tell her something that might help.

"Ah, hard to say. That's like asking which beautiful lady I prefer. I like them all."

"Oh, I see. Then which one of these beautiful ladies is fastest?"

"Easy. The Mustang. The most valuable is that old truck, but I don't really care 'cause I'm not gonna sell. Let me ask you something. If your date arrived to pick you up in one of these babies, which one would turn you on the most?"

"Ah, good question," she said, looking over the options. "I'm going with the little convertible."

"Oh, you like to go topless, do you?"

"Ha, I suppose I do."

"Good to know. By the way, I have asked Regina to fix us a nice dinner tonight. Find something nice to wear and I'll stop by your cottage at seven to get you."

"Sounds good. I was going to spend a little time at the pool this afternoon if you are looking for me."

"Will you be topless?" Their laughter was genuine and for a minute she forgot she was being held captive.

***

They had arranged to meet for lunch at Dino's so they could freely discuss the case. Laurie arrived first and ordered a soft drink while she waited for him. After a few minutes, she started wondering if he was really going show. Fifteen minutes after the agreed upon time, her phone chirped announcing an incoming text message. It was Nate and he was running late, but on his way.

"Hey," he said, as he slid in to the other side of the small booth. "Sorry I'm late. But I have a good reason."

"Yeah, what?"

"Met with Pete. Looks like I'm officially back on the case. Sorta. He needs help with the murder scenes. Mostly leg-work stuff, but could give me cover to poke my nose in other stuff."

"That is good news, but you still have to buy me lunch for being late."

"Is that some kinda rule?"

"Is now. Besides, I have good news too. Found lots of good stuff on Stiano's tie to the Vatican. He visited there twice and met privately with the Pope at least once. He actually stayed at the Vatican. No tax dollars funded his trip, but I found enough related stuff to put the pieces together. It was not a secret trip. In fact he made it a political talking point in his constituent letters."

"Any word on what he spoke to the Pope about?"

"No, but I cross-checked his visit with the timeframes of the victims' complaints and they work well together. But that's not the good news. I took your suggestion and looked for a tie between the politicians and the victims. Stiano was the front man and the other two seem to be the money launderers. I can document a meeting with six of the victims' families and Stiano, but that's where the trail ends. But the other two, shortly after the meeting, made significant contributions to Church. We're talking big money."

"Interesting. Good work."

"But wait, there's more," she said imitating an announcer on an infomercial. "Stiano is the only one of the three who *has* big money. The other two are small potatoes with net worths under a million. Stiano is stinking rich. So I figured he must have been funneling it back to the others."

"And?"

"And let's order lunch first," she said, as she noticed the waitress approaching.

After ordering, she returned to the story. "So, Stiano is no fool when it comes to moving money. If he just gave them money, some red flags might go off. Instead, he has a foundation that supports religious charities. The two money-laundering politicians would give a speech at a spiritual retreat for a $200,000 fee and the foundation would pay the bill. Then, all but $20,000 would be donated to the church. This happened dozens of times."

"Whew. How much in total?"

"Just under $5 million. There's probably more, but that's all I had time to trace."

"What about Stiano and the victims. How did you tie that together?"

"Like I said, I can prove he met with six of the families only . Believe it or not, it was all part of the public record. He took them to lunch at his club and wrote it off as official public business."

"We'll have to make sure it does become official public business. Good work. You also just reminded me about George, the landscaper."

"Who?"

"Frankly, I forgot about him. He approached me the day after the case broke. Said he was a victim and wanted to talk. He wanted to make sure the truth got out. Crap, he's probably thinking I blew him off."

"Can you talk to him now that you are back on the case, or should we let Trista contact him?"

"Good question. Let's eat while we think about that," he said, as the waitress headed their way with a couple of sandwiches.

"That hit the spot," she said wiping her mouth with a napkin. They had eaten in silence, lost in thought.

"Yep. So, here's what I think we should do with George. It would be better to have him go to Trista first, but that will put him in danger. She thinks everything she does will be monitored very closely by the FBI or someone. If George goes to her, he will be in danger. Wouldn't be surprised if he was found dead with suicide or an accident blamed. That'd certainly send up a message to the other victims."

"Yeah, but what if we get his story and feed it to her?"

"You mean unofficially, or by leaking the police report? Either way, we are getting outside the lines pretty far." His facial expression let her know he was not willing to break too many rules.

"How about we do it as an official police investigation, but take our time filing the official report. Maybe we can find a way to have a secret meeting with Trista and George as well."

"That'll be tough, but I think we can do it. I have a few ideas."

"Perfect," she said, looking at her watch. "Since you are picking up the check, do you mind if I run off? I have a meeting in ten minutes," she added with a smile.

He just shook his head in mock disgust and smiled back at her as she left the booth.

Chapter 23

As planned, Senator McDermott arrived home around 6:30. It was still light outside and he had to resist looking around to see if he could see his would-be murderer watching him. Instead, he heeded the FBI's warning and tried to act as natural as possible.

There was also a bit of fear testing his stomach. Even if the bomb squad did find all of the explosives, there was still someone actually trying to kill him. He'd had death threats before, but this was much more than a threat.

He walked around the house trying to keep his routine. He stopped by the kitchen and sorted his mail, set the bills aside to pay later and tossed the junk mail. Grabbing a beer with the hopes it would calm him down, he headed to the bedroom. He had been told the bomb was under his bed and he could not help but sneak a quick peak after pulling the curtains shut.

The curtains were heavy and dark. The agent had suggested he make a show of drawing the curtains so anyone watching would know he was in the bedroom. He had also been instructed to leave the curtains slightly cracked so the bedroom light would show after the sun went down. If they had not arrested the guy by 9:00 p.m., he was to go to the bedroom and get ready for bed.

At 7:30 his phone chirped and he hoped it was good news. It was just the FBI checking in to let him know they were still there, but so far no sign of the hit man. He would likely show after dark and closer to bedtime. He was told to make sure the light was off in his bedroom and to turn on lights in the kitchen and living room. They would call when they had eyeballs on the suspect.

The electronic trigger for the bombs was with the lead FBI agent in the vacant townhome across the street. They needed the bomber to use his cell phone to set the trigger off so they would have solid proof they had the right guy. As soon as he did, he would be swarmed and taken into custody.

For now, it was a waiting game. Hopefully, the results would be worth the wait.

***

Promptly at 7:00 p.m., Kristen heard a car horn honking outside her cottage. She went to the window in time to see Mr. Williams exiting the car and heading to her front door. He had pulled up in the beautifully restored Mercedes convertible she had picked out this afternoon.

He was dressed in nice slacks, a sports coat and a yellow tie. She had understood his request to "wear something nice" as a command to dress like you were going on a date. She glanced at herself in the mirror before opening the door to meet him. The dress she had selected was nothing special except for the low cut neckline that would show the old man a little of her charms. She smiled at the image in the mirror. It had been a long time since she had dressed this fancy for a date.

She waited for him to knock on the door before she swung it open and greeted him with a big smile. "Good evening, you're right on time. Should I have planned to make you wait like an old fashion girl?"

"Well, if you had, it would have been worth the wait, but glad you didn't. You look beautiful, Kristen."

"Why, thank you. You look pretty good yourself. I see you brought my favorite car. I was figuring we could just walk to the main house."

"We could've, but we are not going to the main house."

"Oh? Are you taking me out?"

"Sort of. You'll see. Are you ready?" he asked, offering his arm to lead her to the car.

She took his arm and allowed him to open the car door for her. He was pouring on the old school charm and she enjoyed the show. The car turned right and headed to what she assumed was the main entrance to the estate. She could not see the entrance, but had seen a few vehicles come and go in that direction. She assumed that would be the hardest way to escape, so she had not really thought much about the entrance.

He slowed the car and took another right away from the entrance on a less traveled road that went into a wooded area. After a minute of slow travel on the bumpy road, the forest opened up to reveal a beautiful small lake with a distant mountain in view and the beginnings of a pastoral sunset. It was the type of site that took your breath away and she felt him glance over to see her reaction.

The car came to a gentle stop and she looked over at him. "This is beautiful."

"Yes it is. I thought you'd like it, and since the weather was going to be so perfect, I decided we would do dinner by the lake," he motioned with his hand behind her. She spun around to see a quaint cabin overlooking the lake. "This is called Sunset Cottage. Sometimes I wish the main house was down here."

"Wow, and dinner on the porch while we watch the sunset. You really know how to show a date a good time."

"Dinner should be ready, so let's eat and enjoy the sunset."

***

The caller ID on Joel's phone simply said "payphone." He had hoped Bert, aka, Seagull, would contact him before the end of the day. He knew Trista's story for the Saturday edition was already put to bed, but he really wanted something to give her for the Sunday article that would be widely read.

"Hello?"

"I'm calling for Eagle."

"This is Eagle," Joel replied. "And I assume you're Seagull," he said awkwardly, wondering if this espionage crap was really necessary. Better safe than sorry, so he'd play along.

"Yes. This doesn't feel right. I don't like this kinda sneaky stuff," Bert complained.

"I know, me neither," he said in as calm and reassuring voice as possible. "Unfortunately, we need to be careful to protect you."

"So, I don't know where to start."

"How about we start with me asking a few questions. Then we can see how it's going."

"Okay."

"Are you in a safe location where you will not be overheard?"

"Yes, for now," Bert answered. "Do you know how hard it is to find a payphone these days?"

"Yeah, I do. We will get you a special cell phone to use at some point, but for now, this will have to do. So, how long have you worked at the Senator's office and what do you do for him?"

"Three years. I do policy stuff. I know how to read and write legislative stuff and I advise the Senator on what bills really say instead of the public spin."

"Everything going okay at work?" Joel asked trying not to sound to accusative. "I mean, you're not coming forward because you're having trouble at work, right?"

"No, everything's fine at work. I have other reasons."

He paused hoping Seagull would continue, but he didn't. "Sorry to press, but we gotta know why you are doing this. If your intentions are dubious, you could just be using the paper for your own agenda."

"Yeah, I understand," the younger man replied. "My reasons are personal and private. For now, let's just say I grew up Catholic here in DC and knew all three dead priests."

"Ah, okay," Joel stumbled. "That's good enough for now. Let's talk about the Senator. Your note said his hands were as dirty as the priests. What did you mean by that?"

"Stiano is not only helping cover up the priests' abuse of those kids, he is also guilty of abuse. He used to share these kids with the priests. That's why he has helped cover this up. If they went down, so would he. I'm surprised the guy didn't kill him, too."

"Wow, didn't see that coming. Can you prove this?"

"Yes. I have evidence that the priests were essentially blackmailing Stiano."

"Really, what kind of evidence?"

"Pictures and a note," Bert replied quickly. "It is not signed, so I did not know who was doing the blackmailing until the priests were killed. After that, and seeing Stiano actions, I knew exactly who had been blackmailing him."

"How did you get these pictures and will you share them with us?"

"I was in the Senator's office looking for a file he had on a piece of legislation I was supposed to be writing a report on. I found a file in his side drawer where he sometimes stashes files when he has a visitor. When I opened it, I saw the pictures. I actually hurled in his trashcan when I saw them. After I got my act together, I didn't know what to do, so I took pictures of the photos and the letter with my phone. That was three months ago and I didn't know what to do until now."

"Holy crap," Joel exclaimed. "Can you send me the images?"

"I can, but shouldn't I just go to the police?"

"Normally, yes, but the Senator has the FBI keeping this case from being explored by the DC police. He must have some insiders at the FBI. I'm not sure who we can trust right now. There is one cop we do trust and he is working with us behind the scenes. He's the one you sent the anonymous email to. We'll share this with him."

"What will you do with this?"

"Good question," Joel acknowledged. "We're gonna to need to do our homework before we go public with this. We need to verify your evidence with other sources. We'll probably want to turn up the heat on the Senator gradually. Did you see the *Post* article this morning?"

"Yeah. Didn't go far enough. Lot more to the story. Why not expose what the priest did to us?"

"We know, but this is like a poker game and we aren't ready to show all our cards. The police we are working with want to make sure there is enough evidence before they jump back in the case. Otherwise the FBI could just sit on this evidence. We have to have so much evidence it can't be swept under the rug."

"Well, maybe I'll just resign and watch this all unfold. Not sure I can work close to this bastard any longer."

"No," Joel said a little too eagerly. "We might need you to keep an eye on him. For now, just send me the images and try to act normal. We don't want to spook him just yet."

"Okay, but I'm not sure how long I can take it."

***

In the landscaping business, you work until the sun goes down. Nate had reached George Knowles on the phone and they had agreed to meet for a drink at 8:00 p.m. Laurie met him there at 7:30 to help stake out a good table. The place had cleared out when the after-work crowd went home for dinner. Laurie was waiting in the corner booth and waived him over.

"Does this mean I'm buying again because you beat me here? I'm not late," he noted, looking at his watch.

"Actually, you were buying anyway. Your meeting, your tab. I'm just a guest," she said with a smile.

"Do you always set rules that work in your favor?"

"When possible. So, what does George look like?"

"Large, make that very large, black guy. Looks like he could have played for the Skins. Might be a little grubby, he's coming straight from work."

They ordered a beer and chatted about the case while they waited. At ten minutes after eight, she pointed toward the door. "That him?"

"Yep." Nate stood up so George would see him and waved the man over. "George, this is Laurie, she works with me."

"Hello. Sorry I'm late. Bitch finding a place to park a truck pulling a trailer around here. I think I'm a half mile away."

"Wow, I bet. Hard enough finding a regular spot. Thanks for making the effort."

"Somethin' I gotta do. Frankly, I had almost given up on you. Figured you must have thought I was nuts or something."

"Yeah, sorry about that. We got kicked off the case by the FBI and you got lost in the shuffle."

"Should I be talking to the FBI instead?"

"No," they both said in unison.

"We're back on the case now, so it's good." Nate looked at Laurie before continuing. He was unsure how much he should share with this man and was hoping to get some sort of signal of agreement from her. She nodded slightly and he took that as agreement. "George," he continued, "there's a lot going on with this case that you gotta know."

"Like what?"

"The FBI, we think, has been ordered to sit on this case and keep the truth from coming out."

"Why? That doesn't make sense."

"No it doesn't, but it is deep and complicated. Did you see the *Post* this morning?"

"No, I left pretty early."

"There's a paper box on the corner. I'll go get a copy," Laurie said, as she scooted out of the booth.

"There is a reporter working on a conspiracy story that involves the priests and a US Senator," Nate explained. "We think the Senator has pulled some strings with the FBI to keep the truth hidden. We have found ties between the church and the Senator."

"Are you telling me this isn't over? I'm not living a lie anymore," George said in a raised voice. He looked around, and took a deep breath before starting up in a much quieter voice. "There was some deep joy in my heart when I heard how the priest had been killed. I don't want to bottle that back up. It has been too long."

"We're gonna make sure the truth gets out," Nate assured him, "but we have to play our cards right or it could blow up in our face. We can't just let out what we know just yet, because we have to make sure we have enough to convict the bastards."

"The bastards are dead."

"Not all of them. There are at least three members of congress with dirty hands and probably someone at the church."

Laurie returned with the paper and put the lead story in front of George. "That story is just the tip of the iceberg. Read it and we'll get you a beer," Nate said, motioning to the waitress.

Ten minutes later George finished the article and let out a big sigh. His eyes were watering and Nate could tell he was feeling a mixture of emotions. "That's some shit, man. This has been going on for a long time. Damn Senator is involved. Shit," George said, lowering his head trying to hold his emotions inside.

His beer arrived at the right time and the three sat in silence until George could take a long draw off his beer. "When you are ready, we'd like to hear your story. From the beginning" Nate added.

"Sure," he said, taking another large breath. For the next 30 minutes, they took notes as George recanted a long and sordid story of child abuse. As he spoke, they could see the strength and resolve growing within him. He would be a very credible witness at the trial.

"Thanks, George, for having the courage to come forward. I'm sure that was difficult."

"Not as difficult as keeping quiet the past 18 years. So, what's next?"

"We'd like to set up a meeting with you and this reporter," Nate said, tapping the article. "If you come forward to the FBI they will find a way to discredit you and make it look like you are just trying to set up your lawsuit against the church. She will keep your name out of it for now but we can use your information to push the Senator to do something that we can use to hang him."

"I like the sound of that," George responded.

"George, do you mean that?" Nate said with concern. "'Cause I don't want you to do anything stupid."

"Naw. I'm just a big teddy bear. I could never hurt anyone. I believe in turning the other cheek. Funny, despite the bad memories, I still go to Mass every week and try my best to be a good Christian."

"Good for you. This town could use a few more folks like you," Laurie chimed in.

The big man stood and reached into his pocket for his wallet. Nate waived him off and grabbed the check the waitress had placed on the table. George smiled and said, "Thanks. I better head home."

They watched as the George departed. "What now?" she asked.

"You mind typing up a statement? We need to get George to sign it later. Also, dig into George's case and make sure it all pans out. Maybe there is a direct chain of events that connects George and Stiano."

"Sure. You going to set up a meeting with Trista?"

"Yep. I have no idea how to pull that off, but I'll figure something out."

***

Senator McDermott's phone chirped to life and he looked at his watch before answering. 9:05. It was the FBI agent telling him that they had the suspect in sight and that he should start the process of going to bed. He was to take his time and do his best to be patient. The worst thing that could happen would be to spook the bomber before he tried to trigger the bomb.

Twenty minutes later, he clicked off the lights in his bedroom and lay on the bed fully clothed. He held his phone in his hand and nervously waited for the all-clear signal. The next thirty minutes felt like thirty hours. Finally, his phone rang and he was told they had the suspect in custody. The plan had worked perfectly.

"Agent," the Senator commanded. "Make him tell you where Miss Carr is and go save her. She saved my life and we must find her."

"Yes, sir. That's exactly what we plan to do."

"Oh, and thank you. The FBI will be properly congratulated for your efforts. Keep me posted on Miss Carr."

Chapter 24

The morning had come too early for Trista and she had to hit the snooze button a second time. Normally she was a morning person, but her brain had refused to be quiet and her sleep had been very restless. When the third alarm sounded, she turned it off and sat on the side of the bed waiting for her eyes to clear.

Nate had texted her last night and suggested a run at 6:00 a.m. It was already 5:50, so she was going to be late. She texted him to let him know she was running ten minutes behind.

When she opened her front door, he was already there stretching. She also saw the black security car that had become her personal chauffer and bodyguard. She nodded a 'good morning' greeting to the man and smiled at Nate.

"Good morning, sunshine," he said in jest. "Rough night?"

"Yeah. Lot on my mind."

"A nice run will help clear your head. Ready when you are."

She stretched for a few seconds and said, "Okay, let's get this over with." With that she turned and started to jog down the sidewalk. He quickly caught up to her. They waited to speak until they had gone a couple blocks and were sure no one had followed them.

"I met with a guy last night you need to speak to."

"Yeah, who?

"Name's George Knowles. Nice guy, landscaper by trade. Catholic. Very credible and believable. Says he was abused by the three dead priests and his family was paid big bucks to keep quiet."

"That'll help fill in some holes in the story. I suspect others will come forward as well."

"They usually do. Once one brave soul steps up, the others tend to follow. The more, the better. Your story becomes a lot more credible with multiple victims coming out."

"Can I speak to George, or do you think that would be too dangerous?"

"I'm working on that. Yes, it is too dangerous, but I'm trying to figure out a way to have a secret meeting. He really wants to talk and if you don't talk to him, it will be obvious I fed you the information. I'm still working on the details, but I'll set it up soon."

"Joel is going to be my go-between with our pal Bert. He does go by Bert. Met him briefly when I visited the Senator's office yesterday. Long enough to slip him a note with Joel's contact info. Told him it was too dangerous to talk to me."

"Did he contact Joel?"

"Not sure," she replied with annoyance in her voice. "This crap is just getting started and it is already a pain in the butt. I can't talk to you, Joel, or anybody."

"Hang in there. We'll get through it. Besides, I have more and unless you want to run a few extra miles, I better tell you." He reached into his pocket and pulled out a folded piece of paper and discreetly handed it to her. With hardly a glance, she slipped it into to pocket of her shorts.

"So, is that it, or did you want to tell me some more?"

"That is a description of how the money made it from the Senator, to the church and assumedly to the victims. Laurie is scary good at digging stuff up without a subpoena. This is not part of the official police investigation, so run with it however you like."

"Great! That should be a couple of stories all by itself."

"Laurie's looking for a connection between George and the Senator's money. She already has proven that Stiano met with six of the victims. If she can link George to him, we'll have the Senator by the balls."

They finished their run without another word, lost in their thoughts. It was not even 7:00 a.m. and it had already been a successful day.

***

The sisters had been left alone for several hours. The man known as Jake had generally given them food and water when he left for such a long time. This time, they had nothing except the four walls of this room that had been their prison cell for several days.

They missed their mommy and were huddled together sleeping when loud noises outside the room woke them. Men's voices were yelling in the distance and, as the voices got closer, the girls stood against the back wall. Mini hid behind her older sister, who was trying to act brave.

As the voices became clearer, they recognized that the men were calling their names. Unsure what this meant, and still disoriented from being asleep, the girls remained quiet until the men were outside their door.

"Sarah, Mini! It's the police. We're here to help you."

"In here!" Sarah yelled in response. "We're in here!"

"Okay, great to hear your voice. Stand back from the door so we can kick it down."

The girls stayed pressed against the back wall as the men kicked the door several times before the doorframe split and the lock gave way. The men entered with guns in hand, but aimed at the ground so as not to scare the girls. "It's okay, girls. You're safe now," said the first man who entered.

A female police officer pushed her way into the room. "Hey girls, I'm Kathy," she said in a soft calm voice as she slowly approached. "Are you gals okay? Anything hurt?" The two girls shook their head. "Great! Let's get you out of here," she said, extending her hand toward Sarah. To her surprise, the girls recoiled and pressed themselves against the wall.

"Where's Mommy?"

"Some other police officers are going to find your mommy right now. If you come with me, you can wait for her at the police station."

Slowly, the girls relaxed and Sarah reached out to take the officer's hand. It was hard to trust anyone after living on the street, especially after what happened the last time they had accepted help.

"Thata girl. Let's get you out of this place."

***

They woke to the sound of a helicopter that sounded suspiciously close. The old man sprung from the bed with amazing agility and grabbed the phone on the small desk against the wall. After punching in a few numbers, he asked, "What the hell is going on?"

Kristen could not hear the voice on the other end, but could tell something was very wrong by the old man's expression. "Get your clothes on, now," he yelled.

"What's wrong," she asked, as she rolled naked out of bed and started to reach for her clothes.

"Just get dressed and hurry," he replied, as he pulled on his own pants.

Less than a minute later they were jumping in the Mercedes convertible as the sound of the helicopter roared from a short distance away. Before pulling away, he reached into the glove compartment and pulled out a pistol. "What's going on, you're scaring me," Kristen shouted.

"We are under attack and need to make a run for it." She did not like the look of concern on his face.

"Attack? By whom?"

"Not sure," he replied, as he threw the car into gear and sped off down the dirt road headed back toward the main house. He stopped at the edge of the tree line and waited for the chopper to circle back around to the other side of the compound. Then, he gunned the engine and sped off taking a right away from the house and towards what she assumed was the main entrance.

She turned and glanced back toward the house to see if they had been spotted and saw several men racing about in what appeared to be military uniforms. She could not tell if they had escaped notice and was not sure if that was a good thing or a bad thing. Were these men here to save her, or were they here to kill everyone?

The car raced along the main road through heavy woods. The sporty car took a series of curves like a champ but came to a sudden stop as the entrance gate came into view. The gate was a large and substantial combination of brick and iron with a guardhouse. On the other side of the entrance she could see a dozen police cars and several officers pointing their guns toward the guardhouse.

When the police saw the car, they all seemed to redirect their aim toward it. Over the police PA system came a command. "This is the Tennessee State Police. Put down your weapons, open the gate and come out with your hands up."

The old man took the gun from his lap and released the safety. "What are you going to do?" Kristen asked with fear in her voice.

"Sorry, my dear, but I'm afraid you are my ticket out of here." He pointed the gun at her head and she gasped.

"What are you doing?"

"Just cooperate and we'll get out of this. I need to take you hostage for a few minutes." He edged the car forward towards the gate. Now, several dozen guns, including Mr. Williams', were trained on her. Tears of fear started to roll down her cheeks.

When the car was twenty feet from the heavy gate, he stopped. She could see a guard in the house crouched down to hide from the police. Mr. Williams nodded to the guard and the guard reached up and flicked a switch, which caused the gate to slowly swing open.

Both sides seemed to freeze for a few seconds waiting to see what would happen next. "Clear a path," yelled the old man, "or she dies." After a few seconds of no movement, the man yelled even louder, "Now!"

With that, the police slowly started to move. A few of the police cars started and backed away to clear a path. The old man edged the car slowly ahead until he was sure he had a clear path to escape, gunning the engine to race past the last several cars. In a few seconds he would be clear and the chase would be on.

She made a split second decision that this needed to end now, one way or the other. In one quick move, she ducked her head under the aim of his gun and grabbed the wheel of the car, turning it sharply. The old car slammed head-on into the last police car with surprising force. The last thing she remembered was slamming hard against the dashboard.

***

After a shower, Trista decided to check Twitter to see if Joel had tweeted an alert for her. Sure enough, there it was, time-stamped at 7:05 a.m.

Looking for another good day of sunshine in good old DC.

While Joel wouldn't win any awards for his tweeting abilities, he had done an excellent job of following instructions. She quickly finished getting ready for work and headed out front to her security detail. The black car was across the street from her townhouse and she looked both ways before crossing the road and climbing in the back.

As soon as her door shut, the electronic locks snapped closed. "I need to go to the office," she announced as she reached for her seat buckle. The car started forward down the narrow street and she settled in for the ride.

After reaching the *Post*, she headed to the 4th floor bathroom before heading to her cubicle. There were two staff members holding an impromptu meeting just outside the bathroom making it too difficult to grab Joel's information from under the large flowerpot. She entered the bathroom without interrupting their conversation and by the time she exited, the hallway was clear. She extracted the single sheet of folded paper and headed back to her cubicle.

After reading his note about the conversation with Seagull, she signed on to her computer and started to write the story for Sunday. She had decided to write the story now and then go to both Stiano and the church to get comments. By getting the story down on paper, she could more easily convince the subjects to talk. It would also allow her to funnel a copy to Joel in case she needed a backup plan.

By 11:00 a.m. she was done with a good first draft and ready to approach the Senator. First, she printed out a copy and went to the 4th floor bathroom to leave a copy for Joel. When she returned to her desk, she opened Twitter and tweeted, *I'd rather be headed to the beach to enjoy the sun, sand and water.*

Her first call was to the Diocese to see if Archbishop Charron was available for comment. To her surprise, the phone was answered on the second ring. After identifying herself and explaining what story she was working on, the nice lady turned a little cold and unhelpful. She was able to get her to agree to pass her name and number to the Archbishop with a request to call her back before her 4:00 p.m. deadline.

As expected, there was no answer at the Senator's office, but Trista had other ways of tracking down politicians over the weekend. She made a few calls to contacts and within the hour, the Senator's Chief of Staff had called her. She was told the Senator was not in town and had gone back to his home state of Indiana for the weekend and would not be available for press calls.

"You may want to get in touch with the Senator to at least let him know we are running a story linking him directly to the three Catholic priests and the child abuse allegations."

There was a moment of silence on the phone line. "Can you send me a draft of the story?"

"Sure. But the story will run with or without his comments, so make sure he calls me before 4:00 p.m."

"Will do." With that, the phone line went dead and she quickly sent out the draft as promised to the chief of staff. She had decided to hold back the pictures of the Senator with the little boys and the subtle blackmail angle. Instead, she decided the money was the best part of the story to pursue first.

Next, she needed to meet with her editor and make sure he was alerted to the story. He was on the phone when she appeared at his door and he waved her in while cutting off his conversation abruptly. It took thirty minutes to convince him the money angle was strong enough to run with for the Sunday story. She did not show him the pictures Joel had funneled her from Seagull, but she did mention that she had evidence that the Senator was directly involved in the child abuse scandal, it just needed to be verified still.

"Trista, I gotta tell you, this has to be solid stuff. We're getting pressure form the Senator to back off. We can't go forward until we have verified all the stories. Understand?"

"Yes, sir. And, thank you for not backing down. I'm not sure where this story is going, but I think there's a lot more still to come out."

Her stomach was rumbling for some food and she decided to head home for lunch. There was nothing else she could do here except wait for return calls and she could do that at home. The black car was waiting as she walked out of the door. There were a million black cars exactly like this one in DC, so she looked for the AGS sticker on the front bumper to make sure it was a car from Akers and Gerow Security.

It was the right car, but a different driver than earlier. As soon as her door shut, the electronic locks were engaged and the car started to slowly pull away from the curb. "I'm headed back home, please."

"Actually ma'am. I'm just going to drive around for a few minutes while we talk."

"What? Who are you?"

"I'm George Knowles. Nate asked me to talk to you about the dead priest."

"Where is my security?"

"They are with Nate following us a ways back. We only have a few minutes, so we might want to get started."

"Okay. I understand you were abused by the priest as a boy. Was it all three of the priests?"

"Yes." For the next 10 minutes George gave a brief account of the pattern of abuse and how the three priests has passed him around.

"George, were there others? Other men besides the priest?"

"Ah, I guess I forgot about that. Must have blocked it out. There was another guy. He was friends with Archbishop Reilly. Only saw him a few times. Can't remember much about him."

She pulled up a picture of Senator Stiano on her phone and passed it forward to George when he stopped for a traffic light. "Was this the other man?"

"Not sure. I never got a good look at him. It was always a dark room with him. Could be. Just donno."

"I think it best that we not use your name just yet. The press will be all over you. But, eventually, you'll have to come forward. You okay with that?"

"Yep, I'm ready now."

"Have you told anyone else besides Nate?"

"Just my wife. Figured she had the right to know."

"Okay, but if you can keep it quiet for a few more days, I think I can leverage this information to make a few bad men squirm."

"Okay, but I don't want to wait long. This should have been over years ago. I'm glad those bastards are dead, but I wish they had been forced to face the music."

Chapter 25

Debbie was back in the room with Agent Brown from the NSA. He seemed a bit more upbeat than past meetings. She sensed something had happened or was about to happen and everyone except Amir would be happy.

"We have something we need you to do." She just looked at him and nodded her head waiting for him to continue. "We need you to push his buttons and make him squirm a bit. It's a bit dangerous, but we'll be there if you get in trouble.

"What we want you to do is to turn into the overbearing girlfriend," Agent Brown said with a half-hearted smile. "Start pressing him about what he does at work, talking marriage, telling him you think he's the one and stuff like that. Just tell him you've been thinking a lot about him these past few days and realizing how much you love him."

"Okay, but I don't get it. How's that going to help?" she asked.

"We think he is in love with you. We had some experts look at your text exchanges and other interactions and think there is a real affection he has for you. The problem, his problem, is that the closer it gets to the deadline for his attack, the harder it is to say goodbye. If he did not have affection for you, he would have dumped you by now so he could focus on the mission.

"By trying to move your relationship to the next level, we think it will make him react. Hopefully he will get sloppy and make a mistake. If you play it well, this could crack him enough to break him."

"I'm not sure I can pull that off. He's not who I thought he was."

"So, let me be blunt. You do this and we have assurance from the Ambassador that your record will be wiped clean. If you don't, you will be deported and fired. Your government might even file charges."

"Since you put it that way, I'm in. When?"

"Now," he replied, reaching into the breast pocket of his jacket and extracting her phone. "Text him now and let him know the good news about being back in town. If he can see you tonight, set it up."

Ten minutes later, she had arranged to meet him for dinner at her place. They took her phone away and another agent came in to coach her on what to do and how to act. This was all moving very fast, but it was better than sitting in her room as a prisoner.

***

Mini and Sarah had waited long enough at the police station for their mommy. They had been left in a small waiting room outside one of the administrative offices, well away from any bad guys who might filter through the station. At first, someone had been watching them, but about an hour ago, they had turned on the TV and left them alone.

Sarah had decided it was time to find out why there had been no word about their mother. She opened the door to the office and saw three officers busily working and talking on the phone. One pleasant lady looked up to see Sarah and motioned her to hold on for a second while she finished her phone call.

"Did you need something, sweetie?" the lady asked in a pleasant tone.

"Where's my mommy?"

"You know, I'm surprised we haven't heard yet. Let me check." She picked up the phone and spoke to someone and was put on hold. "They're checking. Did you need something to eat or drink?"

Before Sarah could answer, the lady started talking on the phone again. The expression on her face turned from pleasant to something Sarah did not understand. "Is Mommy okay?" she asked.

The lady officer took a deep breath before answering. "Sweetie, your mother has been found down in Tennessee. Unfortunately, she was in a bit of a car accident. I think she is okay, but they had to take her to the hospital."

Sarah had toughened up after almost a year on the streets. Her mom had taught her how to survive and how to deal with problems. She had also instilled in her that you always have hope. The lady had not said her mom was dead, so there was still hope. "We want to go see her," she said, flatly.

"Let me see what I can do," the officer said, returning to her pleasant tone.

***

At 3:30 her cell phone rang. She did not recognize the local Washington, DC number. "This is Trista," she answered, calmly.

"This is Senator Stiano."

"Thanks for returning my call, Senator. I wanted to get a comment from you . . ."

"I know what you want, but I have nothing to add to your little make-believe story. I'm calling to let you know I've filed a defamation lawsuit against you and the *Post* and should have an injunction issued in the next few minutes. If that story runs, your career is over."

"Thank you for the career advice, Senator," she said in as sarcastic of a tone as she could muster.

"Look here, young lady, I'm a US Senator and you're a junior reporter, you'd be well advised to listen to me. You are jeopardizing US relations with a foreign entity. I believe that is covered under the Patriot Act." The threat was clear. He'd have the NSA detain her, with no rights, if she did not back off.

Her slight hesitation in responding to his threat seemed to embolden the Senator. "Good. I thought you were pretty smart. Now run off and find some news about nuclear power to write about." With that, the line went dead.

She stared at her phone for a few seconds before mumbling, "screw that bastard" under her breath as she marched off to her editor's office. It would be good to have Joel with her, but best to leave him out of this for now.

She walked through the door of the editor's office without asking to come in. "You must have heard," he said looking up at her. "I have legal looking into this now. If we can't get an answer soon, we'll have to push the story."

She nodded, thankful he had not already pulled the article. She had been ready for a fight, but maybe he was not as wimpy as she thought. "He threatened to declare me an enemy combatant under the Patriot Act and have the NSA pick me up."

"Really, no shit? He must be desperate. If we get clearance to run the story, can you run that as a quote?"

"Sure, but let me write it down before I forget the bastard's exact words." She grabbed a pen and started to write down the Senator's exact words.

The editor's phone rang and he picked it up while she tried to focus on her conversation. The situation had suddenly blown up and she noticed her hand was shaking as she wrote. When she was done, she looked up to find the editor staring at her.

"What?" she asked.

"That was Mr. Potter. Legal was in his office. They expressed concern, but he said to run the story. He said that we probably need to leave the NSA threat out for now, but document it. He said unless you recorded the conversation, don't print the threat."

"Gotcha. I'll have it on your desk in 30 minutes."

"Make it twenty."

Chapter 26

After submitting her story just before the deadline, Trista was told to report to Mr. Potter's office. He greeted her warmly and checked to make sure she was holding up okay. "So, after the paper hits tomorrow, you may be in eminent danger. I'm not sure if he'll be cocky enough to send the NSA after you, but he might. If not them, then he might just put a hit on you."

"You really know how to sugar coat things."

"Yeah, sorry. Not much time to beat around the bush. We need to hide you and even I should not know where you are. If he does call the feds in on you, we will not be able to lie if we know your whereabouts. Do you have a place to go that no one would expect?" he asked holding up his hand. "Don't tell me where."

"Yes, I think so."

"Good. It's a few hours until dark. We'll sneak you out of here after that and you can make it to your hideout. Do you have cash?"

"Some. Twenty bucks, maybe."

He reached into his pocket and pulled out a roll of twenties. "This is about $300. Should be enough to get you where you need to go. No credit cards or cell phones, except the one I gave you. Only call if you have to. You should leave your phone here so the GPS will not know where you are."

"How do I get my stories sent in?"

"That phone has a hotspot. That should be good enough to submit stuff for the short run."

"How long do you think I'll need to hide?"

"Hopefully only a few days. Before we leave, you might want to send out a few messages on your phone. Tell a few people that you are staying at the *Post* and will not be home for a while. That might give us some cover when we get you out of here."

After returning to her cubicle, the gravity of the situation hit her. A US Senator had threatened her like she was a terrorist and her boss wanted her to hide out. This was more intense than she had expected, but she gave herself a mental pep talk and started making plans for her hideout.

She packed a bag with all her business tools and information she needed. Her laptop, the files related to the story and a few personal hygiene items she had in her desk.

She had a plan, but it was sketchy. Sometimes the best place to get lost is to stay close to home. She'd leave a trail indicating she was headed north and instead she would simply disappear into the background in the DC area.

She sent emails to Nate and her editor telling them she going to stay at the *Post* 24/7 until she felt more safe and then she went online and left another trail. A search for New York City services for abused and battered women revealed several services and a few help lines. She called one of the help lines from her office phone and had a very helpful conversation with a woman. In thirty minutes, she had set up a meeting for tomorrow to start the process of getting her temporary shelter to protect her from her abusive husband.

Next, she went to the Amtrak website and searched train schedules from DC to NYC. She thought about booking a ticket, but decided that was too obvious of a clue. She had to leave a trail to make them think she was going to NYC, but she did not want to make it too obvious.

At 7:30 p.m. it was dark and Mr. Potter walked by her office and casually said, "good evening" as he dropped a folded note at her feet and kept walking. She waited a few seconds before reaching for the paper and unfolding the note. It said:

Meet me in the garage, floor G1, in five minutes.

She stuck the piece of paper in the shredder and started to gather her stuff. She had condensed her purse and other belongings down and had everything in one knapsack. Traveling light would be best.

The elevator doors opened on G1 and she stepped out and looked around. Seemingly out of nowhere, a car started to move towards her slowly. She felt like running but held her ground hoping it was Mr. Potter. The car stopped just past her and the trunk and driver's door both popped open simultaneously. The publisher hopped out and motioned to the trunk. "Get in. I'm going to drive you out of here and pull down a backstreet somewhere and let you out. When I pop the trunk, get out and get lost. Do it as quickly as possible."

She hopped in the back end of the large sedan and tried to get comfortable. She looked up at him as he poised to close the trunk. "Good luck and be careful." She did not say a word, but gave him a reassuring smile as the lid closed and her world went black.

As far as trunks went, she was sure this one was better than most. Even so, it was still a rough ride. Every bump felt like she had run into a wall. The twenty minutes she was inside the black hole felt like hours. Finally, the car came to an abrupt stop and the trunk lid popped open. She quickly hopped out and shut the lid before walking briskly away.

By the time she turned to look back at the car, the taillights were disappearing around the next corner. He had let her out on a residential street and she quickly slinked down an alley and cut over to the next street. It appeared to be one of DC's "good" neighborhoods and she felt reasonably safe. Twenty minutes later, she hailed a cab and put more distance between her and those who wished to stop her.

***

Debbie had invited Amir over for dinner at her place. Homeland security had installed hidden cameras and microphones everywhere to make sure they captured every word and movement of the evening. She was too nervous to have actually cooked, so takeout was the choice for the night. She had dinner all set up on the kitchen counter when she heard the knock at her door.

She took a deep breath before opening the door and let it out slowly trying to relieve her tension. Swinging the door open quickly with a big smile on her face. "Hey, love," she exclaimed, as she lunged forward to hug him. He wasn't prepared and they almost fell over backwards.

"Easy there. Mind if I come inside before you attack me?" he said, smiling.

"Sorry. I just missed you."

"Missed you, too."

She moved into him and wrapped her arms around him while pressing her body close. Seconds later, they were locked in a passionate kiss and for a moment she was transformed back a week when all was right about this man.

"Shall we take this back to the bedroom?" he asked.

"After dinner. Eat first, make love later"

Over dinner, she explained the fictitious story of where she'd been for the past few days before launching into overbearing girlfriend mode. "So, what have you been doing while I was away? I missed you so much."

"Just worked, nothing special."

"It occurs to me I don't know much about your work and it seems to me that it's about time you let me into your life. Tell me what you do."

"I have told you. I work for the World Commodities Council."

"Yeah, but what do you do?"

"It's complicated. Why the sudden interest?"

She was ready for this question. "Well, I've had a lot of time on my hands these past few days and I've been thinking, a lot, about us. I think what we have is special and decided I need to know more about this guy I'm falling in love with."

"You think you are falling in love with me?" he said with a confused look on his face.

"Yes, I am. And, I think you are falling in love with me, too."

"Look, Deb. We do have something special, but it can't last."

"Why not?"

"We are from two different countries and neither of us are from this country. Our cultures are completely different and I'm not sure either of us would survive in the other's country. And they are not going to let us stay here forever."

She had not been prepared for this logical answer, but she refused to let it derail her. "We can figure that stuff out. We are meant to be together."

"Maybe, but..."

He stumbled for an answer and she pounced on the void. "We can and we will. Now, let me into your world. I need to know more about the man who will someday be asking to marry me." The fear in his eyes was real and obvious. She let the silence linger as he struggled trying to decide how to respond.

"Okay, what do you want to know?" he said in a defeated tone.

"Tell me about your day, the people you work with, what you are working on. Hell, I don't even know any of your friends or family."

The conversation lasted through dinner and into the night. He had been very willing to share details, even if many of them were fabricated as part of his cover. She realized after about an hour, this was a conversation they had been avoiding because they both feared what he had said earlier about their different worlds. This was an uncomfortable truth.

By the end of the discussion, they were both numb and confused. Instead of heading to the bedroom for their normal end of the evening activities, she simply fell asleep with her head on his chest. He needed to sleep on this new stage of their relationship and she realized all her old feelings of love and lust were gone. She was very glad not to have to fake it with him for the sake of the NSA.

***

When Senator McDermott found out that Kristen was in a Nashville hospital and that her two young daughters were stranded in a DC Police station, he started to work the phones to fix the situation. After a few phone calls, he had secured three airplane tickets to Nashville and arranged for the police to bring the girls to Reagan International to meet him.

It was after 10:00 p.m. before the plane touched down in Nashville. The girls had slept most of the way, for which the Senator was thankful. They woke up just as the plane touched down and seemed startled a bit by the strange surroundings. He imagined they were not used to flying and waking up next to stranger would upset anyone.

From what he'd been told, the last time they had accepted a ride from a stranger had not turned out well. The police had assured them they were in good hands, but he could understand their fear. If the girls had not wanted to see their mommy so badly, he doubted they would have agreed to come with him.

The only thing they had been told was that their mother was in the hospital because of a car wreck, but she was going to be okay. The Senator assumed they were not likely to believe such fairytales until they saw her for themselves. He owed it to Kristen to help.

As they walked through the airport, the Senator held their hands. "You know, girls, I had two girls about your same age. Their names were Teresa and Laura. You would have liked them." They did not seem to catch the past tense of his statement.

The three rode in silence in the back of a large black SUV on their way to the hospital. The Senator's phone rang and he barely spoke but listened carefully to the caller. After he hung up, he tried to casually look over at the girls only to find them staring intently at him. "What?" he asked, trying to act like nothing was the matter.

"Is Mommy okay?" Sarah asked, bluntly.

The Senator was impressed by this young lady. He knew he could not deceive her into believing her mommy was okay, so he decided it was best to tell the truth. "Well, we hope she is okay. She was in a pretty bad accident and she was knocked unconscious. She has not woken up, but the doctors are hopeful," he added, even though that was not what he'd been told.

"Can we see her?"

"Yes. We'll go to the hospital and see her and if it is okay with the hospital, you can sleep in her room tonight. You should be there when she wakes up." The girls simply nodded their head and looked away, apparently satisfied with his answer.

An hour later, he was still working with the night manager in the ICU to get a bed rolled into the room for the girls to sleep. This was completely against the hospital's policy, but he was a US Senator and was not going to settle for anything less.

When they had first arrived in the room, he had looked at her for a long time and watched the girls lovingly stroke her arm and examine the bandages wrapped around her head. Maybe it was just his empty heart telling his head what it wanted to hear, but he saw his lost family before him. They had perished in Joplin almost two years ago, but the similarities in ages and appearances were remarkable.

After he got the girls bedded down in the room, he slipped into the uncomfortable armchair and drifted off to sleep in a few minutes. The morning would take care of tomorrow's problems. Humans can only handle so much before the body needs to be rejuvenated.

***

At the opposite end of the hospital, in the private room with a guard standing just outside the door, was old man Williams. His injuries had been less severe than Kristen's and if not for a heavy dose of sedative, he would be awake and angry. His one uninjured leg and his unbroken arm were both in restraints. Despite the assurance of the doctor that it would be weeks and probably months before he could walk unassisted, the FBI had insisted on the restraints and the guard.

Around midnight, the nurse stopped by and was allowed to enter the old man's room after having her hospital issued badge quickly examined by the tired state trooper who had been on duty since 8:00 a.m. that morning. The badge was real, but the tiny picture, if examined closely, revealed that she was not nurse Elizabeth Geldmacher.

The nurse examined the IV machine that was slowly dripping fluid into the old man's veins. As soon as the door completely shut behind her, she extracted a syringe from the pocket of her scrub and injected the contents into the IV tube.

Before the lethal dose entered the old man's body, she turned off the monitor that would alert the real medical staff that his heart had stopped. After less than a minute inside the room, she left, giving the guard a friendly smile as she headed back in the same direction from which she had entered. She slipped the badge over her head and left it on the counter at the nurses' station before escaping through the stairwell where she had a lab coat stashed. Exiting through the lobby, no one noticed her at all.

Chapter 27

The first light of the new day was showing when Trista woke from her latest catnap. It had not been a restful night, but she had not expected her first night sleeping on the streets of DC to resemble anything close to a "good night." Well, technically this was far from the streets of DC.

She had spent most of the night hiding her trail. She had changed cabs three times and even bought a t-shirt at an all-night drug store to give her a different look. She considered it overkill, but better safe than sorry.

She had finally ended up at her destination around midnight. She needed a friend she could trust. Someone who would help her in this scary situation, yet someone her pursuers would not suspect. Shelly was just that person. They had worked together at the *Post* before Shelly found a sweet job as a media relations manager for a big corporation.

Trista had visited Shelly a few times after she had left the *Post* and moved to the Virginia suburbs. She had even helped her move a year ago. They had often shared lunch in the *Post's* cafeteria, but otherwise had very little contact that was traceable.

Trista had slept in Shelly's carport last night because it was too late to have imposed on her. Besides, the houses in the neighborhood were very close together and Shelly's large German Shepard would have woken up the neighbors. Fortunately, it had been a mild evening and the carport gave her some protection from the spring night.

Her plan was to wait until Shelly was up and fully awake before knocking on the side door that entered into the kitchen. If she timed it just right, the dog would be in the fenced in backyard and not notice her or hear the knock at the door. About 6:00 a.m. her plan worked perfectly, except for startling Shelly enough to make her drop her mug of coffee on the kitchen floor.

"Sorry about that," she said, helping pick up the pieces of the shattered mug.

"It's okay, you just startled me. What the hell are you doing here at 6:00 a.m.?"

"I need a huge favor. Have you seen my recent story in the *Post*?"

"No, I only get the Sunday paper."

"I grabbed yours when it was delivered this morning," she said, pointing over to the kitchen table where she had dropped it when first coming in amidst the coffee chaos.

Shelly reached for the paper and quickly scanned the bylines. It only took a second for her to notice that the lead story was written by Trista Hadden. She looked at her friend. "Wow, lead story..." Her voice tailed off as she read the headline. "Whoa..."

Ten minutes later, she looked up from the paper and said, "Holy shit, Trista. That's a big story."

"Yeah and not everyone is glad to see these facts came out."

"I can imagine."

"That's kinda why I'm here. I need to lay low for a while. There's a lot more to the story and until all the facts are out, I need a hideout."

"Sure. I have an extra bedroom."

"Shelly, this is a lot to ask. You have to understand that there is some danger. It is not just the Senator that is pissed at me. Also the church and possibly the FBI."

"The FBI! What for?"

"It's complicated, but there is some conspiracy stuff going on that is not in the article. The FBI is helping cover this up. I doubt they will connect us in their search, but you never know. The friggin' FBI is pretty good at digging up leads."

"Not as good as you, evidently. That's some story to break. Probably win you a Pulitzer."

"I'm just hoping to live long enough to accept it. This is dangerous, so feel free to ask me to leave."

"Not a chance. Stay as long as you like. I get a free copy of the book, autographed."

"Deal. Thanks, Shelly. Suppose I can get a shower and some clean clothes?"

"Sure. Are you hungry? I can make us something while you're getting cleaned up."

"That'd be great. Thanks."

***

Mornings come early in a hospital. About 6:00 a.m., the night nurse came in to make her last check of Kristen. The Senator woke, but thankfully the girls stayed asleep. When the nurse left the private room, he noticed a uniformed police officer outside the room. As a Senator, he was used to security, but he thought this was an unnecessary step.

He decided to go in search of a cup of coffee. "Good morning, officer," he said as he left the room. "There's really no need for a guard outside the door, is there?"

"Good morning, sir," the officer said, recognizing the Senator from the picture he'd been shown at his briefing. "We had an incident last night, sir, and we are not taking any chances."

"Incident?"

"Yes sir. The man in the wreck with Miss Carr was murdered last night. Or at least we think he was."

"What? What happened?"

"Might have been a professional hit. Best we know someone posing as a nurse killed him and disconnected all the monitors so no one knew for hours."

"Do you think they'd really come after Miss Carr, too?"

"Doesn't seem likely, but we're not taking any chances. They're going through security footage now. We should know more later."

In a few minutes, he was back in the room with a hot cup of coffee. He wanted to be there when the girls woke up. He stood beside Kristen's bed and looked at her sleeping, or at least that's the way he chose to describe her current state. She was a bit younger than his deceased wife, but she resembled her more than he wanted to admit.

He reached down and took her hand in his. It was warm and made her seem alive instead of the pale-faced corpse-looking person in the bed. He thought about the death of his wife. He hadn't had time to grieve and be with her to say goodbye. The tornado, he had been told, killed his wife and daughters instantly and without suffering. It was a good story that he had chosen to believe.

He was so lost in his thoughts that he missed the first two times she squeezed his hand. On the third time, he jerked back to reality. He bent over and whispered her name in her ear. For the first time in a long time, he asked God for a favor. It wasn't a prayer, but it was clearly a throwback to his former days of believing in God.

When her head turned and she started to moan softly, he pressed the call button to summons the medical staff. Within a minute, the door opened and both a doctor and nurse appeared. "I think she is waking up," he said in a whisper, trying not to wake the children.

The staff went to work checking her vital signs and trying to wake her. The commotion woke the children and he was there to hold them while the staff worked on their mom. A minute later, her eyes cracked ever so slightly and she twisted. The doctor motioned for the girls to come closer and the Senator helped them out of their bed and brought them closer to their mother.

"Mommy," pleaded Sarah. "It's Sarah and Mini."

She turned her head toward the girls and tried to blink her eyes clear. "Mommy's here girls. Everything will be okay." Her voice had been but a whisper and the words were not very clear, but the meaning was clear. She was back and knew they had been rescued.

The doctors explained that she was very groggy from the painkillers that had been administered. Waking up after a car wreck was going to be painful and they did not want her to do so without pain meds. It would be a slow process, but this was a good sign and everyone was either smiling or crying. The Senator was doing both.

***

Nate had texted Trista to see if she wanted to run. There was no answer and that caused him concern. The last he had heard, she was spending the night at the *Post*, but he had hoped she would answer his text back so he'd know she was okay. Not being in control of the situation was something he hated.

He looked out of the window to see if her security detail was out front. It was not, so he assumed they were with her at the *Post*. Frustrated, he decided he just needed to get on with his day. It was Sunday, and he was not planning to work, at least on official business.

He slipped on his heavy robe and slippers so he could venture out to the street and pick up a paper. Even though he knew what the lead story was going to be, he wanted to see it in print. That would help this entire situation feel more real. Slipping a doorstop, actually a real brick, against the door jamb to prevent the door from shutting and automatically locking him out, he looked around for any danger signs before stepping completely out of the door.

It was maybe twelve feet from his door to the paper box, but that was enough time for the man to slip out of the crack between Trista's door and the next unit. When Nate turned back toward his townhome, he saw a gun pointed at him from the man's side. He froze and stood tall with the paper in his hand. The two men stared at each other for a second before the man spoke.

"Let's go inside."

Nate didn't bother to respond. With his hands held up to his shoulders, he clutched the newspaper and pushed the door open. This morning had not started off well and he sensed that the day might not be any good either.

Once inside, the man told Nate to sit at the small kitchen table. Tossing the paper on the table, Nate obeyed. "Who the hell are you?"

"Doesn't matter."

"Seems relevant to me. What do you want?"

"Now that's relevant. I want you to put a stop to that," he said, pointing at the paper.

Nate glanced at the top headline, *Senator Tied to Church Cover-up.* "What, newspapers? Isn't the Internet making them go away anyway?" he said in his best smart-ass tone.

The man walked behind him and out of Nate's sight. "You know what I mean." The blow from the handle of the man's gun struck Nate on the back of the head hard enough to make him blackout for a few seconds.

He awoke on the floor and looked up at the man through bleary eyes. "What the hell did you do that for? I assume you already know I'm a cop. You just added twenty years to your sentence."

"I don't have time to chat. You can either make your girlfriend stop writing this crap, or a bump on the back of your head will be the least of your worries." With that, the man kicked Nate's mid-section with such force he was sure a rib or two would be broken.

By the time Nate pulled himself together, the man was gone. There was no sense looking for him, or even filing a police report. The good news is that they would not have come after him if they had gotten to Trista. For now, she must be safe. He was willing to take a few blows to find that out.

Pulling himself up slowly to a stand, he headed to the freezer and grabbed a bag of frozen corn for the welt on the back of his head. He'd cracked a rib before and knew that was going to hurt for a while.

***

Father Charron, as always, was in his office before 7:00 a.m. He enjoyed the solitude of the early morning and generally used this time to read and answer his emails and letters. There had been many letters and cards since the three priests had been murdered and he had painstakingly answered each and every one. Catholics everywhere were hurting and many had reached out to him for spiritual guidance.

When his private line rang, it startled him and broke his peaceful morning. He knew any call this time of day was not good news. "Hello?" he said picking up the phone after two rings.

"Have you seen the *Post* this morning?"

"Good morning Senator," he said in a calm voice intended to sooth an obviously angry Senator Stiano. "I have not."

"Well the lead story is about us! Somehow they have tied me into this mess. What have you told them?"

"Senator, I have told them nothing. I have not spoken to anybody regarding the case since Agent Murphy first contacted me. What information do they have?"

"They know about my meetings with the families and about the money we contributed. How the hell could they find that out unless you told them?"

"I assure you, Senator, it was not me. Frankly, I do not even know what you are talking about. I was unaware you were involved in the matter."

"Involved? I saved the Church. Don't try to make it sound like I did anything wrong. This mess would have been much worse if we had not stepped in. Now, we are being blamed."

"I assure you Senator," he said, using his calm voice to ratchet down the emotions of the conversation, "we are not blaming you for anything."

"Well someone is out to ruin me and I expect you to support me. The press is going to be all over you today and I better hear you defending me or this is gonna get ugly."

"Senator, the Vatican has instructed us not to respond to any press inquiries until further notice. It would be inappropriate for me to defend you in the press."

"You can expect a call from the Vatican authorizing you to do it. That's my next call."

With that, the phone went dead and Father Charron replaced the receiver. He decided he better read the *Post* before the Vatican called.

***

Debbie woke first and gently eased out of bed, trying not to wake Amir. He rolled over and shifted in bed, but did not seem to wake. She looked down at him, admiring his half-exposed naked body. They had always slept naked and she was really going to miss this virile man who suited her in bed better than any man ever had.

In the kitchen, she quietly made coffee. Her mind was racing and she was torn between emotions. This man was a terrorist, but the feelings she had for him before she knew that were hard to push away. Part of her wanted to go back to the bedroom and make love with him one more time and part of her wanted to run.

Having a broken heart was hard enough, but playing the man you loved, especially since he still loved her, was an enormous burden. She had been able to push the pain aside last night as she fulfilled her obligation to the NSA, but this morning the pain washed over her. She sat her mug of coffee down and gave into the violent sobs that had boiled up inside her.

Thirty minutes later, she had fallen asleep, exhausted from the emotional discharge. He had found her there on the couch, asleep with a full cup of coffee next to her. Her eyes were puffy and he sensed something was wrong, but attributed it to a bad night's sleep. Before waking her, he poured them each a cup of fresh coffee.

"Hey babe, good morning," he said, gently touching her face.

"Oh, hey," she said, managing a smile.

"Whatcha doin' out here?"

"Woke up early and didn't want to wake you. Guess I fell back asleep."

"Everything okay?"

"Yeah," she said, giving him the best smile she could. "Lot on my mind after last night."

"Yeah, me too. Not really sure where we go from here."

The NSA had instructed her to keep pushing to see how far he would let her into his plot. He had just given her a big opening and she decided to go for it. "I want in. I want to be part of your world. I know you are involved with something big that you are scared to share with me, but I can take it. I want to help, I want to work with you on whatever it is."

"No, you don't. At least I don't want you to. It is not something I'd want to drag you into."

"Amir," she said, sternly. "We took a step last night. I don't think there is any turning back. Whatever it is, I'm in. If you're in, I'm in. It's as simple as that. Let me be part of your world. Let me help."

"No. I could never do that."

She looked him in the eye to see if there was any weakness in his resolve. If there was, it was well hidden. There was only one card left to play. It would either work, or she would have fulfilled her duty to the NSA.

She said nothing, but her body language spoke volumes. She got up and went to the bedroom and started angrily gathering his clothes.

"Wait. Don't be like that. I'm only thinking about you."

"Sounds like you are not ready to let me into your life."

"Yes, I am."

She did not respond verbally, but thrust his clothes into his arms and pointed toward the door. "We are a good team, Amir. Shame you are not willing to trust me. You need to leave." With that, she headed to the apartment door and yanked it open.

"Wait! Okay."

"Are you going to trust me?"

"Yes, but you have to trust me. We have to do this my way."

"Your way is not working for me so far. Are you going to let me help you, or are you going to keep treating me like your little play toy?"

Their eyes locked on each other and he said nothing. She could tell he was about to break, but needed one more push. She gave him her most disgusted look and yelled, "Get out!"

"Okay, wait. I'll trust you completely. But I hope you'll still love me once you know."

"You'll have to take that chance." She shut the door. "You talk while I make us some breakfast." Normally, she was only in charge in the bedroom, but for now she was in charge of the entire relationship and he would tell her whatever she wanted.

"My job is a lot like yours," he started, sitting on a stool in the kitchen as she cooked. "I work for my government, the Saudi government. I'm on a special assignment here in America to promote the best interests of my country, just like you."

"You're saying you are a diplomat?"

"Sort of, anyway. I just work more behind the scenes than in official diplomatic channels."

"Are you a spy?" she asked in a tone she hoped didn't sound judgmental.

"No, I'm more of an activist. I do not steal information for my government, but I take actions that that help my homeland."

"I don't get it," she said pretending to be confused. "What does your country need help with here in America?"

"America is a threat to my country and Islamic law. We cannot fight them on the battle field, so we must outsmart them."

"How? I don't get it," she said with a confused look on her face.

"By making them see what is actually going on. America is in denial about what's going on. The world is in a religious war between Muslims and the infidels. My job is to help America understand this by fanning the flames of war."

She wanted to remind him that she was an infidel, but contained herself. "How does Saudi Arabia benefit from this? I don't get it."

"America thinks my country is a friend, but we could never be their true friend because they are an abomination of Islamic law. If they think they are in a religious war, they will not blame us. Instead they will attack Iran, Syria, Iraq and other Islamic states. This will allow us to become the strongest nation in the Islamic world while weakening America."

"So you are trying to get America to fight other Islamic nations so yours will be stronger? Shouldn't your country be on the same side as other Muslim countries?" She was genuinely confused now.

"We are the only true Muslim state. My country is the only place you will find true Islamic law. Other Muslim countries just use the law to seize money and power. Those countries are not our allies; they are our competitors. They are our enemies and we will use America to defeat them. The enemy of your enemy, is your friend," he added with a smile.

"So, how are we going to stir up this religious war? What's the plan and how can I help?" She still did not understand completely, but knew the NSA needed to find out more about the plan.

"My job is to create Internet chatter that alerts the Americans that a threat is coming. There are others working on other aspects of the plan. I do not know details, but it will happen on May 1st. You and I will be in Cape May and should be safe."

"Safe? From what?" she probed.

"I'm not sure. I assume it is an attack on Christians somewhere. I did some snooping and found a large Christian event here in DC on May 1st over at JFK. It might be that, but I don't know for sure."

"Will it be a bomb?" She was trying to stay calm and make him think she was okay with all this.

"Not sure. I'm not part of that. I'm just making sure America thinks it was terrorists from Syria who do it. I've been laying the groundwork by pretending to be a terrorist in some chat rooms. Then, when it all goes down, they will believe it when I claim responsibility. Well, not me, but the Syrian terrorist I'm supposed to be."

She wanted scream that he was a terrorist and was not just pretending. When she was sure she had enough to satisfy the NSA, she kissed him long and hard to show support for his mission, but in reality, it was a goodbye kiss. "I have to go to work, but we'll talk more tonight."

"You okay with all this?" he asked as he gathered his things to leave.

"We're a team, babe. I told you to trust me. Now beat it so I can get ready for work."

With that, it was over. Another chapter of her personal life had ended and once again it was in disappointing fashion. She had really thought Amir was the man for her, but this little terrorist thing had killed off any hope for her. Tears filled her eye as she climbed into the shower to try to wash away the pain.

Chapter 28

She really needed to talk to Nate and Joel to get the latest for her next story, but the risk of a phone call, email, or any other communication was a concern. Senator Stiano was also on her list of people to talk to, but she really feared calling him. After debating with herself for ten minutes, she decided now was not the time to get timid.

To get to Stiano, she needed to go through his chief of staff. She called him and insisted on getting the Senator's personal cell phone number. She got it, but was asked to wait a few minutes so the Senator could be warned first.

Ten minutes later, she was on the phone with Stiano and she knew he was probably trying to trace her untraceable cell phone. She'd have to make this quick before the Senator's people could figure out how to locate her position.

"Hello, Senator. I wanted to get your comments on a story I'm working on," she said as simply as she could.

"Look here, young lady. I thought I told you to leave this alone."

"Senator, I have a picture of you with one of the victims of the priest molestation. It appears you were also molesting these innocent children. Is that true?"

There was a long silence on the other end of the phone. She waited patiently, but was not going to wait forever. "How about we get together and discuss the issue?" he suggested.

"Senator, last time we spoke, you threatened to have me detained under the Patriot Act as an enemy combatant. I considered that an abuse of power. Are you still planning to have me detained for doing my job?"

"Of course not. I just want to talk. Your facts are incorrect and I'd be happy to discuss things with you so you can get the story right."

"With all due respect, Senator, I think I understand what happened pretty well. I just want to know if you have any comment on the evidence I have that you not only helped the church cover up these child abuses, but also participated in the molestations."

"I did neither. You are mistaken."

"I'm looking at a picture of you Senator with a little boy in a compromising position. In addition, I have a witness ready to testify that you molested him and then convinced his parents to take money instead of pressing charges." She was embellishing a bit, but knew that it would make the Senator squirm. There was silence on the other end of the phone and she waited for his response.

"I suggest we meet and discuss this matter." His voice was calm and calculated. "I'm sure you'd like my side of the story before you go to press."

"I'd be happy to meet with you Senator, but after you threatened my freedom . . . "

"I'll come by and pick you up and we can talk in my car so we can talk privately."

The thought of getting into his car did not make her feel safe, but she might be able to twist things a bit. "Okay, under two conditions. First, I bring my security man with me. Second, I get to record the entire conversation. And, just so you know, getting rid of me will not stop this story from being published. Others have this information and will publish it if something happens to me."

"I cannot agree to your terms. I just want to talk, off the record."

"Senator, I am the record. I don't do *off the record*. I can either put you down as refusing to comment on these allegations, or you can give me a statement."

"Okay," he started, but paused to form his thoughts. "The allegations being made by an uninformed reporter are ridiculous and insulting. I have no knowledge of, nor have I taken part in, any activity that could be considered child molestation or the cover up of such a heinous crime. This type of politically motivated attack is reprehensible and illegal. I have asked the FBI to look into this matter and will bring the full weight of the American justice system down on the *Post* and the source of this misinformation. This type of political attack cannot be tolerated in a free society."

"What makes you think this is a political attack?" she countered.

"As you know, I'm Catholic and this is an election year. Trying to tie me to the current troubles of the Church is an obvious election tactic to discredit me."

"Do you have any proof of this?"

"This matter is being investigated by the FBI and I am not able to comment at this time."

"Thank you for your time, Senator. Anything else to . . ." The phone line went dead before she could finish the sentence.

***

The welt on the back of Nate's head was not too bad. He'd had worse. His tender rib was another story. Breathing was painful and so was most every move he made. The Advil would kick in soon and he would just power through the pain until it did. He did not have time to worry about a little discomfort.

For the fourth time that morning, he sent Trista a text. Not hearing from her pissed him off, but he knew it was probably because she had turned off her phone to prevent being tracked. He was really more worried than pissed, but he was much better at being mad.

The chirping of his phone made him forget his pain and anger. The caller ID showed Laurie's name, which was odd since it was Sunday. He answered before the second ring.

"Hey, Nate. How 'bout I buy you a cup of coffee?"

He had already had enough coffee, but he sensed she was really just saying she needed to talk to him. "Sure. Where?"

"I'm just around the corner from you. I'll pull up out front and get you in two minutes."

Minutes later he jumped in her small Nissan and she sped off without a word. "What's up?"

"They found Trista."

"What? Who?"

"The FBI. Agent Murphy to be more precise. He's heading to pick her up now. We need to get to her first. I'm assuming you can't contact her."

"Been trying all morning. She probably ditched her phone. Should I ask how you know all this, or do I not want to know?"

"I'm dating a guy who works as a tech at the FBI. He was told to trace a call between Stiano and Trista. Not sure how they knew when to do it, but they got her. He said it wasn't easy because it was a secure phone, but he is scary smart."

"Is he smart enough to know he broke the law by telling you?"

"Yeah, but he knows what's going on. He's on our side."

"So, where is she?"

"Out in the suburbs. Must be staying with a friend. I just have an address. Funny thing is, my friend gave Agent Murphy the wrong address, just one house over, but it might buy us some time and help her see it coming."

"I like your boyfriend."

"Yeah, you would. You can buy him a beer sometime."

"You got it. So, do you have a plan?"

"Nope, gonna have to play it by ear. Can you get someone to see if there is a landline at this address?"

Ten minutes later, he was calling someone he did not know to have a very strange conversation. "Hello. This is Nate Romano. You don't know me, but I'm friends with Trista. May I speak with her?"

"Sorry, you must have the wrong number. There's no one by that name here."

"Okay, I understand. But if you see her, please tell her to expect some visitors very soon. There are some people she does not like headed your way."

"Really. Like I said, she is not here."

"I understand. If she was, I would suggest she go out the back door and meet me on the street behind your house. I'll be in a white Nissan. I think that is Greenfield Lane."

"It is, but there is no Trista here!"

"I understand. Sorry to bother you."

He hung up and looked at Laurie. "She's there, but her friend did a nice job of protecting her."

"You think she'll meet us?"

"We'll see."

***

"Trista, I just got a really strange call."

"Yeah, from who?"

"Some guy named Nate something."

"Romano?"

"Yeah, that's it. Said there were some people on the way here for you."

"What? Who?"

"He didn't say. Just said you wouldn't like them."

"Shit. Did he say anything else?"

"He said you should go out the back and meet him on the street back behind. He's in a white Nissan. What's going on Trista?"

"Shelly, I told you this was dangerous. I'm guessing the FBI is coming for me. The Senator has told them I am somehow compromising national security. He threatened to have me declared an enemy combatant under the Patriot Act. That means they don't have to give me my rights."

There was a silence that fell over the room. Neither of them knew what to say. Trista walked to the window and parted the curtains to peek out. The street was quiet. She knew she had to leave, but it still felt safe here.

"What are you gonna do?" Shelly asked.

"Leave. I cannot put you in danger."

In two minutes she had collected her things and was ready to go. She took another look out of the window just in time to see a black car pull onto the street about a block away. She gave Shelly a quick hug, thanked her for the help and slipped out the back door.

The neighborhood was well established and so was the shrubbery. It was thick enough to cover her departure, but not too thick to navigate. The hard part would be to find a place to hide and wait for the white Nissan without alerting the neighbors. She could not stand out on the street and wait in plain sight.

There was a perfect clump of bushes on the corner about 50 yards of open space away. She would be exposed for a while, but the risk seemed worth it. She quickly walked down the street trying not to attract attention and ducked into the bushes. She could see both ways on the street and if trouble was spotted, she could quickly go deep and be completely hidden.

She didn't have to wait long. A small white car made the corner and traveled down the road at a moderate pace. When it got close enough for her to see Nate in the front seat, she partially emerged so he could see her. The car sped up and came to a quick stop right beside her. The back door popped open before it even came to a stop and she literally dove in.

The car door shut behind her as the car surged forward. Nate's hand was on her back holding her out of sight. She looked up and gave him a smile. "Thanks for the warning. You don't think they will hurt my friend, do you?"

"No, but the guy next door might be in a rough spot." She gave him a confused look. "The FBI thinks you were in the house next door. Seems they got some bad intel. Where's your cell phone?" She reached into her pocket and retrieved it. "Take the battery out. That's how they found you."

"Potter said it was secure," she said, as she removed the back panel.

"It does not have a GPS," Laurie explained, "but it still uses cell towers. If you stay in one location too long, they can triangulate your approximate location. If you have to use it again, just keep moving and they probably won't be able to pinpoint your location."

"Where we going?"

Nate and Laurie looked at each other before he responded. "Not sure. We were in a hurry to get you out of there and hadn't figured out anything further."

"Well thanks. Hate putting you guys at risk, but I really appreciate the help. I really need to submit my next story. After that, enough of the story will be out and they might back off." They drove on in silence as each tried to think of a safe place to hide. She pulled out her laptop knowing she needed to write. "Either of you got anything new I need to know about?"

"We now have a tie between Stiano and 15 of the victims," Laurie replied.

"That's good. I need something to confirm Stiano was one of the molesters to really seal the deal."

"Here," she said grabbing a file she had tucked between the seats. "First page should be a list of the victims and their current contact information. Give one of them a call."

"Wow, you're amazing."

"Just keep that to yourself. I probably bent a few rules pretty far to get that information."

"Gotcha. Shit, how can I call them? I can't use my cell."

"I have a plan. Remember George?"

"Yeah, but he could not confirm Stiano abused him."

"True, but he'd probably be willing to contact the other victims and set up a meeting. He can say it is just to discuss the death of the priest and the legal obligations of the confidentially agreements they signed. Then you pop out and ask them about Stiano."

"Huh," she said, considering the plan. "I like it. Having them all together might give them the strength to come clean. Let's go see George."

***

Kristen was doing much better. She was fully awake and had even tried to eat a little lunch. She still had a serious headache and was a bit woozy from the pain meds. Senator McDermott had spent the entire day at her side with Mini and Sarah.

She had been reluctant to discuss things with the girls around, so when the police came by to get her statement, he had quickly taken the girls for a walk to get some fresh air. When they had returned, she had squeezed his hand and giving him a smile. "Thanks for your help. Wish I could vote for you or something."

"I've run my last election. Besides, you saved my life. I should be thanking you."

"Okay, then. Can we call it even, Senator?"

"Only if you call me Terry from now on."

"Deal."

The door to the room opened and in walked her doctor. He started to get up and leave to give her privacy, but she grabbed his hand and gestured for him to stay. He nodded and moved to the end of the bed to give the doctors room to examine her.

A strange feeling settled onto him. He had not felt this way for a while and he was confused, but whatever it was seemed to make him happy. He watched the girls as the doctors spoke to their mother. As smile came to his face as he realized what he was feeling. He felt like he was part of a family again. It was nice to have someone to care about.

The doctors were impressed by her rapid recovery and told her that they would observe her one more night and then let her go tomorrow if all was still looking good. More tears and smiles filled the room. The girls jumped on the bed and hugged their mother. He was glad no one was paying any attention to him as he wiped the tears from his eyes. He felt alive again and it was a wonderful feeling.

Chapter 29

The meeting with George was fruitful. He was more than happy to help and vowed to get the meeting set up for the next day. He even decided to host the meeting at the church, although he did not tell the church staff what the meeting was about.

After they left George with the list of other victims, Trista explained she needed a place to write. Her editors would want another story from her and she did not want Stiano to think he had silenced her. She might have thought differently if Nate had told her about the thug who visited him and bruised his ribs. He had managed to prevent her from seeing him wince as pain shot through his body on several occasions.

They found a quiet coffee shop to hang out in while she wrote the next lead story for the Post. Laurie texted with her boyfriend to see if there was any fallout from the raid that was intended to capture Trista. Agent Murphy and his team had searched every house on the street. Likely that was a gross abuse of police power, but he had subtly threatened each owner to let him in willingly.

Nate spent the time pretending to read a newspaper while watching the street for any potential danger. He had planned an escape route just in case, but all remained quiet. After an hour, Trista looked up and said, "I'm done. How should I send it in? My phone has a hotspot."

"If we are ready," Laurie advised, "we should do it while on the move. Just get it all ready to send and then we can send it and go dark again. Best to do it while on a remote road or low-end residential street where there are no cameras for them to spot our car."

"Okay, let's roll."

Nate took over the driving and in a few minutes he found a back street with older homes that did not look like the type to have security cameras. In less than a minute the email was sent to her editors with the next article and they were off the grid again.

"Nothing to do now but wait for George to do his thing," Trista remarked. "Let's find a cheap hotel and some dinner. Maybe we can even get some sleep."

"I'm on it," Nate replied as he maneuvered the small car around several potholes that filled the streets. After two minutes he glanced in the rearview mirror and saw that Trista had already fallen asleep. He was proud of her and how tough she was in the face of great danger. Now it was his turn to keep her safe.

Laurie was next to him in the front seat. He looked over at her and smiled. "Thanks for your help on this." She simply smiled back and turned to look out of her window. His feeling for her had changed in the past 24 hours. She had gone from a cute co-worker to a respected colleague. Whatever amorous feelings he had felt towards her earlier, were now replaced with professional respect.

The cheap hotel Nate had stumbled across would work well. He went in while the ladies stayed in the car and paid cash for a room with two double beds. They'd get some sleep and kill as much time as they could before needing to move on. The meeting George was setting up was scheduled for 4:00 p.m. the next day. After seeing the shabby condition of the hotel room, he was hoping they would not have to spend too much time in this pigpen.

While the ladies got settled in the room he turned on the 19 inch tube TV that looked like a leftover from the 80's. He wanted to check the news outlets to see how the coverage of Trista's story was progressing. The local stations were all covering it and the story had progressed from the church's cover-up to focus on Senator Stiano's involvement.

He flipped to CNN and saw a live interview with Stiano. The ladies stopped what they were doing and focused on the TV. Stiano was in full damage control, sticking to his claim that this was a politically motivated attack on his character and the accusations would prove to be false.

After the clip of the interview was over, the coverage switched to a panel discussion featuring two well-known partisan spin-doctors and another familiar face – Bishop Charron speaking on behalf of the church. They stayed glue to the TV as the spin-doctors both trashed Senator Stiano. Neither political party wanted to have anything to do with a child molester.

"I agree, Senator Stiano needs to resign," echoed the second spin-doctor. "This is exactly why our Constitution requires a separation of church and state. Corruption is inherent in all governments and in all religions. When you combine the two institutions you create a state where corruption is not only inevitable, but also powerful. When these institutions operate separately, they can act as a type of checks and balance on each other. When they are combined, they create fertile ground for men to abuse their power under the guise of moral superiority. We must keep church and state apart. We have to have a separation, or the few in power will use religion to suppress the masses."

"Do you agree, Bishop Charron?" asked the moderator. "The Catholic Church is a combination of church and state, isn't it?"

"The separation of church and state is an American tradition. Religious freedom was one of the main reasons our founding fathers came to America. It is not a worldwide tradition. The Catholic Church can hardly be compared to the United States government. While the Vatican is considered an independent sovereignty, it is first and foremost a religion. Outside Vatican City, we have no authority to govern people, except as their moral compass which they voluntarily embrace."

"But Bishop Charron," the first spin-doctor started, "didn't the church, in this situation, use its status as a foreign government to justify an intervention by a US Senator? Sounds like a combination of church and state to me."

"First, we need to wait for the facts to come out in this case before we jump to conclusions. This country's legal system is based on presumed innocence, so I suggest you not condemn Senator Stiano until he has had his day in court."

"Bishop Charron," started the moderator, "Are you suggesting that the facts reported in the *Post* today, that detail Senator Stiano's involvement with funneling money to the same families alleged to be involved in the abuses, are incorrect?"

"I'm suggesting this case is far from complete and we should not rush to judgment. Let's let the facts come out and allow the justice system to do its job. While I think we all agree that a separation of church and state is a great protector of human rights, I think we'd also all agree that mob rule, energized by inflammatory media coverage is just as harmful to human rights."

"Can't argue with that," acknowledged the moderator. "With that, we'll take a break. Stay with us for more coverage of this breaking story."

The room was silent as they took a moment to process what they had heard. Trista was the first to speak. "Wait until they find out Stiano was actually abusing the kids and covering his own ass as much as he was covering for the church. If he is getting this beat up for paying off some families who had been wronged . . ." Her voice trailed off.

"That's why he is so desperate to stop you," Laurie added. "If George comes through and we get confirmation that he was one of the abusers, it's over for Stiano."

"Let's hope that happens," Nate chimed in. "If not, we are going to be on the run for a while. We've been breaking a few laws ourselves and if we do not take him down hard, we are gonna have to start answering questions. So far, I think we can avoid any serious legal troubles, but we are walking a thin line. Time is not on our side."

"At least the news coverage is not about three persons of interest on the run related to this case," Laurie added. "I'm guessing the FBI is trying to keep this quiet because they know they are on thin ice as well. If the press started asking them why they are looking for us, it would be a difficult conversation."

"I need a beer and some food," Trista said changing the subject. "I'd rather not sit in this crappy hotel room and eat pizza out of a box. Do you think we are safe to go out?"

Ten minutes of debate later, they decided it was worth the risk to find a quiet spot to have dinner.

***

Senator McDermott had offered to take the girls out for dinner, but they had refused to leave their mom's side. After what they had been through, Kristen couldn't blame them. Instead, the kind Senator had ordered a pizza delivered to the room and they sat around the hospital room enjoying the closest thing to a family dinner any of them had had in quite a while.

They discussed what would happen when Kristen was discharged. She did not have a home to go to and the hospital could not release her until they had made arrangements for her to have a place to go. He had insisted that they stay with him. Kristen had hesitated until the social worker told her that it was either that or the kids would have to go into foster care until she had a place to live.

Her headache was mostly gone and the few other injuries seemed irrelevant since she was alive and the girls were okay. She was not sure why the Senator was being so kind to them, but he was a very nice man and she sure needed help right now.

Later that evening, the girls had gone to sleep and he told her he was going to get a hotel room. She hated to see him go, but sleeping in a hospital room chair was not ideal. She was glad to not be sleeping on the street, but it was also hard to forget the beautiful cottage Mr. Williams had set up for her. Part of her regretted not giving in to the old man's way of life.

She pushed that thought out of her mind as she looked at the girls sleeping. Before Terry left, her curiosity got the best of her. "Terry, what gives? How come a US Senator is taking such an interest in us? You've been so kind, but why?"

"It's not complicated, He started. "You remind me of my family."

"Really, I'd love to meet..." Before she finished her sentence, she knew something was wrong. The expression on his face had changed and his eyes watered. "What's wrong, Terry?"

"Remember the bad tornados that hit Joplin a few years ago? I was in DC, serving my country and the citizens of Missouri. My family stayed in Joplin because we thought it was better for the kids. Safer than the big city of DC. But, the tornado took out our home, actually the entire neighborhood. I lost my entire family that day."

"That's horrible," she said as tears welled up in her eyes.

"They were a lot like you and the girls. You even look like my wife and your girls are about the same age as mine were."

"Terry, I'm so sorry. I'm not sure I could cope with that."

"Ha," he chuckled. "I don't think I have done very well coping. I was a very devout Christian before all this. Now, I have not only turned away from the church, I have coped by making it my mission to remove religion from the entire country. All that's accomplished is alienating my friends and colleagues. I'm so hated that it's only because of you that I'm still alive. Frankly, you might be the only person in America who's willing to be a friend."

"I could say the same to you. Not many people looking to be friends with a homeless lady with two small girls. Seems we have a lot in common." She watched him shake his head, obviously choked up and unable to speak. She smiled at him and squeezed his hand. "It's gonna be okay Terry. Thanks for being my friend."

"I better leave," he said, as he stood.

"Wish you didn't have to, but that chair does not look very comfortable."

"I could also use a shower and a shave. Glad you are doing better. You get a good night's sleep and I'll break you out of this place tomorrow."

As he turned to leave, she called after him, "Hey, Terry. Thanks. For everything."

To her surprise, he leaned over and kissed the top of her head. "You get some sleep. See you in the morning."

She watched the door shut behind him before closing her eyes and succumbing to sleep.

Chapter 30

None of them had slept well. Not only was the hotel noisy with guests coming and going all night, but the mattresses were probably 40 years old. It had been an awkward night, at least for Nate. He had shared the bed with Trista, but with their relationship cooled, they had avoided even touching each other. In addition, he was fully aware of Laurie's presence. Whatever feelings he had felt for her over the past week had been changed, but having her in the room, was simply weird.

Nate was the first to wake up. He decided to go out for coffee. When he returned 20 minutes later, Laurie and Trista were up and watching the morning news.

As expected, the lead story was still about the Senator and the church. There was a mention of Trista's latest article, but otherwise no new information. With any luck, tomorrow's news would be the other shoe dropping on Senator Stiano when Trista exposed his involvement in the actual molestation.

They sipped their coffee and bided their time. They decided to rotate through the shower and then get out of this nasty place. Better to be mobile than stuck in this hole. By ten a.m. they were on the road again with Nate driving, Laurie in the passenger seat and Trista in the back seat.

The hours crawled by as they waited for the four o'clock meeting. Nate used a pay phone, which had been hard to find, to check in with George. The meeting was all set and most of the families had said they would be there.

Nate made sure they got there early and found a good spot to watch the attendees arrive. By five after, he had counted twenty-six people who had arrived and entered the church. On his direction, they exited the car and made their way to the church door, looking around for trouble as they covered the 50 yards between their car and the door.

Once inside, Nate led the way toward the back of the building that had several classrooms along the hall. George had told him which room and when they entered everyone stopped what they were doing and stared at them. It was obvious they were not one of the affected families.

"Can we help you?" asked the lady closest to the door.

George emerged from the crowd and said, "They're with me. Let's get started. First, thanks for coming on short notice. As I explained on the phone, we all have something in common. We were all part of the scandal that broke after the priests were killed. Now we need to stick together because one nightmare is over but another is getting ready to start."

The crowd stayed silent and listened as George continued. "The press is going to be all over us and there will likely be a trial. The gag orders my parents signed all those years ago died with the three priests."

"No, it didn't," said a booming voice in the doorway, as Senator Stiano entered the room. "You all made a deal to never discuss this. The dead priests don't change any of that."

"Looks like we have an uninvited guest," George said as he moved closer to the Senator, looming large over the much smaller man. "Does everyone know who this is?"

"Yeah," said a young man. "He's one of them. I wondered why Jonathan didn't kill him too. Maybe we should now," he said, closing in on the Senator.

"Hold on," said George raising his large hand. "Are you saying this man molested you?"

"Yeah. More than once," replied the young man. "Made me do things to him after the priest had fucked me."

"Really. Anyone else here get abused by Senator Stiano?" Three or four admitted to it right away and soon almost all chimed in. "Well, that should make a good story in tomorrow's paper. Can you still make deadline, Trista?" he said turning away from the Senator and looking towards the three visitors.

The Senator looked at Trista with contempt on his face. "What are you doing here? Stirring up more lies?"

"I'm just a reporter here covering a story. Got it all on video to make sure I get the facts straight," she said showing him her phone. "Assuming these people agree to stand by their statements, I think we now have evidence that you were one of the abusers and not just simply an overzealous member of the church."

"You bitch," he said, as he charged towards her. Nate stepped in his way, but did not notice the knife in the Senator's hand until it was a split second too late. He twisted at the last second to try to avoid the knife, but the blade pieced his clothes and gashed his side enough to make him bleed heavily. The crowd gasped and Nate staggered enough to leave an opening for the crazed Senator to get to Trista.

Seemingly out of nowhere, George's big hand grabbed the Senator by the collar and pulled him away from her. With the other hand, he grabbed the Senator's wrist and twisted it until his elbow became dislocated and the knife dropped to the floor. Next, he body slammed the Senator hard to the floor and put his large knee in the middle of his back to hold the screaming man in place.

"Thanks, George," said Nate, coming forward with his handcuffs.

"You okay?" asked the big man.

"Yeah. Mostly missed me. Mind if I cuff the bastard?"

"Help yourself. I might have broken his wrist," he said as the Senator screamed in agony as Nate cuffed him.

"No worries, George. He'll live to see his trial."

"Freeze! FBI," announce a suited man holding a gun aimed at Nate.

"It's over, Murphy. I have a room full of witnesses that can identify Stiano as one of the men who molested them. You are officially off the case."

"Like hell I am," he said, stepping towards Nate.

Nate rose to meet his advance and grabbed his wrist to raise the gun toward the ceiling and out of harm's way. A shot rang out and ceiling plaster rained down on the screaming crowd. Agent Murphy freed himself and aimed the gun at Nate, but before he could pull the trigger, George landed a punch to the side of his head. The gun and Murphy fell to the floor.

"Thanks, George," Nate said, retrieving Agent Murphy's handcuffs and using them to secure the unconscious man.

"He okay? Hit him pretty hard. Sometimes I don't know my own strength."

"He's still breathing, but he'll probably wake up with a big headache." He looked the room over before deciding what to do next. "Laurie, call this in and help me secure the scene and get statements from these nice folks."

"May I have your attention please," he said, addressing the crowd. "I'm sorry for the commotion. Is anyone hurt?" Seeing no response, he continued. "We are going to need to get a statement from each of you, so please do not leave until we do so."

"Bishop Charron," gasped one of the family members. Everyone turned to see the priest leaning awkwardly against the door jam.

Trista and Laurie grabbed the Bishop by the arms and led him carefully to a chair. "What happened Father?" asked Laurie.

"I saw the Senator as he was coming into the building. Tried to stop him, but he pushed me down a flight of stairs. Sorry I couldn't stop him from getting here, but looks like you have it under control, Detective Romano," he said, motioning to the two men lying on the floor in handcuffs.

"Actually, George gets the credit for that," replied Nate.

"I might have hit them harder if I'd known what they did to you, Bishop Charron," George added.

"Actually George, I think it is time to turn the other cheek. For all of us," he said addressing the assembled families. "This has been a bad chapter in the history of the Church and on behalf of the Vatican, I want to offer my deepest apologies to everyone. This should never have happened and I pray each of you will find a way to get past this. Even the Church is subject to the sins of man. You have my promise that this will not happen again, to anyone."

An hour later the crime scene had mostly been cleared. The only people who remained were Laurie, Nate and George. Trista had left to write the ending to the story, the prisoners had been taken away and Bishop Charron had been taken to the hospital reluctantly.

"Well, glad that's over. Without you two," he added looking at Laurie and George, "this might not have had a happy ending." They shook hands, thanked each other and left the church.

***

It was late when they arrived back in DC from Nashville. The girls were asleep with Kristen carrying Mini and the Senator carrying Sarah. He led the way to the guest room and helped her slip the two girls between the covers of the large bed. They stood back and watched them sleep for a few minutes.

"You must be tired. Can I get you anything before you turn in?"

"It has been a long day. I can't thank you enough for being there for us."

"Actually, I should thank you. It feels very good to have someone to take care of again. We'll talk more in the morning. I'm an early riser and do not have any meetings until tomorrow afternoon. Just let me know when the girls get up and I'll make my famous animal shaped pancakes for breakfast."

"Thank you," she said, as she moved in and wrapped her arms around him. He returned the embrace and they stood still enjoying the feeling. He did not know what would happen next, but for now, his life was on an upswing. He suspected the same was true for Kristen

***

Nate had suggested he grab some take-out and bring it to her place for dinner. Trista had readily agreed, but he was not sure if this date would be a new beginning, or the end of their relationship. Now that the story had been fully exposed, their relationship was at another turning point.

"Room service," he yelled as he enter her townhome and started up the stairs. She met him at the top of the steps with two cold beers in her hand and a big smile on her face. He noticed her casual, yet flirty attire, with a scoop neck blouse over a pair of jeans that fit just right. He took this as a good sign.

"Hey there. Beer?" she said holding out a bottle.

"Absolutely. I'm thinking we earned this." He took the bottle and raised it to clink hers in a mock toast. "You done good, Trista. Hope you don't forget us little people."

"You're silly," she said as she moved in for a hug. "Just doing my job, just like you were. It was fun, maybe a little too fun, working together for a change."

"As much as I'm enjoying this hug, a little softer might keep my stiches from popping." He still hadn't told her about his broken ribs from the thug who kicked him."

"Oh, sorry. How about your lips? Are they available for a little loving?" she said lifting her face up towards him.

He didn't bother answering. Instead he leaned down and they met in a passionate kiss. After a few long and enjoyable seconds, they broke apart. He looked at her smiling face with her eyes still closed. "Does this mean we are back together, or are you just looking for a one night stand?"

"Ha, I don't do one night stands. What kinda girl do you think I am?" she added with an exaggerated southern drawl.

"I think you are one helluva woman. I'd love it if we could pick up where we left off. I hated this last week," he said referring to their relationship being put on pause.

"I think that sounds like a good idea. Sorry I made our relationship such an issue for this story. Turns out it was not that big of an issue. I figured this story would take months to unfold."

"I thought the same thing. Let's just be glad it all happened so quickly. Ready to eat?" he said holding up the bag from the local sub shop and trying to change the subject.

The rest of the evening had been spent rehashing the events of the past week. Nate sensed a change in her, but was uncertain what that meant for their relationship in the long run. For now, he was happy to be back to normal. Tomorrow would take care of itself. Tonight was the time to enjoy the moment.

Epilogue

The justice systems can be slowed down when rich, powerful people want it to be. It took over two years to finish the trial, but in the end, George and the other victims got the verdict they wanted. Senator Stiano was convicted on all counts and would likely die in prison one way or another. Even before the criminal trial was completed, the civil suit was ready to move. If all went well, the Senator's vast wealth would be gone and the victims would be set for life.

Amir was arrested the day after he had confided his mission to Debbie. In return for his freedom, he had shared all he knew with the NSA. What he had not bargained for was being dropped off in Saudi Arabia, his native country, instead of being allowed to find safe asylum. He was never seen or heard from again. Debbie was allowed to stay in the United States and continue to work for the German Embassy. She met and married an American lawyer and still lives in the DC suburbs.

Senator McDermott, moved back to Missouri and took Kristen, Sarah and Mini with him. They were married a year later and even had a child together. The Senator made amends with his church and withdrew the lawsuit against the YMCA and the City of Charlottesville before it went to trial. While a decision on the case would have been interesting, he decided it was time to move on.

Father Charron was promoted to Archbishop and continues to serve the church in that capacity. He was able to institute some mandatory counseling for all priests and created a policy for preventing future cases of child abuse that was adopted by the Vatican and mandated throughout the church. He was offered the opportunity to move to Rome and join the Vatican staff, but declined; he did not want to be that far removed from the people he loved to serve.

Trista and Nate lasted another year together before her fame sent them in different directions. She moved to Atlanta to host her own show on CNN after finishing writing the book that Hollywood was now making into a movie. Nate had not wanted that lifestyle and they both knew it was just a matter of time before they needed to go their own separate ways. Both Nate and Laurie were offered jobs with the FBI and both accepted.

www.ingramcontent.com/pod-product-compliance
Lightning Source LLC
Chambersburg PA
CBHW030423290526
45786CB00001B/110